Performance and Professional Wrestling

Performance and Professional Wrestling is the first edited volume to consider professional wrestling explicitly from the vantage point of theatre and performance studies. Moving beyond simply noting its performative qualities or reading it via other performance genres, this collection of chapters offers a complete critical reassessment of the popular sport.

Topics such as the suspension of disbelief, simulation, silence and speech, physical culture, and the performance of pain within the squared circle are explored in relation to professional wrestling. Chapters by both scholars and practitioners are grouped into seven short sections:

- Audience
- Circulation
- Lucha
- Gender
- Queerness
- Bodies
- Race

A significant re-reading of wrestling as a performing art, *Performance and Professional Wrestling* makes essential reading for scholars and students intrigued by this uniquely theatrical sport.

Broderick Chow is a Lecturer in Theatre at Brunel University London, performance practitioner, and amateur weightlifter.

Eero Laine is a Visiting Assistant Professor of Theatre at the University at Buffalo, State University of New York.

Claire Warden is a Senior Lecturer in Drama at De Montfort University.

Performance and Professional Wrestling

Edited by Broderick Chow, Eero Laine, and Claire Warden

Routledge
Taylor & Francis Group

LONDON AND NEW YORK

First published 2017
by Routledge
2 Park Square, Milton Park, Abingdon, Oxon OX14 4RN

and by Routledge
711 Third Avenue, New York, NY 10017

*Routledge is an imprint of the Taylor & Francis Group, an informa
business*

British Library Cataloguing in Publication Data
A catalogue record for this book is available from the British
Library

Library of Congress Cataloguing-in-Publication Data
Names: Chow, Broderick.
Title: Performance and professional wrestling / Broderick Chow,
   Eero Laine, and Claire Warden.
Description: Milton Park, Abingdon, Oxon; New York: Routledge,
   2016. | Includes bibliographical references and index.
Identifiers: LCCN 2016002736 | ISBN 9781138937222 (hardback) |
   ISBN 9781138937239 (pbk.) | ISBN 9781315676401 (ebook)
Subjects: LCSH: Wrestling. | Wrestling—Social aspects. |
   Performance art.
Classification: LCC GV1195 .C487 2016 | DDC 796.812—dc23
LC record available at https://lccn.loc.gov/2016002736

ISBN: 978-1-138-93722-2 (hbk)
ISBN: 978-1-138-93723-9 (pbk)
ISBN: 978-1-315-67640-1 (ebk)

Typeset in Bembo
by Apex CoVantage, LLC

Contents

Figures

Contributors

Keiko Aiba is a Professor in the Department of Global and Transcultural Studies at Meiji Gakuin University.

Janine Bradbury is a Lecturer in Literature at York St. John University and specialises in American literature and culture.

Broderick Chow is a Lecturer in Theatre at Brunel University London, performance practitioner, and amateur weightlifter.

Morgan Daniels teaches British history at Queen Mary, University of London, and lectures in history and media at Arcadia University's London Center.

Stephen Di Benedetto is Chair of the Department of Theatre Arts and Associate Professor of Theatre History at the University of Miami.

Carrie Dunn leads the Sports Journalism program at the University of East London. She is the founding editor of *The Only Way is Suplex*, a website about professional wrestling.

Jon Ezell is Assistant Professor of Journalism at Tennessee Technological University.

Stephen Greer is a Lecturer in Theatre Practices at the University of Glasgow.

Jamie Lewis Hadley is a London-based performance artist and former professional wrestler. He completed his MRes in Theatre and Performance at the University of Plymouth.

Nina Hoechtl is an independent researcher and artist. From 2014 to 2016 she was a Postdoctoral Research Fellow at the Institute of Aesthetic Research, Universidad Nacional Autónoma de México.

Charles Hughes is the Director of the Memphis Center at Rhodes College.

Eero Laine is a Visiting Assistant Professor of Theatre in the Department of Theatre and Dance at the University at Buffalo, State University of New York.

Heather Levi is an Assistant Professor of Anthropology at the College of Liberal Arts, Temple University.

Sharon Mazer is Associate Professor of Theatre and Performance Studies at Auckland University of Technology.

Nicholas Porter is a PhD candidate in American Studies at Saint Louis University, Missouri.

Laura Katz Rizzo is Assistant Professor and BFA Coordinator in the Department of Dance at Temple University. She is also an author, performer, and choreographer.

Claire Warden is a Senior Lecturer in Drama at De Montfort University.

Nicholas Ware is a PhD candidate in Texts and Technology at the University of Central Florida.

Hamlet doesn't blade

Professional wrestling, theatre, and performance

Broderick Chow, Eero Laine, and Claire Warden

At one point in Kristoffer Diaz's Pulitzer Prize–nominated play, *The Elaborate Entrance of Chad Deity*, Chad Deity explains: "In wrestling, you can't kick a guy's ass without the help of the guy whose ass you're kicking."[1] Here, Diaz, through his character, gets to the central contradiction of professional wrestling – it is a performance form that is both intensely physical, even dangerous at times, yet at its core it is a cooperative, theatrical effort between two performers.

By engaging professional wrestling explicitly through the fields of theatre and performance studies, the chapters in this volume develop an updated methodology for the study of professional wrestling. Much of the existing pro wrestling scholarship has employed theatrical parlance or loosely acknowledged the theatricality of professional wrestling. Beginning with Roland Barthes's semiotic analysis of the "spectacle of excess" in his 1957 *Mythologies*, theatre and performance have often been employed in studies of wrestling largely as a way to mark the form as somehow other than sport, but only rarely as a particular performance form.

Both Sharon Mazer's *Professional Wrestling: Sport and Spectacle* (1998) and Nicholas Sammond's collection *Steel Chair to the Head* (2005) act as guarantors for this diverse study. Mazer's ethnographic study of the form is rooted in deep observational readings that, nearly twenty years later, stands as a model of critically engaged performance scholarship. While some of the critics of the book observe the limits of ethnographic performance research, such critiques might even more so reveal the trouble of studying a performance form based in and so heavily reliant on deception as its primary mode of performance. Sammond's *Steel Chair to the Head* offers a number of perspectives on professional wrestling that undergird this volume, including a keen eye towards the performance of race, class, and gender. Sammond's introduction to the volume, "A Brief (and Unnecessary) Defense of Professional Wrestling" places wrestling among other popular US art forms while engaging various storylines through a variety of analytic lenses.

However, delivering a steel chair to the head is a gesture no longer practiced in the more concussion-conscious, PG–world of World Wrestling Entertainment

(WWE; formerly WWF, World Wrestling Federation), a sign perhaps that a re-evaluation of professional wrestling is needed. And while this collection engages professional wrestling from the perspective of theatre and performance, it can also be placed in what might be called a developing interdisciplinary field of professional wrestling scholarship – notable academic entries to this this field include Scott M. Beekman's *Ringside: A History of Professional Wrestling* (2006), Heather Levi's *The World of Lucha Libre: Secrets, Revelations, and Mexican National Identity* (2008), and R. Tyson Smith's *Fighting for Recognition: Identity, Masculinity, and the Act of Violence in Professional Wrestling* (2014). This growing interest in the characteristics and conventions of professional wrestling is as evident in books for general audiences as for those for overtly scholarly ones, as evidenced by David Shoemaker, whose *Inside the Squared Circle: Life, Death, and Professional Wrestling* (2013) has brought a more literary treatment of the subject to a wider audience.

In all of these studies, the central figures are the wrestlers themselves. Indeed, at the core of the professional wrestling event is a live connection between performer and audience. While many people experience professional wrestling on television or through various media, the entertainment form itself would not exist without the stadiums full of active participants. That is to say, professional wrestling is first a live performance. While there are no printed scripts, professional wrestling does rely on ongoing storylines and conflicts among characters. But it is a particular kind of performance in that it is both intensely physical and relies heavily on various aspects of spectacle (costumes, pyrotechnics, acrobatics, and unusually shaped bodies – to be emulated, admired, or mocked) that are overlaid with an over-the-top theatricality that animates and drives the narrative forward.

Professional wrestling is a live, theatrical performance, yes. Perhaps most importantly for this volume is the attempt to show that professional wrestling exemplifies, in its own intense little world, many of the central concerns of theatre and performance studies. Since the establishment of the field of performance studies in the mid-1960s, scholars such as Richard Schechner, Erika Fischer-Lichte, and Marvin Carlson have established a continuum between "theatre" and "performance" that is epitomized in Schechner's notion of the "entertainment–efficacy braid," whereby performances that tend towards ritual (marriage ceremonies, coming-of-age rites) have effects in the "real" world, and those that tend towards representation and entertainment, namely theatre, do not. The continuum between entertainment and efficacy, especially among practitioners of theatre and performance, can often seem more like a chasm, especially in the context of bodily violence.

A simple illustration of this deep divide can be found in the act of "blading," wherein a wrestler will discreetly make a cut in their forehead with an otherwise concealed razor blade. The wound is self-inflicted and the actual cutting of flesh is hidden from the audience, but the blood that flows is the wrestler's real blood. It is a perhaps strange act to perform, but is an act that is not isolated to the wrestling ring. Take for instance performance artist Marina Abramović's 2010 interview with the *Guardian*, where she states:

> To be a performance artist, you have to hate theatre [. . .] Theatre is fake . . . The knife is not real, the blood is not real, and the emotions are not real. Performance is just the opposite: the knife is real, the blood is real, and the emotions are real.[2]

Excusing the force of Abramović's rhetoric, most theatre people might agree with her assertion. And many wrestlers might as well. After all, Hamlet doesn't blade.

But what, then, is pro wrestling, a form where the contest is "fake" but the knife or razor, at least, is certainly real? Professional wrestling represents a special case in that it is at once scripted, theatrical, and fake, and improvised, performed, and real. We might even suggest that it is this blurring that positions it as it is in some estimations. If one were to focus only on performance, wrestling would be a stunt show or just a simulated fight – somewhere between circus and performance art. Alternatively, to focus solely on the theatricality of professional wrestling might lead one to a common enough assumption that R. Tyson Smith characterizes satirically as thinking of pro wrestling as a "shirtless variation of the community theatre parodied in Christopher Guest's *Waiting for Guffman*" or as a "Kafkaesque blend of *Jerry Springer* and *Jackass*."[3] As a theatrical/performance form that is widely derided, what might professional wrestling's elision from theatre and performance studies tell us about theatre and performance studies?

Such considerations demonstrate the need for a theatre and performance studies approach to professional wrestling. After all, the issue of what is false, true, and merely playing true (or playing false) has been active in the discipline since its inception. In many ways, professional wrestling provides a particularly visceral illustration of the questions and seeming divide between theatre and performance studies illustrated by objects onstage. Performance artist/activist Guillermo Gómez-Peña cites an email exchange with Richard Schechner, who writes:

> In performance art the "distance" between the really real (socially, personally, with the audience, with the performers) is much less than in drama theatre where just about everything is pretend – where even the real (a coffee cup, a chair) becomes pretend.[4]

In professional wrestling the chair is always a chair but it is also something more than a chair. That is, the chair can be used to sit, but it comes imbued with latent violence; it interrupts feuds; it enacts an in-ring power struggle; it

4 Broderick Chow et al.

is a banned weapon. To borrow from Schechner's description, in professional wrestling the coffee cup or the chair (or the table or the ladder) move back and forth between the "really real" and pretend.

The problem of the fake and the real in pro wrestling is posed by the French sociologist Christophe Lamoureux in his 1993 ethnographic study of *le catch* (pro wrestling) events in the Parisian *banlieues* (suburbs). Lamoureux considers wrestling in terms of Émile Durkheim's conceptualisation of ritual. As Durkheim shows, "when it becomes recreational, ritual threatens to disappear because it loses its symbolic charge" ("*lorsqu'il devient récréatif, le rite est menacé de disparaître parce qu'il perd de sa charge symbolique*").[5] Lamoureux thus finds *le catch* a perplexing case, since it continuously risks "bringing about points of rupture in voluntarily creating confusion between what is true, false, and clearly pretense" ("*[le catch] prend délibérément le risque d'opérer à des points de rupture en créant volontairement de la confusion entre le vrai, le faux et le faire-semblant*").[6] In other words, wrestling is not purely ritual, but nor is it "an enclosed (theatrical) universe with its own logic" ("*cet univers clos, replié sur sa propre logique*"). In the event of wrestling, the oscillation between belief and doubt is so great that it cannot be suggested that, unlike rituals, which perform a function in the real, the participants leave transformed. And yet, Lamoureux muses, people still find meaning in it.

The professional wrestling audience is an active audience. Wrestling audiences are particularly adept at not only parsing the theatrical aspects from performance, but perhaps more interestingly, are very capable of holding them in mind at the same time. Professional wrestling then sits simultaneously as performance and as theatre. The performers are actually doing the things we see them do, but their motivations for doing them are highly theatrical. To be a wrestling spectator is to both admire the technique and determination of the performer and to suspend one's disbelief regarding their character and the plot.

These audiences participate in a uniquely liminal experience; professional wrestling's refusal to accept easy demarcation extends and augments the ideas of liminality so intrinsic to performance studies as a discipline. It is both theatre and performance, with violence as both its primary method and its thematic concern. Professional wrestling does what theatre cannot do or can only do by means of illusion: enact violence in a live performance. But despite the fact that pro wrestling is so clearly theatre, there is also something in it that is *more* than theatre, that goes beyond the purely representational, demonstrating the impossibility of a pure theatricality. Professional wrestling, then, is excessive to theatre and to the combative, competitive sports that it emulates. Professional wrestling is always more than theatre, more than sports (and maybe simultaneously less than both of these more established, acceptable modes of entertainment). At the centre of this liminal experience is the wrestling body: an excessive body, a body built for spectacle. Unlike martial arts that strive for efficiency of movement, professional wrestling embraces the overtly theatrical – telling stories through outsized physical gestures that upon review only resemble some physical struggle due to the overt performance of agony.

This volume is organized around a number of central themes that emerge at the intersection of wrestling and performance: *audience, circulation, lucha, gender, queerness, bodies,* and *race.*

The experience of the *audience* in professional wrestling may seem entirely different from the typical theatregoer's experience. However, the three authors in this section (Jon Ezell, Claire Warden, and Stephen Di Benedetto) demonstrate that interrogating the pro wrestling audience resonates with questions central to theatre and performance research: mediatization, participation, and the way in which *mise-en-scène* affects audience response. As a global performance form, the *circulation* of professional wrestling is embedded in modern media, economics, and artistic forms. Eero Laine and Nicholas Ware address this important contextual issue by examining the current business of sports entertainment and the history of wrestling video games, respectively. In the section *Lucha,* Heather Levi's and Nina Hoechtl's chapters examine the unique position of lucha libre in politics and performative identity in Mexico and the United States. Wrestling has often been critiqued for its *gender* representations, as well as the imbalance in the ratio of male-to-female wrestlers on a typical card. Keiko Aiba's and Carrie Dunn's chapters on women wrestlers in a typically male-dominated industry (in Japan and the UK, respectively) explore possibilities for the performance of wrestling to challenge normative representations of gender. Similarly, while wrestling to an extent relies on stereotypical portrayals of hegemonic masculinity, its performance practice provides numerous possibilities for the exploration of *queerness.* This section looks at three key figures who embody pro wrestling's queer potential. Janine Bradbury discusses the ambiguous queer performance of Goldust (Dustin Runnels) and his valet and "director" Marlena (Terri Runnels). Stephen Greer argues that the performances of Welsh wrestler Adrian Street embodied the emergence of alternative masculinities in the context of larger changes in both attitudes towards gender and sexuality, as well as work and labour. Laura Katz Rizzo's discusses how Bernard Hermann (aka Ricki Starr) enacted and embodied (and possibly commodified) queerness in his elaborate performances of a ballet dancing wrestler. The chapters by Broderick Chow and Jamie Lewis Hadley foreground the *bodies* that are central to the wrestling event. Chow takes up the figure of the muscular "body guy" through wrestler George Hackenschmidt, and Hadley interrogates changing performances of pain in and out of the ring. Professional wrestling's ability to speak into and about current socio-political issues is central to the *race* section, in which Charles Hughes negotiates racial violence in the history of southern wrestling, Nicholas Porter uncovers the post-colonial history of the British scene, and Morgan Daniels argues that flags become theatricalised national identifiers.

Sharon Mazer's epilogue brings some sense of conclusion while opening up new questions about the implications of this field for performance studies and the efficacy of using the tropes of professional wrestling as a way of understar i-ing contemporary academia. Together these provocations attempt to reshape and reimagine the potential intersections of pro wrestling and performance, uncover the place of pro wrestling studies in the dynamic intellectual space of modern academia, and open up new ways of understanding this established, popular, and globally recognised sport-art.

Notes

1   Ibid.
2   Sean O'Hagan, "Interview: Marina Abramović," *Guardian*, October 2, 2010, accessed December 1, 2015, http://www.theguardian.com/artanddesign/2010/oct/03/interview-marina-abramovic-performance-artist.
3   R. Tyson Smith, *Fighting for Recognition: Identity, Recognition, and the Act of Violence in Professional Wrestling* (Durham: Duke University Press, 2014), 39.
4   Guillermo Gómez-Peña, *Ethno-Techno: Writings on Performance, Activism and Pedagogy* (New York: Routledge, 2005), 38.
5   Christophe Lamoureux, *La Grand Parade du Catch* (Toulouse: Presses Universitaires du Mirail, 1993), p. 49.
6   Ibid., 53.

Part I

Audience

Chapter 1

The dissipation of "heat"

Changing role(s) of audience in professional wrestling in the United States

Jon Ezell

On a Saturday morning in April 1981, a visibly agitated Terry Funk appeared at the WMCT Channel 5 studios to deliver a message to announcer Lance Russell and the people of Memphis about their hometown hero, Jerry Lawler:

> I have got a date. I have got a time. And I have got a place. This is a personal invitation – sealed right here – to Jerry Lawler to ask him to meet me by himself with nobody else involved at an area that I know, he knows, and you will know. And I want you to bring the camera down there, but I don't want a referee, I don't want the police, I don't want the fans, I don't want money for this. [. . .] I want to see if he's got the *guts* to come down there! The *guts* . . . like I don't think a lot of people have around here, and I'm talking about the fans, Lance. I'm talking about you!

In the footage that aired the following week, Russell waits outside the ring in an empty Mid-South Coliseum chatting with an unseen film crew. He explains to viewers that Funk demanded the 11,300-seat venue be completely emptied because Memphis fans and officials gave Lawler an unfair advantage. Funk suddenly arrives, accosts Russell, enters the ring, and curses Lawler. He continues to berate Lawler and express joy at the absence of Lawler's fans, several times turning away from the camera to shout and gesture toward empty stands. Lawler appears in the distance in full ring attire – white singlet, tights, cape, and oversized crown. "Look at that fool! Look at that idiot! Don't you realize there's nobody here? You *jackass!*" Funk's insults echo for seconds. Lawler, unfazed, proceeds to the ring at a stately pace and disrobes. The wrestlers lock up and brawl around the ring and floor, wrecking sections of seats and tables where the members of the live audience should be. For about six minutes, they move in and out of the foreground, behind and around objects, playing to an absent audience while ignoring the lone video camera operator and running play-by-play from Russell. Grasping a shard of a broken table, Funk tries to blind Lawler, but the plan backfires. Funk shrieks and collapses. The camera changes angle (the lone edit of the film) to focus on the shard buried in Funk's eye as the other participants exit and the film abruptly ends.[1]

At a time when televised wrestling was a means of selling tickets to live events, this made for dubiously compelling advertising. There is a sense of anxiety and absurdity in the absence of a live audience; the sounds of the men shrieking and screaming reverberate like attempts at echolocation. That professional wrestling, as a genre of performance, requires a live audience seems obvious. This negation of the audience goes further in that it serves to confirm Blau's assertion that the audience completes the theatrical experience

> through a break in memory, so that we're not quite sure who is giving the command. At this ontological level, there would be no theater to imagine if the audience were not, from its inception, there in the shadow of thought – if not its final, its initiating cause.[2]

When compared to contemporaneous footage of the packed Monday night shows from the same building, this performance conveys only ambiguity regarding its possible reception by presumably atomized televisual spectators, and thus an uncertainty about the roles *they* should play. In isolating the wrestlers from a physically present audience, the performance calls into question the roles of both the live and televisual audiences in professional wrestling's "ecologies of performance," a term coined by Baz Kershaw to convey the web of interdependent relationships within performances and between performances and their environments.[3] It is with an eye toward the structural changes in the industry of professional wrestling, particularly in the shift from an industry driven by ticket sales to one built upon commodification of the televisual product, that this chapter will outline the consequent changes in the relationship of spectator to spectacle.

Duncan and Brummett argued that television imposed its own logic upon spectator sports, adding narrative structures and focusing on intimate details of individuals involved. Rather than framing a football game as team competition for its own sake, announcers focused on individual stories and histories that fit a standard set of narrative frames; cameras would combine panoramic shots with close-ups of individual faces of players and spectators.[4] From this study of mediated sports we might extrapolate two reasons for wrestling's early success as a televised spectacle: building a narrative about competition and emphasizing the individual experience are fundamental to professional wrestling performance, and it can fit the time and budget demands of television production.[5] The small television screen, better suited for the close-up than the panorama, could effectively convey wresting's athleticism, drama, and personalities in the ring. This is exemplified by the sudden, nationwide celebrity of George Wagner, whose Gorgeous George persona presented a pompous affront to postwar masculinity and ushered in a short-lived national boom for televised wrestling.[6] By the mid-1950s, televised wrestling already began to develop several characteristics of its televisual presentation: larger-than-life characters, interview segments for character and storyline development, commentary from one or more announcers who described both the physical logic of combat and the details of psyche and spectacle, and the presence of the live audience as an authenticating back-drop and sometime participant.

Examining the impact of televisual media on live performance, Auslander made several observations about the relationship between live performance and mediated reproduction beneficial to the present discussion: cultural forms based in live performance must increasingly depend upon mediated reproduction (and those institutions controlling it) for economic survival; live performance and live audiences will come to resemble their mediatized representations; technologies of mediation and reproduction will begin to augment (or encroach upon) live performance; and liveness of performance is ontologically reliant upon mediated forms.[7] After first outlining the structural transformation of the professional wrestling industry toward mediatization and monopoly, I will then explore how practice of performance and the roles of the audience have become increasingly mediatized and distanced from the immediacy and spontaneity of traditional live performance.

From the mid-1950s until the early 1980s, professional wrestling was a regional genre. Promoters set up rings in television studios or compiled footage from weekly matches. These territorial promotions generated revenue almost entirely through ticket and merchandise sales, travelling along a circuit defined by the reach of the local stations that aired their programs. This system began to unravel by the early 1980s, as some promotions began using cable television as a national platform, distributing programming with production values and star power that territorial promotions were simply unable to match. The Monday Night Wars of the 1990s structurally transformed the business in two ways: from an industry built around ticket sales to one built on pay-per-view buys, advertising, and cable distribution agreements – in the end, to a functional monopoly that continues to this day.[8] Where the territorial system utilized mediated forms to persuade the television audience to become the live (co-present) audience, the WWE has monetized the television audience directly: the live, physically present audience is now an element of production rather than its means.

To imagine past audiences, cautioned Blau, risks nostalgia for a cultural unity that was likely never there.[9] Thus any attempt to elaborate on the traditional roles of the professional wrestling audience is immediately complicated by the ontological elusiveness of the audience itself. Despite the diversity between and among audiences, regions, performers, and time, some approximations and generalizations can be made regarding the role of audiences in the context of professional wrestling performance.

The presence of a live audience is fundamental to the performance of a dramatic and compelling wrestling match. Wrestlers traditionally learned to listen to audience reactions and improvise in order to manipulate heat, build tension, and logically work toward a satisfying conclusion. Aside from knowing how the match would end, little else was planned. This was partially necessity – competitors traveled separately and avoided associating with one another – and partially preference for adapting to each audience and staying in the moment. Comparing planned and improvised approaches, Justin Credible argued that choreographed matches are performed identically with wildly different responses from one night to the next, and that match length, when working a series with some-one, can vary widely depending on the needs of the event and the crowd's response.[10] Professional wrestler Colt Cabana, when asked about adapting to differing live audiences, insisted on the need for the performer to remain fluid when setting the tone and pace of the match: "It's not the audience's job to enjoy my wrestling, it's my job to listen to how they're responding and change what I'm doing accordingly."[11] As described by deGaris, working a match does not mean controlling the audience, nor does it mean letting the audience dic-tate the pace or outcome of the match. "In effect, the crowd tells the wrestlers the story it wants to hear. It's up to the wrestlers to listen and react."[12]

This interactive spontaneity is an aspect of the craft of professional wrestling that is disappearing for reasons emanating from the bottom and top of the industry and rooted in the mediatization of the form. As early as the mid-1980s, performers in WWF (the World Wrestling Federation) were choreographing and memorizing matches, most famously in Randy Savage and Ricky Steam-boat's WrestleMania III match.[13] A preference for coordination with produc-tion staff and the national scale, particularly of main event matches, provided incentive for such rigidity. This degree of control has spread from major pay-per-view main events to weekly live television, especially for less experienced performers or for matches with complex sequences of spots. Executives moni-tor live broadcast feeds, dictating direction to announcers, technical personnel, and referees, who may tell wrestlers to work a rest hold during commercials, change the direction of the match, or to wrap it up.[14] Once behind the cur-tain, talent and producers can dissect the performance from the perspective of the television audience rather than the audience in the building. Thus, the live mediated production process serves for panoptic control and critique of the performance even as it unfolds – allowing for the internalization of the medi-atized gaze. For matches being recorded rather than broadcast live, multiple "takes" of a botched maneuver or sequence may be filmed in front of the live audience, whose response may be "sweetened" in post-production to compen-sate. The emphasis on the mediated product rather than the live performance coincides with the economic prioritization of ratings over ticket sales, to the extent that wrestlers are, at times, advised to completely refrain from interacting with the live audience for the sake of making good television.[15]

As Dell's interviews with wrestlers and female fans of the 1950s indicate, being ringside offered spectators the excitement of seeing and being seen, of screaming and displaying rage in a rare public context where such expression was socially permitted. Audience members – some of whom became regional celebrities – conspicuously competed to be the loudest and occasionally crossed the line to commit real physical violence.[16] Wrestlers and fans attributed the behavior both to the desire for attention from the presence of television cam-eras and to mimicking the unruly fans seen on the screen.[17] Getting heat from the audience is fundamental to the performance of professional wrestling, but its conversion to physical violence is this sort of breach of the paratheatrical boundaries of spectatorial performance that I would now like to briefly explore.[18]

Attacks from fans were not an uncommon risk of doing business for effective heels in the territorial era. Whether the heat came from cruelly taking unfair advantage of a sympathetic protagonist, working slowly to maximize tension and frustrate the crowd, or simply from insulting the town, it was often described as a necessity for emotional involvement in a match, story, or character. Successful heels took pride in their ability to work a crowd to the boiling point, which was accounted for both in ticket sales and scars. As Ole Anderson recounted in his autobiography:

> The people who usually got involved in altercations were generally the wrestlers on top who had a lot of heat. I got sliced open by a fan in Greenville. I was stabbed several times during my career, but it was that Greenville incident that made national headlines.[19]

Wrestler and trainer Danny Davis likened such transgressions to a positive performance review:

> There were times where we'd come out and we'd have bricks thrown through our windshield and, you know, that's how serious people took it back in the day. And I'll be honest with you, I miss those days, because they were wonderful times in my life [. . .] I knew I was doing my job.[20]

Whether we conceptualize such forms of participation as attempts to span the distance between the spectator and spectacle or as expressions of agency and protest against domination, they have become so rare as to be virtually unheard of in the modern era.[21] This is partially an effect of the erosion of kayfabe. Although the integrity of professional wrestling as a legitimate sport was disputed throughout the twentieth century, believable performances and the tradition of kayfabe kept the question alive. National prominence from the 1980s onwards allowed even casual fans to infer some degree of wrestling's inner workings.[22] Vince McMahon's 1989 admission that wrestling was not a "legitimate sport" was perhaps less significant than the growth of the dirtsheets, tape trading, and Internet fan communities by the late 1990s. As Mazer's study of late 1990s wrestling fan culture described, insider knowledge became a form of cultural capital, fueled an obsession with behind-the-scenes information, and recast the promoter/owner – rather than any heel – as the ultimate antagonist.[23] Former WWE executive Larry Matysik described this as a basic reversal of the psychology of wrestling.[24] Narrative scope and production values increased, and dramatic boundaries expanded beyond the squared circle to the promotion or the entire industry. Storylines stretched out and blurred the line between fiction and reality. This creates the possibility for complex and all-encompassing narratives (e.g., McMahon's feud with Steve Austin in the late '90s; Daniel Bryan's road to WrestleMania XXX), but it can also decrease the significance or convolute the stories of individual wrestling matches themselves. The multi-platform intertextuality (or hypertextuality) of the modern, post-kayfabe wrestling industry has complicated the process of generating heat – especially "real" anger – in the traditional sense of match psychology, although fans will perform emotional involvement as a way to participate.[25]

WWE visits major population centers in the United States once or twice annually, meaning that when current fans watch wrestling it is usually on a screen rather than in person. It is therefore understandable that attending a *Raw* event is not altogether different from watching the show. The set, made entirely of screens, dwarfs the ring. In addition to displaying entrance videos, vignettes, and commercials, it visually amplifies the performers, approximating the televisual intimacy and prolonged talking segments that constitute the home viewing experience.[26] Noticeable crowd silence and disengagement during TitanTron malfunctions suggests the dominance of mediatized representation over live presence in physical, perceptual, and economic terms.[27]

As live production strives to recreate the mediatized experience for the live audience, so does the live audience endeavor to emulate audiences on television.[28] Despite some regional differences, *Raw* audiences generally behave like audiences on past episodes – they pop or boo for entrances, they spout catchphrases, they start chants that are or are not related to the match, they pop for big moves, they bring signs, they take photos. "Smarts" and casual fans may cheer and boo different performers, but in the repertoire of responses there is a continuity informed by prior televisual experience and dictated by the current ecology of performance, where live audiences' immediate responses have less influence on the performance than responses from mediated audiences (e.g., ratings, stock price, social media).[29]

This diminished influence on the immediate performance does not imply that the live audience cannot disrupt, interrupt, or influence broader creative direction. For example, Daniel Bryan's "Yes!" movement evolved from a cheer to a disruption to an official storyline. The "Yes!" chant began as an ironic solo victory celebration in January 2012 and became a meme on wrestling blogs by the next month. "Yes!" signs and gestures began to appear in audiences by March. After a major loss in April, the chants became impossible to ignore, and the company capitalized, exemplified in a scene from the April 16, 2012, episode of *Raw*. From the perspective of the floor seats a camera faces the TitanTron as it displays a vignette of Daniel Bryan dressed in an official "Yes!" shirt chanting "Yes!" in the face of Kofi Kingston. All visible audience members are staring at the screen and chanting in unison.

The proliferation of the "Yes!" chant is an example of live emulation of the televisual experience, and its eventual recognition, incorporation, and commodification proved that live audiences had some power, or at least a sense of it. The image of thousands of fans thrusting their arms in the air and chanting "Yes!" made for compelling television, sold merchandise, and planted seeds for storylines and meta-storylines that established Bryan as a people's wrestler held back by WWE executives. This general narrative resulted in multiple events being hijacked by audiences unhappy with how he was booked, most notably in the 2015 Royal Rumble.[30] After Bryan was eliminated and it appeared that Roman Reigns – being positioned as the top babyface – would win, a remarkably loud chorus of boos droned for the remainder of the match. The boos swelled to a crescendo as Reigns mounted his babyface comeback, and thundered through the pyro. The Internet and social media erupted in vitriolic rage, and #CancelWWENetwork spent a day at the top of Twitter. This was "go away heat," but because there was nowhere to go, the next evening's *Raw* pulled the second-highest rating for 2015, and WWE Network subscriptions continued to increase through the next quarter.[31]

Whether Reigns's performance proceeded as scripted because performers lack the autonomy to adapt to the audience, or because the complexity of the match prevented deviation from the plan, its tone-deaf conclusion demonstrated that the imaginary audience is not always the one that shows up. Returning to the empty arena where this chapter began, this incongruity between the imagined and the real appears the moment Lawler emerges in king regalia and is mocked by Funk before the match begins. At various points in the brawl, the wrestlers gesture toward empty seats and sections, reflexively seeking connection to imaginary audiences in the room and watching at home. An imagined fan sits on the couch, sees the familiar hero in the familiar arena surrounded by the unfamiliar emptiness, is compelled to fill it, to commune. The emptiness fixes the gaze, foreshadowing the coming dominance of the televisual form over the live, when almost all professional wrestling will be experienced primarily by watching screens in relative isolation. As a form to fill the emptiness, to push back, to bear witness to the battle, the live audience, in its absence, asserts its multifaceted importance to the territorial era. Bouncing through the emptiness of the room, the voice of Terry Funk is twice diffused in the high reverberation of the empty space. His shrieks and moans, remediated through the television speaker, and at some point becoming ridiculous, presage the dissipation and dispersion of heat in the mediatized, post-kayfabe era.

Notes

1 "Terry Funk," *Corey Maclin Presents Classic Memphis Wrestling: Outside Invaders*, compiled from footage of *Championship Wrestling* that aired across several weeks in April 1981 (Charlotte, NC: Highspots Video, 2009), DVD.

2 Herbert Blau, *The Audience* (Baltimore: Johns Hopkins University Press, 1990), 41.

3 Baz Kershaw, "Oh for Unruly Audiences! Or, Patterns of Participation in Twentieth-Century Theatre," *Modern Drama* 42, no. 2 (2001): 133–154.

4 Margaret Carlisle Duncan and Barry Brummett, "The Mediation of Spectator Sport," *Research Quarterly for Exercise and Sport* 58, no. 2 (1987): 168–177.

5   Gerald W. Morton and George M. O'Brien, *Wrestling to Rasslin': Ancient Sport to American Spectacle* (Bowling Green, OH: Bowling Green University Popular Press, 1985), 47.

6   David Shoemaker, *The Squared Circle: Life, Death and Professional Wrestling* (New York: Gotham Books, 2013), 49–53.

7   Philip Auslander, *Liveness: Performance in a Mediatized Culture*, 2nd ed. (London: Routledge, 2008), 10–72.

8   Scott Beekman, *Ringside: A History of Professional Wrestling in America* (Westport, CT: Praeger, 2006).

9   Blau, *The Audience*, 29.

10 Justin Credible, "Pro Wrestling 101 – Calling a Match," *YouTube video*, 7:39, posted by "Justin Credible," January 27, 2014, https://youtu.be/fg9SMHHuLf0.

11 Colt Cabana, phone interview by author, June 24, 2015.

12 Laurence deGaris, "The 'Logic' of Professional Wrestling," in *Steel Chair to the Head: The Pleasure and Pain of Professional Wrestling*, ed. Nicholas Sammond (Durham: Duke University Press, 2005), 207.

13 George Steele, interview by Sean Oliver, *Kayfabe Commentaries Timeline Series: 1986 WWE as told by George "The Animal" Steele*, DVD, directed by Sean Oliver (Bayonne, NJ: Kayfabe Commentaries, 2012). Steele stated Savage relied on extensive notes, but accepted that wrestling seemed to be heading in that direction for the WWF. Larry Matysik, *Drawing Heat the Hard Way: How Wrestling Really Works* (Toronto: ECW Press, 2009), 133. Matysik claimed NWA imports, skilled in improvisation, complained about having to memorize short, uninteresting matches in the WWE.

14 Kurt Angle, interview by Rob Feinstein, *Kurt Angle Shoot Interview*, DVD, directed by Rob Feinstein (Langhorne, PA: RF Video, 2008). Angle recounts an early match where Vince called changes via the referee.

15 Bryan Alvarez, "Todd Martin and Lance Storm," *Figure Four Daily*, podcast audio, August 22, 2013, http://www.f4wonline.com/aug-22-figure-four-daily-bryan-alvarez-todd-martin-and-lance-storm-talk-summerslam-wwe-title-change.

16 Chad Dell, *The Revenge of Hatpin Mary: Women, Professional Wrestling, and Fan Culture in the 1950s* (New York: Lang, 2006), 105–109.

17 Ibid.

18 Kershaw, "Oh for Unruly Audiences!" 133–154; Bruce Wilshire, "The Concept of the Paratheatrical," *TDR: The Drama Review* 34, no. 4 (1990): 169–178.

19 Ole Anderson and Scott Teal, *Inside Out: How Corporate America Destroyed Professional Wrestling* (Gallatin, TN: Crowbar Press, 2003), 99.

20 Danny Davis, interview by Jim Ross, *Ross Report*, podcast audio, May 27, 2015, http://cdn46.castfire.com/audio/522/3426/25262/2497032/2497032_2015–05–21–003132–7770–0–8544–2.64k.mp3.

21 Blau, *The Audience*, 26; Kershaw, "Oh for Unruly Audiences!," 133–154.

22 John Hitchcock, *Front Row Section D* (Middletown, DE: TV Party! Books, 2015), 29.

23 Sharon Mazer. "'Real Wrestling'/'Real' Life," in *Steel Chair to the Head*, ed. Nicholas Sammond (Durham: Duke University Press, 2005), 67–87.

24 Matysik, *Drawing Heat the Hard Way*, 24.

25 Colt Cabana, phone interview by author, June 24, 2015.

26 Auslander, *Liveness*, 184.

27 Dave Meltzer, "Notes from the 9/28 Raw Show in Buffalo," *Wrestling Observer Newsletter*, October 6, 2015.

28 Auslander, *Liveness*, 27.

29 Kershaw, "Oh, for Unruly Audiences!," 133–154.

30 Dave Meltzer, "Royal Rumble 2014," *Wrestling Observer Newsletter*, February 3, 2014.

31 Brandon Howard, "2015 Year-End Stats: Star Ratings, TV Ratings, Attendance & More! (WWE, NJPW, NXT, ROH)," Voices of Wrestling, last modified January 13, 2016, http://www.voicesofwrestling.com/2016/01/13/2015-year-end-stats-star-ratings-tv-attendance-wwe-njpw-nxt-roh/.

Chapter 2

Pops and promos

Speech and silence in professional wrestling

Claire Warden

Nicholas Sammond describes the "squared circle" as an innately visceral space: it is "brutal and it is carnal. It is awash in blood, sweat and spit."[1] The history of professional wrestling confirms the validity of Sammond's statement; the most iconic moments (from Stone Cold Steve Austin's bloodied grimace to camera at WrestleMania XIII, or Shawn Michaels leaping on to Razor Ramon from the top of a ladder at WrestleMania X, *ad infinitum*) are generally the most somatically arresting. Initially, then, it might appear that such a physicalized space, akin to the ancient gladiatorial coliseum, offers little room for articulate speech. Certainly Roland Barthes's seminal description of professional wrestling as a "spectacle of excess" partly substantiates this claim, the spectacle dependent on dazzling visual imagery. Indeed, to the non-wrestling fan, it is the simulated pain (engendering the wearisome "Isn't it all fake?" question) or the seemingly unrestrained violence (causing mothers everywhere to worry about their children performing Tombstones in concrete playgrounds) that puts them off.

But these readily accepted images of professional wrestling obscure the vital importance of the speech act. This is old news to the wrestling fan, of course, captivated over the years by the storylines, the arguments, the ardent appeals for fan support, amazed by the engrossing verbal dexterity of wrestlers, commentators, managers and announcers. However, such textual interventions are rarely theorised and often seem disconnected from the physical excess that defines the spectacle of professional wrestling – wrestlers speak, put the microphone down, fight, win, pick the microphone up again. Wrestlers are often defined as "good workers" or "good on the mic." The best, of course, are both, but the two are read as different (though symbiotic) sides of the pro wrestling performance game. This chapter seeks to reattach the physical and the linguistic, claiming that the two act in tandem. More than this, speech acts and bodily actions are inextricably tied together. Indeed, I claim, both a Powerbomb and a scripted piece to camera are physical acts. I follow Judith Butler's lead; in *Excitable Speech* she affirms "language is our name for our doing: both 'what' we do (the name for the action that we characteristically perform) and that which we effect, the act and its consequences."[2] Spoken language is intricately bound up with the body, a fact we unconsciously acknowledge every day when we open our mouths and use our larynx, lips, tongue and diaphragm to articulate our thoughts. We can only speak through our bodies. Butler pushes this further, saying: "what if language has within it its own possibilities for violence and for world-shattering?"[3] Language here is a performative act, not merely a descriptor but an utterance bringing something tangible into existence. Although Butler is using this concept to examine language as an *oppressively* violent system, I want to rework it in a professional wrestling context. Language in professional wrestling does not so much describe situations, acting as an intermediary between spectator and spectated. It is instead, following Butler, a dynamic system of action, a system that, in some contexts, "presumes not only that language acts, but that it acts *upon* its addressee in an injurious way."[4] While recognising the diverse variety of speech acts in professional wrestling, I want to use Butler's conclusions as a starting point to claim that the squared circle is a space of physicalised speech, of speech that "does" rather than "describes."

Promos

In order to justify this claim, I am going to examine the conventions of professional wrestling's two most regularly utilised speech interventions: wrestler's promos and commentator's narratives. Promotional spots (promos) can be read as dialogue or monologue, illustrating the personality traits of the character and setting up storylines. They can even, as CM Punk's now legendary 2011 "Pipe Bomb" promo revealed, actively undermine the very institution of professional wrestling. My example is an obvious one – Dusty Rhodes's "hard times" promo from 1985 – but rather than simply accept it as an extraordinary piece of storytelling or focus on its political potency, I want to analyse the linguistic reasons for its success, breaking it down as a theatrical vignette. The reason this promo is so successful lies in Rhodes's total command of linguistic patterns and structures. During the course of the promo Rhodes switches from third person ("Dusty Rhodes, the American Dream") to first, simultaneously establishing his character and locating himself in the middle of the action. He speaks to four different people or groups of people: first, the interviewer who welcomes him back; second, the people in the crowd whose acousmatic sounds act as an almost musical backdrop to Rhodes's promo; third, the audience at home, through the camera; and finally, his rival Ric Flair, whom he criticises as having "no respect, no honour." He uses a different cadence for each. Most noticeably, when he is talking about Flair, his tone quietens, layering his challenge with a real sense of menace. When he speaks through the camera, the modulation is quite different: the tone is heightened, he explicitly associates himself with the spectator by acknowledging not only his own "hard times" but the "hard times" experienced by workers across the United States (this political solidarity seemed to capture perfectly the context of the 1980s). He uses distinct gestures, reaching towards the camera as if creating a physical bond, visually illustrating "my hand touching your hand."[5] This is not only a verbal moment of solidarity but also a somatic one, overcoming the detached mediation of the television screen. Here, the physical and linguistic work in tandem, as in a Bertolt Brecht play where the concept of *gestus* unites the non-verbal gesture and the political comment. In a popular culture form so often disregarded as an opiate for the masses, it is rather disconcerting to find Brechtian *gestus* lurking in the structures of a promo.

Rhodes's promo is a seminal moment in professional wrestling performance and evidences his tremendous on-mic abilities. But it also typifies an old-school, kayfabe style. Shortly after this, professional wrestling was confirmed as a work, and the straightforward, emotive narrative storytelling of Rhodes's promo began to look rather passé and dated. However, promos continue in contemporary WWE and they are not unique to wrestlers; indeed some of the most linguistically complex work historically comes from figures held up as managers or promoters, figures usually employed for their ability to verbally represent wrestlers (though, in Vince McMahon's case at least, sometimes unable to resist getting into the ring). Similar to Rhodes (but using an altogether different style), a character like Paul Heyman – currently managing "The Beast" Brock Lesnar but with a long, illustrious career in pro wrestling, particularly as manager of rival promotion Extreme Championship Wrestling (ECW) – uses particular linguistic trickery to further storylines. Take, as one example among many, a segment aired as I was in the process of writing this chapter in June 2015: Lesnar's apology to Michael Cole and John Bradshaw Layfield, the commentators he beat up months earlier. The visuals of this segment are vital: Lesnar shakes hands with a terrified Michael Cole before putting him in a "joke" headlock. At this point, the central action of the segment, Heyman is not even on screen. However, Heyman's promotional work turns this segment from a potential shamefaced humbling of The Beast into a war cry for the forthcoming Battleground pay-per-view. First up is his description of Lesnar's opponent Seth Rollins, an opponent who, Heyman repeats, has been "protected . . . protected . . . protected" on his way to the top. As so often with Heyman's promos, there is a sense he is speaking in shoot rather than kayfabe parlance; he is acknowledging that Rollins has enjoyed pushes throughout his career while others have fallen by the wayside. This promo, like the jokes in the *Shrek* movies, for instance, points to WWE's dual audience – the smarks[6] who get the in-jokes and the children who don't but laugh anyway. Heyman's description of Rollins shows a particular linguistic dexterity, listing a range of uncomplimentary terms from "slinky, slimy, disgusting" to "repulsive, repugnant, dirty." Even transcribing parts of his list it is easy to see Heyman's speech patterns: the alliterative couplets, the additional assonance of *sli* and *re*. He builds on this in his direct address to Rollins, not only reminding the audience of the date and venue of Battleground – ever the pro! – but describing Rollins's expected future humiliation as prompted not by McMahon's millions, not by "J&J security who beat you, Kane who wants to eat you, or the WWE Universe who's dying for someone to defeat you" but by Lesnar himself.[7] The cadence of this promo, presented by Heyman in his typical deliberate tone, is perfect, creating a sense of linguistic movement and dynamism that reaches climax at the end when he presents the "future WWE World Heavyweight Champion": Brock Lesnar. This short description of one arbitrarily chosen Heyman promo reveals the central importance of language in professional wrestling. It also, however, pinpoints the inherent violence of speech acts; the "beat," "eat," "defeat" behaves as a rhyming challenge – the consonants and vowels are harsh and their repetition feels as savage as three well-timed suplexes.

Commentary

Until relatively recently the contributions of the commentary team, importantly heard by the television audience alone (with fairly regular exceptions) could be split into narrator and colour roles, the former providing play-by-play narration, the latter (often a heel) intervening in the in-ring storyline. These roles are less defined in the modern product, yet most commentary includes an element of straight descriptive explanation and more emotive remarks. Their contributions bring a vital acoustic layering to the professional wrestling experience. Two examples to illustrate the way these interventions function: the first is taken from a 1992 Royal Rumble match. For the uninitiated, a Royal Rumble is a match with upwards of twenty competitors who enter the ring at timed intervals. The winner is the one who stays until the end and the only way to get rid of opponents is to fling them over the top rope. The announcers in 1992 were Gorilla Monsoon, the play-by-play guy, and Bobby "The Brain" Heenan, probably the greatest colour commentator, who had been associated with heel Ric Flair in the months leading into this match. The start sees the British Bulldog in the centre of the ring waiting for the first opponent. Monsoon carefully explains that no wrestler drawn 1–5 (that is entering the ring first, second, third, fourth or fifth) has ever won a Royal Rumble match. With his vested interest in the result, Heenan expresses his impatience as he waits for the match to start, repeating "come on, come on!" His acousmatic interjections actively elevate the tension and excitement. When a bemused Flair comes through the curtain Heenan is furious, shouting "no, damn it" as Monsoon repeats his statistic. Heenan's insincere apology – "I'm going to have to apologise to the people. I don't think I can really be objective" – sets the tone for the match. The narrator is not going to interpret the action or objectively explain the moves; indeed, his personal connection with Flair ensures that his language will be explicitly partisan.

Throughout, Heenan refuses the call the match and, instead, plays up his relationship with Flair. At the end, three wrestlers are left: Hulk Hogan, Sid Justice and Flair. Justice eliminates Hogan, much to the chagrin of the latter, who proceeds to grab Justice's arm over the top rope. Flair takes advantage of the situation by attacking Justice from behind, throwing him out of the ring and winning the match. The two styles of narration commentary turn this three-man finale into a historic moment in professional wrestling history. First, the whole match has been framed by Monsoon's statistical claims: no one has ever been victorious after entering the Royal Rumble so early. Here, on the one hand, is the objective voice of reason (Monsoon). But this is coupled with Heenan's response; in his excitement he can only shout "yes, yes, yes" as Flair celebrates in the ring.[8] The two oppositional linguistic formats work symbiotically here, turning a simple move (throwing a guy over the top rope) into a moment of historical significance. Heenan's response perfectly reflects the context. Flair had been signed from rival company WCW the year previously. Heenan was charged with ensuring that the crowd realised the importance of this match for Flair, trying to establish himself as the "Real World Champion." His response – "yes, yes, yes" – captured both the excitement that Flair had won the belt (and stayed in the Royal Rumble for a record amount of time) and also a sense of surprise that the WCW (World Championship Wrestling) champion could arrive at the WWF (the World Wrestling Federation) and win. Heenan expresses both these sentiments in his simple linguistic response. One of the most prominent wrestling online forums, the *Bleacher Report*, claims this event as a "work of verbal storytelling art,"[9] a far cry from the image of professional wrestling as violent excess.

The second example turns to commentating legend "JR" Jim Ross at the King of the Ring pay-per-view in 1998. It is a Hell in a Cell match between The Undertaker and Mankind (Mick Foley). From the off the two exchange blows on top of the cage. As they make their way across the top, the wire mesh weakens some sixteen feet above the ring below. This (accidental or perhaps planned) slip creates a heart-pounding sense of danger. Suddenly The Undertaker grabs Mankind's hair and tights and flings him on to the Spanish announce table below. Ross's commentary is the stuff of legend:

[The Undertaker grabs Mankind and launches him down into the Spanish announce table]

JR: Look out, oh no! Good God Almighty! Good God Almighty! That killed him!

[Crowd noise]

Jerry Lawler: Oh my God!

JR: As God is my witness, he is broken in half![10]

It is an iconic wrestling moment. But what makes it so powerful? Certainly the fall itself is remarkable. The danger of the situation is already established by the bulging mesh. Unusually, however, The Undertaker does not tease the move; the wrestlers do not teeter on the edge of the cage for a while, selling punches that might or might not see them fall to the ground below. Instead Mankind's bump comes entirely out of the blue. Coupled with this is Ross's commentary. Somewhat ironically, it is at this moment when language almost breaks down entirely, that the speech act becomes most potent. To an even greater extent than Heenan's "yes, yes, yes" interjections at the end of Royal Rumble 1992, language here seems unable to really capture the significance of the physical act; Ross can only respond with incredulous blasphemy and two predictions that Mankind must surely be dead. It is purposely over the top, suggesting that this is an unusually dangerous situation – which in reality it certainly was! – even in the violent world of professional wrestling. In a sense language is here freed from its moorings and retains a liveness that Butler describes in her analysis of Toni Morrison's writing. When language seeks to capture an event, Butler suggests, it commits a violent act and "loses its vitality."[11] Ross's utterances do not shut down interpretative potential but instead create a sense of openness that we, as audience members, can invest in. His words do not describe the action (indeed they suggest the failure of language to communicate such an extreme physical act) but we, watching on television, grasp the communicative potential of Ross's words. The shock the crowd feels is perfectly articulated by Ross who, for a moment, is transmuted into a fan rather than a commentator. He even uses the parlance of the fan rather than the narrator. He steps out of his communicative structures and adopts our structures instead. It is this linguistic complexity that transforms this single act from an amazing physical feat into an extraordinary seminal moment of professional wrestling history.

Silence

So far this chapter has established the importance of aural language standing alongside, substantiating or subverting the physical action. Such interventions do not simply frame the action, they *are* action. But professional wrestling has always been based on oppositional powers; to borrow the tagline for Wrestle-Mania III, "the irresistible force meeting the immovable object." So what of that alternative to linguistic presence, that is linguistic absence? In many ways, especially if we follow Martin Heidegger's line of enquiry, this is not simply an oppositional relationship as "authentic silence is possible only in genuine discourse."[12]

Focusing on all the elements of professional wrestling performance, Henry Jenkins confirms "wrestling makes you want to shout, and perhaps we have had too much silence."[13] It's a legitimate statement, as I proved at a recent Insane Championship Wrestling event in Sheffield, when I cheered on current Scottish favourite Grado. However, I don't entirely agree with Jenkins's statement. Of course, spectators can cheer their favourite performers, boo poor sportsmanship, interrupt promos with the grating "what?" chant, invest in Daniel Bryan's gimmick with the repetition of "yes, yes, yes." Yet silence remains a vital force in professional wrestling. At football (soccer) matches crowds are now encouraged to engage in a minute's clapping rather than a minute's silence to celebrate the lives of recently deceased legends. This change in tradition is testimony to how hard it is to orchestrate a minute's silence, particularly in large groups of people. Consequently, silence represents one way the audience can "voice" their opinion without the managed interference of the promotion; as every heel knows only too well, if you tell people to be quiet they will generally be as noisy as possible. When it does come, silence, by contrast, is more likely a spontaneous response of a large group of like-minded people. In this noisy, physicalised space, silence is, I suggest, an independent, democratic intervention. Indeed it is actually due to the rowdy atmosphere Jenkins recognises as a defining factor of professional wrestling that silence is so potent; as Mikhail Bakhtin confirms, "quietude and silence are always relative."[14] Silence here is not a signifier of marginalisation or a nod to the old adage that children should be seen and not heard. Rather it is, again returning to Bakhtin, a reaffirming of subjectivity: "in silence nobody *speaks* (or somebody does not speak)."[15] The subjective power (and embodied presence) of the crowd is just as potent when it does not speak as when it does. In fact, I suggest, it is more powerful in silence.

Audience silence appears at two junctures in the professional wrestling experience: when a crowd is not fully invested in an angle or when a real accident occurs in the ring. The latter is relatively easy to explain: shock and concern added together breaks through the conventional kayfabe structures, leaving the crowd unsure about the appropriate aural response. Is the wrestler simply selling the injury or has he really snapped his spine? These silences do not tend to last long; either the wrestler stumbles to his feet to cheers or else is whisked away by the medical team. The former, however, is far tougher for performers to deal with. As Sharon Mazer suggests, "it doesn't matter if . . . [wrestlers] are loved or hated, as long as they are not received with silence and indifference."[16]

In recent years the WWE's creative teams have harnessed the powerful resonance of silence. If, as Lissa McCullough suggests, "the very explosion of verbosity everywhere evident in postmodernity attests to the failure of speech truly to speak – and signals a new triumph of silence *within* speech,"[17] it is no wonder that the WWE, conscious of the troublesome limitations of aural language, have turned to silence as an alternative method of communication. So we've had silent ass-kickers like Lord Tensai and, for a time, Ryback; beasts with managers like Lesnar or Rusev; voiceless machines like the *Raw* general manager who had to be given voice by commentator Cole. Silence is particularly compelling in the contemporary WWE product where protracted verbose interchanges (particularly at the start of *Raw*) seem to be *de rigueur*. Of course this is nothing new *per se*, building on the classic silent wrestler The Undertaker, whose silence (coupled with the visuals of his "dead man" persona) brought delicious terror to a generation of wrestling fans. It is even more potent in lucha libre, where full-face masks prevent speech entirely, compelling the crowd to focus on the wrestlers' high-flying manoeuvres.

One particular angle illustrates the power of silence in modern professional wrestling. In 2010 the WWE established NXT as a training stable for future superstars. As part of this was a competition for a permanent contract with the WWE, a competition won by Wade Barrett. However, a week later Barrett led the seven losers in a takeover of *Raw*, naming the group Nexus. The somatic power of this angle was not accompanied by the conventional speech acts of pro wrestling; instead, silence was used as a powerful narrative device. The segment begins as a straightforward match (albeit the first one to define itself as a "Viewer's Choice" match, a stipulation that obviously "gives a voice" to the audience, even if that voice is orchestrated by the WWE machine) between John Cena and CM Punk. It is a particularly noisy match – Cena enters to deafening cheers, Punk uses loud hard-core punk as his entrance music. The commentators – Cole and the erstwhile Jerry "The King" Lawler – provide useful background material about the forthcoming Fatal Four-Way match and why Punk doesn't have any hair. Cena is about to deliver his signature five-knuckle shuffle when Wade Barrett enters the arena and makes his way to the ring. Gradually the other members of Nexus enter from across the arena. They immediately attack Punk and his entourage before beating up Cena. Cole and Lawler express confusion – "What is this?" "I have no idea what's going on" – challenging the usual position of the narrator as all-knowing. The group turn their attention to Cole and Lawler next, overturning the table and leaving the commentary team in a heap under the desk. At this moment, the usual acousmatic framing disappears and television audiences are left in unmediated (at least in a linguistic sense) confusion. The segment continues: the members of Nexus attack everyone at ringside and smash up the ring, before turning their attention back to Cena. The absence of commentary is obvious and disconcerting. In fact, the silence compels the television spectator to heed sounds often masked by the narration – bodies slamming on the mat, incredulous boos from the crowd, wrestlers talking. One silence makes other sounds clearer. The audience is simply left with the image of Cena carried from the ring by paramedics and, in nearly the final shot of the segment, WWE workers pulling the smashed announce table off the lifeless body of Lawler. When cameras do pan to the audience, they focus entirely on single individuals all with their hands to their mouths in silent shock.[18] The silence not only brings a distinct feeling of realism to the segment, but it also leaves the audience unanchored in a sea of violent, destructive images. Silence, so often the enemy of the wrestler, is used here as a narrative device: amid such anarchy and devastation language is also smashed to pieces. As language shatters so do the very structures of the WWE: the ring, wrestlers, commentators, normal configurations of *Raw* (where commentators tend to sum up the final action), and even the typical conventions of television as a medium are all destroyed. In this post-kayfabe, post-truth world, it becomes difficult to astonish a crowd. Such an unusual event as the Nexus invasion reveals the inherent power of silence to shock spectators so used to noise.

These three elements – the physical, the speech act and silence – exist in a performative Gordian knot in professional wrestling, intertwining, interrupting and interweaving to create a palimpsestic aural and visual experience for audience and performer alike. Butler suggests "*speaking itself is a bodily* act,"[19] that verbal articulation (or indeed non-articulation) and the body coexist in a complex amalgam of communicative potential. Nowhere in popular culture is this clearer than in the squared circle.

Notes

1 Nicholas Sammond, "Introduction: A Brief and Unnecessary Defense of Professional Wrestling," in *Steel Chair to the Head: The Pain and Pleasure of Professional Wrestling*, ed. Nicholas Sammond (Durham: Duke University Press, 2005), 7.

2 Judith Butler, *Excitable Speech* (London: Routledge, 1997), 8.

3 Ibid., 6.

4 Ibid., 16.

5 "Dusty Rhodes Talks about 'Hard Times,'" *Mid-Atlantic Wrestling*, October 29, 1985, accessed June 30, 2015, https://www.youtube.com/watch?v=9py4aMK3aIU.

6 A portmanteau of "smart" and "mark."

7 "Brock Lesnar's Apology," *RAW*, June 22, 2015, accessed June 30, 2015, https://www.youtube.com/watch?v=XnYq_kgdA_Q.

8 Royal Rumble 1992, WWE Network.

9 Justin LeBar, "Breaking Down Why Royal Rumble 1992 Was Pinnacle of Storied Event," December 27, 2013, accessed June 29, 2015, http://bleacherreport.com/articles/1902849-breaking-down-why-royal-rumble-1992-was-pinnacle-of-storied-event.

10 http://www.wwe.com/videos/the-undertaker-throws-mankind-off-the-top-of-the-hell-in-a-cell-king-of-the-ring-16346646.

11 Butler, *Excitable Speech*, 9.

12 Martin Heidegger, *Being and Time*, trans. Joan Stambaugh (New York: State University of New York Press, 1996), 154.

13 Henry Jenkins, "Never Trust a Snake: WWF Wrestling as Masculine Melodrama," in *Steel Chair to the Head*, ed. Nicholas Sammond (Durham: Duke University Press, 2005), 64.

14 Mikhail Bakhtin, *Speech Genres and Other Late Essays*, trans. Vern W. McGee, ed. Caryl Emerson and Michael Holquist (Austin: University of Texas Press, 1986), 133.

15 Ibid., 134.

16 Sharon Mazer, *Professional Wrestling: Sport and Spectacle* (Jackson: University Press of Mississippi, 1999), 24.

17 Lissa McCullough, "Silence," in *The Routledge Encyclopaedia of Postmodernism*, ed. Victor E. Taylor and Charles E. Winquist (London: Routledge, 2001), accessed June 29, 2015, http://www.academia.edu/3674817/_Silence_in_Routledge_Encyclopedia_of_Postmodernism.

18 "The Nexus's WWE Debut," *RAW*, June 7, 2010, accessed June 30, 2015, https://www.youtube.com/watch?v=vVVtqoqzgNw.

19 Butler, *Excitable Speech*, 10.

Chapter 3

Playful engagements
Wrestling with the attendant masses

Stephen Di Benedetto

While the scales of production in professional wrestling differ from events at the local gym with a couple dozen in attendance to the arena with 20,000, the basic event is designed along the same lines – a promoter gathers a handful of wrestlers, each with a gimmick, ensuring a number of good guys and bad guys, a referee, an announcer, and a script dictating the winners and losers according to serial narrative. These performers "work" the attendants to craft an entertaining evening. Professional wrestling's playful qualities are a means of engaging the senses and intervening in the fan's responses to scripted provocations and athletic acrobatics. It makes use of spectacle as a means of affecting fans who are actively attendant to the action by way of the visual stimulation of lighting, pyrotechnics, costume, and choreography; the aural stimulation of noise, music, scripted dialog, call and response, and the amplified thumps and knocks of the ring; and the touches and tastes of the shared experience of the venue and its offerings. Responses from the attendant masses, who are more than passive audiences but rather active participants, are as important as the athletics. The event sets the scene for active playful engagement for the purposes of generating visceral responses to the action in the ring and beyond as well as inviting active participation by the attendants. An examination of the performance design of a typical match reveals professional wrestling to be a form of play that exercises our desire to transgress the bounds of social etiquette.

A discussion of the deliberate design of the event to engage actively the fans in its dramaturgy necessarily relies upon the seminal explorations by Sharon Mazer on the performative nature of professional wrestling, Nicholas Sammond's essay collection on wrestling considering its historical and cultural aspects, and Henry Jenkins's exploration of the popular cultural appeal of wrestling. These researches establish the nature of wrestling as a performance rooted in historical traditions, which rely on a populist fan base that propels the action of the matches. Taken together they demonstrate the performative virtuosity of the wrestler, the dramaturgical continuity of the serial nature of wrestling plots, and the tie of wrestling performance to the history of theatre-making. By considering the designed elements of production it becomes clear the way in which these aspects of performance and the fan's experience are components that must be considered together to understand its relevance and appeal to popular culture.

Mazer demonstrates wrestling is a distinct form of representation that bridges the gap between sport and performance.[1] The lessons that the genre offers can help performance design scholars describe the ways in which shared spaces can be shaped to elicit predicable responses from those in attendance. Professional wrestling's dramaturgy is important in terms of how narrative propels action, and that action is the armature for creating a relationship between wrestlers in' the ring and the fans interacting. Wrestlers work with each other beforehand and in real time in the ring to set up the choreography according to the scenario dictated by the promoter. The fictions spun by wrestlers promote "heat" to spur on fans. Its power comes not from its veracity as athletic competition, but rather from the crowd's propensity to become enthralled and unable to determine when a "work" becomes a "shoot." This attunement between wrestler and attendant is the foundation of the playful nature of live performance.

We play to get caught up in an experience in a space outside of our everyday interactions. The cultural critic Peter Stromberg's research on play in relation to entertainment posits that our pastimes are a form of play that we treat seriously, and we can become caught up in it and forget that the stakes are not real. This is a form of suspension of disbelief, allowing us to engage with the fiction as if it is real. He explains, "When we think of entertainment, we think in the first instance of a person acting in concert with something stimulating the action or imagination so that the person is engaged, responding to something that has independent form."[2] For example, he observed adults playing *Dungeons and Dragons* who created sound effects and jumped up to swipe their swords in character. Ignoring their mundane environment, they all get caught up in the action of the imagination and respond as if they are carrying out the swordplay. Stromberg argues serious play is a form of human development that enables us to work through experiences in low-stakes situations. Professional wrestling deliberately sets out to create an environment to entice fans to get caught up in the action and respond to action despite knowing the outcome is fixed. As Roland Barthes expresses,

> The public is completely uninterested in knowing whether the contest is rigged or not, and rightly so; it abandons itself to the primary virtue of the spectacle, which is to abolish all motives and all consequences: what matters is not what it thinks but what it sees.[3]

Mazer explains that the wrestling promoter (director/producer) is acutely aware of the takes of crafting an effective performance. Advance publicity prepping the melodramatic feuds between wrestlers on the evening's card and the dramaturgy of the action in the ring is created for the attendants. If they do not get what they are promised, they let the wrestlers know in no uncertain terms:

> The action slows in the ring for a moment, becomes repetitive, static. The fans stand together and take up the chant: "Bor-ring!" In response, the wrestlers immediately accelerate: a wrestler body-slams his opponent and

then catapults from the top rope, and/or they take it out of the ring and into the front rows, and/or a couple of stars race from the locker room to mix things up in the ring. Satisfied that they've been heard, the fans settle back into their seats.[4]

Wrestling promoters create production design elements that invite participation. Laurence deGaris explains,

> The underlying structure illustrated here is that matches must be constructed in a dialogue (or maybe colloquy) between or among the wrestlers and the crowd. Thus, the crowd has a say in constructing the story. The wrestlers are never in total control of the crowd – though they are frequently the manipulators or at least the facilitators. In effect, the crowd tells the wrestlers the story it wants to hear. It is up to the wrestlers to listen and react.[5]

At one local match I was more engaged with the other attendants than the wrestlers because of the low production values and the crowd shouted jokes, made fun of their favorite, and passionately cursed them for dirty tricks to egg them on.

DeGaris's experience as a professional wrestler taught him the delicate balance between executing the moves necessary to propel the narrative of the event and the responses of those in attendance. Without the resulting swell of emotional energy from the crowd the match will not be comprehensible. The choreography is meant to communicate to the crowd: "In a good match, it is made intelligible by the performers, who include it in a consciously and carefully crafted series of signifiers. In a bad match, each movement is unintelligible."[6] Immediate intelligibility is important because convoluted action can confuse the fans and interfere with emotional responses to the moment. Barthes describes,

> The spectator is not interested in the rise and fall of fortunes; he expects the transient image of certain passions. Wrestling therefore demands an immediate reading of the juxtaposed meanings, so that there is no need to connect them. . . . wrestling is the sum of spectacles, of which no single one is a function: each moment imposes the total knowledge of a passion which rises erect and alone.[7]

Promoters understand that the scenario must be carefully planned to ensure the interest through the whole match – this is done through varying the tempo and types of events (one-on-one, tag-team matches, battle royals, etc.). Other entr'actes are introduced, such as the use of fireworks, band performances, or wrestler rants keep the action moving and pace the attendant's emotions to rise and subside before the action is built up to a climax again in the next match. A wrestler knows that

> "Working the crowd" typically means the process of manipulating the crowd to elicit certain reactions. "Working," which is deceptive, is contrasted to "shooting," which refers to either wrestling for real in the ring or telling the truth in interviews and other forums.[8]

In effect the promotion is playing with the crowd, riling them up so as to get them caught up in the action. The more successful they are at working the crowd the more likely they will return to buy more merchandise and partake in new matches. Attendants come to "mess with" the wrestlers and get "messed with" by the wrestlers.

The wrestlers' playground: mapping fan experience

Even though I had heard of *Hulkamania* growing up, professional wrestling is not a form that I ever saw as a child; it was considered déclassé. When invited to my first wrestling match in 2013 I was unsure of what or who to expect. What a shock once I got to the small community college gym in Florida to see a small-time promoter, Future of Wrestling – there were toddlers and whole families! Even after, going to *Monday Night Raw* at the enormous American Airlines Arena a year later elicited fear. Excitement grew as my friend and I approached the venue and scrambled to get in. The crowd was lively, and once we hit the voms masses of people filed past, going to the concession stand for beer or looking to buy T-shirts, signs, and other memorabilia. It was apparent entering into the arena how much time the crowd spent preparing. All across the space were handmade signs with wrestler's catchphrases on them or other messages that might be caught by the cameras. The attendants cut across class barriers and represented a large cross section of Miami. Excitement builds as we mix with the crowd and sit down; niche communities are formed section by section, row by row. An eight-year-old child next to us recounts past episodes to his mother and the guys behind shout at the wrestlers commenting on their physical prowess. All around conversations bubbled about past matches, wrestling gossip, and speculation about the outcome of the night's matches.

How are spectators activated into spect-actors? Much like the ritual call-and-response of a Christmas pantomime we quickly learn the rules of the game. Looking across at the other patrons instructs the ways in which we are meant to participate in the rituals of the event. Barthes describes this process where the "public spontaneously attunes itself to the spectacular nature of the contest."[9] The first time my wife joined me she began shouting out phrases without even knowing whom she was shouting for. We could yell out the catch phrases of The Rock, or we could paint signs and bring them to display to other fans and the cameras exclaiming "Kung Pao Bitch," a taunt The Rock levied at John

Cena one where he declared he should slap him with a piece of Kung Pao chicken. Taunts and cheers are used to indicate whether something is boring or if the heel is a really bad heel! There are individual vocal outbursts and mass choral responses. At a WWE *Smackdown* in 2015 at American Airlines Arena we sat in front a mother and her young son; the mother had quite a bit to say about the action unfolding in front of us.

Throughout the entire card she offered a blow-by-blow analysis and education for her young son, as well as some not so subtle correction of her child's enthusiasm rooting for the wrong wrestler. He offered a feeble attempt to explain why he was rooting for her enemy but his attempt could not outlast the vociferous passion of his mother. Sides are taken, and it matters not if you get caught up rooting for the heel – the other attendants will put you in your place. Sensory engagement such as images, sound, touch, taste, and smell are part of being in the moment of a live event, so as an attendant you are expected to engage in the moment-by-moment stages of each match, jumping up, shouting, and vicariously feeling the wrestlers' injuries. This pushes the crowd to get involved, and by the end of the match the boy behind me kicked and punched the chair in frustration or excitement. It is in this state that the body subverts cognitive processing and lives in the moment – thus the attendant can become part of the crowd.

Annette Hill, a cultural historian, uses ethnographic research to argue that audience byplay is a power relationship between performer and spectator. However her evidence demonstrates the shared interplay between actor and spectator within an environment. She recounts how the wrestler Dan Ahtola uses this knowledge to work his audience:

> They are responding to what we do, we are responding to what they do. If they are quiet, you have to create a situation where they need to scream or clap. It is not about doing a fancy move. That is cheap. I try to create a situation that makes them react. But if they are constantly loud that is like the perfect wave for the surfer. . . . We are totally dependent on what the audience is doing.[10]

The byplay of the crowd to the wrestler builds up the emotional intensity of the moment and encourages the spectators to get caught up. Hill goes further to explain that one fan she spoke with explained: "I felt excited. The crowd did it all, the energy and feeling." Another fan describes how a live crowd intensifies the experience and makes it a larger experience: "A body slam looks much bigger (and sounds much louder) when you see it live. A simple suplex, live, goes from a neat trick to 'how does anyone survive that?' It is so much more impressive live."[11] Our proximity to the sounds allows our attention to be captured and held and enhances our attunement to the tribulations of the wrestlers. This live quality encourages us to engage with other fans, and wrestlers know that they must keep our attention or we will become distracted and turn to watch the crowd.

Attendants are impelled through the exploitation of naturally occurring and manufactured soundscapes to get "caught up." Becoming aware of affect allows us to explore the pre-subjective, visceral forces that influence our response to performance. While the intensity of the crowd and the sounds of the bodies slamming against the mat bridge the divide between ring and arena seating, there are other tactics to bring the action into physical proximity with the crowd; attendants need an interlude to rest passively before getting caught up again. For example, at a *Monday Night Raw* Stephanie McMahon came out of the ring to pick a fight with one of the Bella twins who was ringside among the crowd. McMahon had manipulated the fight unfairly so that one Bella twin got pummeled as punishment for her sister's transgressions. Her sister stood up and confronted McMahon, triggering a fight sprawling across the audience barriers, ring floor, and audience seating. McMahon slapped her as she stood alongside fans. Later the police arrived and cuffed a screaming McMahon, dragged her out of the building along the aisles out the exit into the parking structure. After this drama ensued in front of fans, backstage episodes were broadcast back for them to watch, allowing their attention to shift to a more passive mode of spectatorship. After a respite promoters craft an entrance or new episode to build up the excitement and tension anew.

Ahtola describes the aim of the wrestler engaging with the audience, "Every wrestler knows you should be careful with the audience, you don't want to end up with someone getting hurt or scared, but we do want them to feel alive."[12] Hill recounts how this is played out in performance:

> At one event (December 2012), two guys queued outside the venue so that they could get front row seats to their first match. Even as newcomers they expected fights spilling over from the ring. Right on cue, two professional wrestlers jumped from the ropes into the crowd; one wrestler actually sat on the guy's knee. The look on both of their faces was pure amazement. Even knowing this might happen, the power of the moment captured them completely. They explained the feeling – "you are getting drawn into it."[13]

For a playful crowd, being part of a mass of people adds to the excitement generated by the wrestlers' fantastic feats. Diehard fans recommend that if you want to attend an event, "Never go alone; always bring at least one friend who loves wrestling. The crowd energy is good, but the experience is 2–3 times better when shared."[14] Participation and camaraderie is central to getting the most out of the experience.

Actuating fan response

Scenographic elements are the armature for the wrestlers' improvisation. Staging, costuming, lighting, sound, and projection help create a tempo for the attendant's experience of the evening providing cues to engage or distract fans and set up the scenarios. For example, the setting accentuates focus upon the physical action within the ring; it is lit well and the spectator's gaze can be drawn quickly to the action by dimming the periphery. The surrounding seating is lit in various colors according to the mood or in tune with the colors of the wrestlers' various gimmicks. Mats are changed to show different logos and to set up for other types of acts, or to build alternative stages for concerts or specialty matches. The ring for the WWE matches has a stage and backdrop with a narrow ramp leading to the entrance of the squared ring with announcers situated at the opposite end. This gives the wrestlers several playing spaces to work from, and the production designers several surfaces to project upon. In addition, the Jumbotron is employed up above to provide close-ups of the action to the gallery seats, and to show off-stage action and commercials.

The projection backdrop is used when wrestlers make their entrance. Theme images related to their gimmick are projected with other animations. For example when the wrestler Rusev and his manager Lana make their entrance, Russian flags are shown flapping in the wind and washes of red and white bathe the screen. Another wrestler may have a pyrotechnic display explode from the front of the stage with an accompanying image behind; immediately upon hearing the explosions followed by the theme song, our focus immediately shifts to the entrance ramp and our pulse quickens to ready us for the coming confrontation. Our interest between matches may have waned and the scenographic elements work to refocus our attention. The stage is elevated at the same height as the ring, so it can also be used as a second stage where wrestlers can spar verbally with a wrestler in the ring. A heel may make a partial entrance to shout threats from the stage as the face in the ring defends his honor, or if a fight gets particularly bad a wrestler could flee to this location, separating him from the central combat zone of the ring. Where in the space the wrestler occupies helps convey narrative and can endow power or reinforce weakness depending on the blocking.

The WWE ring is twenty feet by twenty feet, purportedly the largest of all promotions, and serves as a focal point for the attendant's gaze. Evolved from boxing rings, wrestling rings have turnbuckles that are attached to padded steel posts. A mat of thin foam covers a three-quarter-inch to one-inch plywood floor with tension springs and steel beams, and skeletal sheet metal holding it up. The ropes surrounding the ring are strengthened with wire on the inside and an outer coating of foam. The ring/mat is elevated four feet above the ground, making it possible to mask props or performers from underneath. Hard foam mats run along the outside of the ring for when wrestlers are thrown out of the ring or for the action that takes place outside of the ring. Separating the attendants from the wrestlers are foam-covered ring barricades. Sounds are a key factor within the production design. While there are sounds associated with the videos, music, and dialog, the ring itself is designed to amplify the sounds of the wrestlers' bodies hitting the mats. The ring's structure and materials amplify sound to maximize the effects of impacts for attendants; we can hear the thuds on the mat and the metallic clang of a wrestler hitting the metal stairs into the ring. The illusion of violence is accentuated by the corresponding sounds. When present in the space it is these bangs that draw attention away from the physical gestures to the impact of the violent moves upon the body.

Costuming is eclectic since the wrestlers each have individual gimmicks (a wrestler's personality, behavior, attire, and/or other distinguishing traits while performing). Costume design supports character development. The tag team known as the Wyatt family (Erick Rowan, Bray Wyatt, and Luke Harper) is known for its gimmicks related to backwoods cults. Rowan, reminiscent of a moonshiner, is a bald man with long combed beard (à la Duck Dynasty) and wears a sleeveless mechanics outfit, while Wyatt sits on a carved wooden rocker sporting another beard, a fedora, and a short-sleeve, button-up, tropical shirt over a T-shirt; Harper wears a sheep mask. When they enter the stadium they move through a darkened arena carrying a lantern to light their way. Almost instantly as their theme music comes on fans light up their cell phones and wave them above their heads. While gimmicks on the local circuits are developed and costumed by the individual wrestlers, promoters or national promotions also devise gimmicks. Individual gimmicks become iconic and fans have established participatory responses to the entrances of the wrestlers as well as standard verbal responses to the rants delivered by the wrestlers during entr'actes.

The committed involvement of the attendants and their knowledge of how props create effect can be seen in a recent wrestling forum debate about the merits of mass participation and the effect a gimmick might have. Discussion began with the image of a whole stadium putting on sheep masks: Truk83 asks,

> I know this sounds random, but how about the WWE sell lanterns like the one Bray Wyatt brings to the ring. All the fans holding their own lantern would be somewhat interesting to see live on television. It would bring a new feeling to his entrance. What do you all think?[15]

Respondents enthusiastically responded, "That would be pretty sweet and hilarious, imagine, the whole arena goes dark . . . majority of the crowd holding up lanterns."[16] Props and lighting are critiqued as much as the moves and dialog. Fans are immersed in the shared atmosphere and aware of the effect of a promoter's choices upon their experience. These fans are attendant to the scenographic structure that shapes their interaction with the live performers and the others in the arena cheering them on. Theatrical design elements are as much of the performance as the wrestler's provocations.

Wrestling with the attendant masses

Wrestling offers an adult form of play where the rules are clear and those that transgress the rules are punished. Those offended stand up for themselves and good triumphs over evil. Peter Gray, a play psychologist, describes the importance role-play serves in social development. This kind of unstructured, freely chosen play is a testing ground that provides critical life experiences without which young children cannot develop into confident and competent adults.[17] Play is a serious endeavor that has psychological benefits allowing individuals to learn how to negotiate their physical and social environments and to gain sense of mastery over the world. Seen in this light wrestling becomes a simulacrum of the repressed desired to gain mastery over the forces in life that conspire to depose us from our sense of mastery over the whims of life. Those who do not have the opportunity to control their own action and to follow through on their own decisions to solve their own problems according to the rules in the course of play grow to feel that they are not in control of their own fate. Wrestling plays with attendants, helping them become a part of the drama between good and evil and allows them to participate and have an effect upon the action that unfolds in front of them. When the action feels monotonous, attendants can shout and compel the wrestlers to liven it up. When new stimulation is needed another battle is fought, another victim (face) stands up to a bully (heel). When bullies win it is the drama of waiting to see the bully pay that draws attendants. It is a shared space where it is safe to scream at the top of your lungs for your foe to be beaten into submission.

Social play is a natural means of making friends and learning to treat others fairly. Play is voluntary. Play theorists believe that "learning to get along and cooperate with others as equals may be the most crucial evolutionary function of human social play."[18] Choosing to attend a performance event and choosing to take up the participatory invitations offered in the space of the performance creates a playful interchange between performer and attendant. By sharing in the experiences of a match the crowd enters a social contract acknowledging their part in the surrounding community.

From a sporting perspective Norbert Elias and Eric Dunning trace the "civilizing process" of modern cultural history and the place of sports in society.[19] They see repression and sublimation as key factors in normative cultural exchange. Contemporary societies view getting carried away by emotional outbursts as a weakness to be avoided, and as a result we have repressed these emotions to function well in conjunction with others. In Henry Jenkins's estimation, it is not only an intensity of feeling that is cast in the pejorative but also our discomfort of its spectacular display. Sports developed as a means of releasing suppressed emotions in a socially sanctioned public forum. Jenkins argues, "the real-world consequences of physical combat (in short, sport's status as adult play) facilitate a controlled and sanctioned release from ordinary affective restraints."[20] This echoes Stromberg's postulation that we play to get caught up and to get caught up with the crowd frees us from the constraints of our own repressed exuberance, offering a controlled release of our repressed responses to the stresses of civil interaction.

The experience of play is linked to forms of entertainment and the structure of spectacular events affect attendant response in predictable ways. If play is a form of human development used to train us without risk of death, then creating playful events has the potential to be used to shape human behavior and to create shared values. A professional wrestling maneuver actuates perceptual mechanisms; a body slam has the effect of causing wonder; and shock at the violence in turn allows us to interpret the experience and perhaps allows us to think about the nature of violence and revenge. Ultimately constructing events that encourage meaningful interaction between attendants and performers is an act of drawing focus to human beings in action in a space that allows the playful crowd to get caught up. This shaping of the environment for shared experience is a visceral social process that satisfies some social-psychological need within us and is a vital function of how humans learn to interact and respond to others as constrained by the rules of society.

Notes

1 Sharon Mazer, *Professional Wrestling Sport and Spectacle* (Jackson: University Press of Mississippi, 1998).
2 Peter G. Stromberg, *Caught in Play: How Entertainment Works on You* (Stanford: Stanford University Press, 2009), 7.
3 Roland Barthes, "The World of Wrestling," in *Mythologies* (New York: Hill and Wang, 1972), 15.
4 Mazer, "'Real Wrestling'/'Real' Life," in *Steel Chair to the Head: The Pleasure and Pain of Professional Wrestling*, ed. Nicholas Sammond (Durham: Duke University Press, 2005), 72.
5 Laurence deGaris, "The Logic of Professional Wrestling," in *Steel Chair to the Head: The Pleasure and Pain of Professional Wrestling*, ed. Nicholas Sammond (Durham: Duke University Press, 2005), 206.
6 Ibid.
7 Barthes, "The World of Wrestling," 16.
8 DeGaris, "The Logic of Professional Wrestling," 206.
9 Barthes, "The World of Wrestling."
10 Annette Hill, "The Spectacle of Excess: The Passion Work of Professional Wrestlers, Fans and Anti-Fans," *European Journal of Cultural Studies* 18, no. 2 (2014): 186.
11 Arkady English, comment on "What Is It Like to See Professional Wrestling Live?," *Quora*, August 1, 2013, http://www.quora.com/What-is-it-like-to-see-professional-wrestling-live.
12 Hill, "The Spectacle of Excess."
13 Ibid.
14 Anonymous, comment on "What Is It Like to See Professional Wrestling Live?," *Quora*, November 10, 2013, http://www.quora.com/What-is-it-like-to-see-professional-wrestling-live.
15 Truk83, comment on "How about Wyatt Lanterns?," *Wrestling Forum*, July 18, 2013, http://www.wrestlingforum.com/general---wwe/885409---how---about---wyatt---lanterns.html.
16 Zombie Princess, comment on "How about Wyatt Lanterns?," *Wrestling Forum*, July 18, 2013, http://www.wrestlingforum.com/general---wwe/885409---how---about---wyatt---lanterns.html.
17 Peter Gray, "The Decline of Play and the Rise of Psychopathology in Children and Adolescents," *American Journal of Play* 3, no. 4 (Spring 2011), http://www.journalofplay.org/sites/www.journalofplay.org/files/pdf-articles/3-4-article-gray-decline-of-play.pdf.
18 Esther Entin, "All Work and No Play: Why Your Kids Are More Anxious, Depressed," *Atlantic*, October 12, 2011, http://www.theatlantic.com/health/archive/2011/10/all-work-and-no-play-why-your-kids-are-more-anxious-depressed/246422.
19 Norbert Elias and Eric Dunning, *Quest for Excitement: Sport and Leisure in the Civilizing Process* (Oxford: Basil Blackwell, 1986).
20 Henry Jenkins, *The Wow Climax: Tracing the Emotional Impact of Popular Culture* (New York: New York University Press, 2007).

Part II

Circulation

Chapter 4

Stadium-sized theatre

WWE and the world of professional wrestling

Eero Laine

The business of professional wrestling is the business of theatre. Even if on the surface professional wrestling seems anathema to theatrical sensibilities, it is hard to deny the formal similarities. After all, professional wrestling is scripted entertainment performed live in front of an audience by actors portraying characters. Indeed, professional wrestling bears many similarities to other theatrical forms such as vaudeville, melodrama, *commedia dell'arte*, and musical theatre (characters break into fights, not songs). Setting aside the specific content of professional wrestling, however, it is also possible to examine the economic and institutional formations that it shares with more distinguished forms of live performance. In this sense, professional wrestling is an exemplary case study for the ways that theatrical performance is produced, consumed, and circulated widely, even globally. Specifically, WWE can be considered a model, yet surprisingly under-examined, example of a publicly traded, transnational theatre company.

Of course, professional wrestling, and WWE in particular, is more than just a live event. Performances are frequently broadcast, recorded, and otherwise distributed through various media. Treating professional wrestling as theatre does not dismiss these methods of circulation, but rather treats them as appendages to the necessarily live performance event at the core of professional wrestling. Following this tack, this chapter situates professional wrestling as a form of commercial theatre. The chapter begins with a recent example of a storyline that brought corporate interests, fan advocacy, and the connections between fiction and finance into sharp relief. A brief historical overview follows that traces early connections between the wrestling business and show business. Finally, WWE is considered within the constellation of contemporary, commercial, globalizing theatrical entertainments, opening questions regarding the relationship between theatrical entertainment and the media that transmits it.

Corporate plots and active audiences

Daniel Bryan wasn't supposed to be the champion. From the summer of 2013 to the late spring of 2014, the bearded, nice-guy underdog battled in and out of the ring for the chance to be the WWE World Heavyweight Champion. Multiple times a week, in stadiums across the United States and around the world, Bryan would make his way to the ring as a hard rock version of Wagner's "Ride of the Valkyries" blared and thousands of spectators pointed their index fingers in the air and chanted "Yes! Yes! Yes!" And in each performance, Bryan would wrestle valiantly, overcome the odds, and conquer the challenges laid before him with a fast-paced and acrobatic style. More often than not, however, Bryan's hard work was left unrecognized and debased by "The Authority," the wife and husband team of Stephanie McMahon and Triple H, real-life WWE executives who also play more sinister versions of themselves in WWE's sprawling wrestling narratives.

Following the storyline, Bryan was regularly denied opportunities to be champion by The Authority because they considered him only a "B+ player," unsuitable to be the "face of the company." The Authority regularly intervened in matches and set unusual stipulations that prevented Bryan from winning (or retaining) the championship belt. The Authority repeatedly stated that they were concerned that Bryan's unkempt looks would not sell tickets globally and that he didn't project a properly corporate image for the company.

The storyline clipped along for most of the summer, and for many it seemed as if things were turning in Bryan's favor. However, at the end of the summer of 2013, according to sports writer Jonathan Snowden, who interviewed many at WWE:

> Bryan ran into an even fiercer opponent – the stock market. The preliminary numbers for SummerSlam were in – and they weren't pretty. "They didn't buy the attraction," Vince McMahon told WWE investors during a conference call. "And these PPVs are attraction based ... SummerSlam was not the right attraction. That was a swing and a miss." ... Economics, combined with the early return of [leading wrestler John] Cena from a tricep tear, spelled the end of Bryan's run as the top good guy.[1]

In a confluence of reality and fiction that is both exceptional and commonplace in professional wrestling, investors seemed to take the side of The Authority against Daniel Bryan and his many fans. The storyline of the lovable but scruffy wrestler who is derided by management came full circle. However, many fans were extremely unhappy with what they saw as the decision to bury Bryan.

Bryan's very vocal supporters organized themselves as what they called the Yes Movement, referring to the chant that Bryan led as he entered the ring. At various events throughout the winter, the Yes Movement cheered Bryan along, while booing and jeering not only The Authority, but other wrestlers who were promoted over Bryan. This was especially evident at the annual Royal Rumble, where wrestler Batista surprisingly won after a hiatus from the company spent shooting movies. The crowd raucously disapproved, booing Batista and chanting for Bryan. This negative reaction to WWE's booking decisions was compounded by the fact that another fan favorite, wrestler CM Punk, walked out the following day.

Shortly thereafter, fans began "hijacking" live events by booing and chanting disruptively wherever the weekly *Monday Night Raw* performed. WWE could not silence an entire stadium of chanting spectators, and these outspoken and organized fans found themselves in a position to shape the wrestling narratives. The fan movement came to a head in CM Punk's hometown of Chicago, a city with a notoriously loud wrestling crowd. #HijackRaw trended on Twitter as the event approached. Fans who would be in attendance shared proposals for various protest actions to be performed in the stadium, from standing and turning their backs on The Authority to starting distracting and off-topic chants to agreed-upon responses when certain predictable things would take place during the show. Before the event, *Bleacher Report*'s Joe Johnson suggested, "Now, WWE is about to walk into a buzzsaw in the Windy City. Chicago is going to do its worst to destroy the flow of the program mere weeks before WrestleMania."[2] However, WWE was prepared for the many possible disruptions. WWE acknowledged #HijackRaw during the live show and managed to turn the audience's energy around to both support Bryan and to boo and jeer The Authority even more than they had before the show.

In the commercial theatre of professional wrestling, negative fan reactions are all part of the show. Stephanie McMahon states: "What we do is a form of method acting. We try to make the situations as real as possible" and suggested that some even thought they were actually going too far (as in beyond the storyline) in intentionally trying to bury Bryan.[3] If WWE had not gone as far as they had, however, the storyline likely would not have angered as many fans and thus the reactions would have been muted. In the end, the fans felt victorious and WWE sold more tickets – after nearly a year of performances, of shareholder selling, and live audiences protesting, Daniel Bryan won the championship at the annual WrestleMania event in March.

This particular example highlights the ways that professional wrestling – where storylines are told over the course of weeks, months, and even years – is reliant on the live event, the actions of spectators, and the intricate connections between theatrical entertainment and finance. It is easy, perhaps, to dismiss WWE as mere spectacle or, worse, as simply televised entertainment. As Daniel Bryan's championship run illustrates, however, WWE is uniquely positioned in terms of theatrical entertainment. It is at once global, performing for a distributed audience of fans and investors and, at the same time, intensely local, grounded in particular places of performance.

Wrestling business/show business

While pro wrestling emerged from carnivals and athletic troupes of the late 1800s, it became more theatrical (including performances on literal stages) as theatre in Europe and especially the United States was becoming more "artistic," less populist, and ostensibly moving away from commercial interests.[4] Journalist Marcus Griffin describes professional wrestling in his 1937 book *Fall*

Guys: The Barnums of Bounce as "probably the greatest entertainment spectacle today, containing acrobatics, comedy, buffoonery, pantomime, tragedy, interlude, curtain, and afterpiece."[5] Griffin's is the earliest book-length study of the theatricality of professional wrestling, and it directly links theatre and pro wrestling through overlapping aspects of production and the work of the performers:

> There are all the elements of theatre including the producer, publicity man, advance agent, stage manager, and prompter. Like Shakespeare's famed line, wrestlers "suit the action to the word and the word to the action," and thus create in their bouts what is known as heat, or as Pope expressed it, "they awaken the soul by tender strokes of art."[6]

While Griffin perhaps stretches some of his more literary connections too far, his book otherwise includes dramaturgical-like analyses of the various ways matches begin, proceed, and finish; information regarding how wrestling promoters and wrestlers tour and stage their shows; journalistic accounts of individuals working behind the scenes; and other presumed secrets of the trade.

Today, fans and wrestling scholars discuss whether the book had an impact on the industry at the time. Some question whether the book was not actually an expose but perhaps a way of drumming up business for wrestling promoter Toots Mondt. Favorably mentioned throughout the book, Mondt was known for promoting bouts full of flashy gimmicks and sideshow antics. Whether it was a piece of promotional literature for a highly theatrical style of wrestling or not, it is unlikely that the premise of the study – that pro wrestling is more show business than competitive sport – was so scandalously surprising to many at the time.

Indeed, as early as 1930, the *New York Times* reported that pro wrestling had "passed into the status of theatrical classification."[7] The headline read: "Wrestling Placed Under New Status: Commission Rules Clubs Must List Matches as Shows or Exhibitions."[8] It would not be the last time the wrestling industry was "exposed" for its overt theatricality, and it certainly did not greatly alter the way the events were promoted. Just one year after the reclassification, the same athletic commission official (former wrestler William Muldoon) who changed the status of professional wrestling objected to a proposed wrestling event that was to be held in a less than sportive location. His statement for the *New York Times*:

> It would be just as ridiculous for New Yorkers to stage a wrestling match at the Metropolitan Opera or to present an opera in Madison Square Garden as for the Westchester County Centre to be desecrated by a bout of professional wrestling.[9]

It seems, however, that the lack of clarity from organizing bodies did not hurt professional wrestling as a source of entertainment.

David Shoemaker submits that the differences between legitimate sport and theatre "mattered far less in those days than it may today."[10] Shoemaker cites a fan from 1931:

> As far as I know the shows are honest. But even if they're not I get a big kick out of them, for they are full of action and all the outward signs of hostile competition. It is either honest competition or fine acting and in either case I get a real show.[11]

Shoemaker suggests that fans have been in on the ruse for well over a century, which is to say it was never really much of a ruse. A reprinted article in an issue of the *Literary Digest* from 1932 supports such a reading offering the notion that "maybe the chief reason wrestling is popular is that it is not wrestling."[12] By the middle of the twentieth century, professional wrestling had spread to many countries throughout Europe and would also gain especially strong followings in Japan and Mexico. Today, the business connections between theatre and wrestling described by Griffin in the 1930s – the producers, publicity people, and advance agents – are wrapped up in a finely polished, corporate package by WWE, which is based in the United States but frequently holds events throughout the world.

WWE and the commercial stage

As Daniel Bryan's championship run illustrates, unlike other forms of performance and theatre, commercial theatre not only performs for audiences in the theatre, but also for shareholders, economists, and business analysts. The staged production is a product of the market and extension of the corporation while influencing share price and consumer perception of the brand. WWE churns out live performances on a daily basis with a surprisingly traditional theatrical business model. Few things have changed since Sharon Mazer's 1990 article in *TDR*, "The Doggie Doggie World of Professional Wrestling," where she described the perhaps surprising numbers of spectators at live wrestling events, the impressive revenues, and merchandising schemes where "every move in the arena encourages the spectators to purchase products."[13] The basic business practices of professional wrestling (and WWE in particular) have remained the same, even if they have become more sophisticated and expanded significantly (today, WWE has a market capitalization of over $1 billion and its stock price has traded in a range from $7 to over $30[14]). WWE has managed to leverage live, theatrical events into profits in ways that are frequently emulated by both large corporations and arts organizations.

WWE maintains four distinct areas (Media Division, Live Events Segment, Consumer Products Division, and WWE Studios Segment). WWE also makes clear that its performers are at the center of its business model: "Our creative team develops compelling and complex characters and weaves them into dynamic storylines that combine physical and emotional elements. The success of the WWE is due primarily to the continuing popularity of our Superstars and Divas."[15] WWE operates offices around the world and continues to partner with other companies in order to brand and distribute its content globally.[16] Such a business model places WWE in the company of a number of other major corporations focused on theatrical production.

While many corporations profit from live theatrical events, it is notable that WWE is the only publicly traded company that is primarily oriented toward a live, theatrical event. Looking at other publicly traded corporations that produce live entertainment, WWE's closest comparison might be Live Nation Entertainment, the corporation that emerged as a result of a merger between Live Nation, Inc. and Ticketmaster in 2010.[17] While Live Nation Entertainment "operates as a live entertainment company," it does not create its own content, nor is that content theatrical or narrative.[18] Rather, Live Nation Entertainment is what might most simply be called a producing company, which focuses on "Concerts, Ticketing, Artist Nation, and Sponsorship & Advertising segments."[19] The "Artist Nation" is a constructed community offering "management and other services to music artists; and sells merchandise associated with musical artists at live performances to retailers and directly to consumers through the Internet."[20] The model for selling and marketing merchandise and touring events is likely similar to WWE, but again, the content is provided by others.

Of course, Disney has made arrangements to license its characters for *Disney on Ice* and *Disney Live* to Feld Entertainment for some time.[21] And since the debut of *Beauty and the Beast*, Disney and other media companies have also embraced theatrical live entertainment.[22] Such moves prompted the *New York Times* to rather naively pose the question: "has theater become just a derivative cog in brand machinery?"[23] Well, perhaps. Studio executives express surprise at just how much revenue can be generated on in live performances "charging 10 times more per ticket than movie theaters do."[24] While it might be easier to consider Disney and DreamWorks as in the business of theatre in that the live events they produce are performed in theatrical venues rather than stadiums, financially and organizationally there are few differences between them and WWE as they all actively pursue live, theatrical entertainment.

However, it might be suggested that offerings such as the musical version of *The Lion King* and *Shrek the Musical* are just further incarnations of the intellectual property of the corporation. That is, Disney is not primarily a theatre company or strictly a live entertainment company. Disney is a media and lifestyle company that has found theatre to be frequently profitable – even if Disney loses money on a particular theatrical production, the net benefit is greater brand awareness and possibly even a tax write-off for the lost revenue. Even if this is a model that WWE might aspire to, it is difficult to shake the importance of the live event for WWE. Disney could hypothetically shutter its theatrical division tomorrow and remain in business. However, WWE still needs the stadiums and the fans and the chants and jeers – even if WWE's content does not conform to what we might think of as theatre, WWE needs theatre in order to exist, whether it acknowledges it or not.

Conclusion: wrestling with legitimate theatre

Professional wrestling has always had a legitimacy issue. Mazer suggests that "Although pro wrestling is not accepted as a legitimate sport, nor can it be considered legitimate theatre, it intersects, exploits, and, finally parodies both forms of entertainment."[25] David Savran quips that the legitimate theatre is "One of the most loaded metaphors in the theatrical vocabulary, it is constructed in opposition to an imprecisely defined antagonist that would never dare self-identify as 'illegitimate.'"[26] However, if there is such an antagonist, it might be professional wrestling. For most of the past century, wrestlers and wrestling promoters vehemently disavowed the theatricality of pro wrestling while antagonizing those who might endeavor to analyze the form as anything other than legitimate sport. Professional wrestling knows too much about the wrong things (physical violence) and not enough about the right things (say, acting) to be considered legitimate theatre or even the sort of popular entertainment embraced as somehow avant-garde.

But even if professional wrestling is at times proudly illegitimate, its business model is highly theatrical. WWE's first annual shareholder report:

> Live events are the cornerstone of our business and provide the content for our television and pay-per-view programming. Each event is a highly theatrical production, which involves a significant degree of audience participation and employs various special effects, including lighting, pyrotechnics, powerful entrance music, and a variety of props.[27]

Professional wrestling might greatly benefit from various forms of mediatization, but it should be noted that if one were to replace "television and pay-per-view" with *Live in HD* and eliminate the section on audience participation, one might have a pretty good description of the Metropolitan Opera's artistic practice. That is, WWE and the Metropolitan Opera's distribution models are strikingly similar in function, but very different in the ways they are considered. Both attempt to distribute a live, theatrical product beyond the place of performance, but one is classified as media and the other is art.

Given the popularity of the Met's *Live in HD*, it seems that the live event may actually be more important to wrestling than to opera: just a few years after the noted popularity of the live HD performances, Artistic Director Peter Gelb has suggested that the success of the mediatized performances have cut into ticket revenue for live performances.[28] In 2011, the *New York Times* noted that "For the first time in seven years, the Met had balanced its budget, thanks partly to $11 million in profits last year from its HD movie theater transmissions, which had been operating for only five years."[29] While the idea of eliminating the live audience and turning the Met into a film and media company that produces classic works from a soundstage might sound perverse, it is perhaps more imaginable than WWE not performing for live crowds, who are integral to shaping narratives, actively responding to narrative twists and turns, and even choosing champions. That is to say, in light of the *Live at the Met* broadcasts, Lincoln Center itself might be recast as a media event broadcast with a live studio audience – a framing many are willing to take with WWE but that appears counterintuitive with more distinguished or legitimate cultural forms such as opera.

Professional wrestling is decidedly and proudly "lowbrow." It has been studied as a curiosity, a sideshow, and as a crude mirror to society – all of which it certainly is. However, when considered as theatre, it presents the possibility of a globalizing theatrical entertainment, which is at the same time an example of highly profitable commercial theatre. Professional wrestling easily fulfills many established definitions of theatre not only through its performance events, but also through its very business model, which privileges the live event. Yet professional wrestling is frequently not cited as theatre. As professional wrestling foregrounds issues that are central to theatre research, it should not be too bold to claim that professional wrestling belongs in theatre studies. Without the stadiums, the live performances, the outsized characters, and other theatrical content and structures, professional wrestling would lack that which has made it a popular performance form for over a century. Professional wrestling maps a global exchange of performers, styles, and verbal and physical vocabularies. It also offers a way of examining the intersections of theatre and capital through a contemporary case of a publicly traded theatre company that is finding ways to produce and circulate live performance on a global scale.

Notes

1 Jonathan Snowden, "Inside WWE: An Exclusive Look at How a Pro Wrestling Story Comes to Life," Longform, *Bleacher Report*, January 21, 2015, accessed January 21, 2015, http://bleacherreport.com/articles/2283701-inside-wwe-an-exclusive-look-at-how-a-pro-wrestling-story-comes-to-life.

2 Joe Johnson, "WWE Will Face Most Hostile Audience Yet in Chicago on Monday Night RAW," WWE, *Bleacher Report*, February 27, 2014, accessed November 10, 2015, http://bleacherreport.com/articles/1976031-wwe-will-face-most-hostile-audience-yet-in-chicago-on-monday-night-raw.

3 Ibid.

4 See Lawrence W. Levine, *Highbrow/Lowbrow: The Emergence of Cultural Hierarchy in America* (Cambridge, MA: Harvard University Press, 1988); and David Savran, *Highbrow/Lowdown: Theatre, Jazz, and the Making of the New Middle Class* (Ann Arbor: University of Michigan Press, 2010).

5 Marcus Griffin, *Fall Guys: The Barnums of Bounce: The Inside Story of the Wrestling Business, America's Most Profitable and Best Organized Sport* (Chicago: Reilly Lee, 1937), 15.

6   Ibid.
7   "Wrestling Placed under New Status," *New York Times*, April 9, 1930, accessed May 15, 2015, http://query.nytimes.com/mem/archive/pdf?res=9902E5DE1F39E03ABC4153 DFB266838B629EDE.
8   Ibid.
9   "Muldoon Denounces Bouts in Civic Centre," *New York Times*, May 15, 1931, accessed May 15, 2015, http://query.nytimes.com/mem/archive/pdf?res=9C06EED71F38E03A BC4D52DFB366838A629EDE.
10 David Shoemaker, *The Squared Circle: Life, Death, and Professional Wrestling* (New York: Gotham Books, 2013), 23.
11 Ibid.
12 Joe Williams, "The Hippo Hippodrome," *Judge*, reprinted in *Literary Digest*, February 6 (1932): 41.
13 Sharon Mazer, "The Doggie Doggie World of Professional Wrestling," *TDR: The Drama Review* 34, no. 4 (1990): 102.
14 "World Wrestling Entertainment, Inc. (WWE)," Yahoo! Finance, accessed June 26, 2015, http://finance.yahoo.com/q?s=WWE.
15 WWE, "Corporate Overview," WWE.com, accessed November 2, 2015, http://corpo rate.wwe.com/company/overview.
16 Ibid.
17 "Who We Are," Ticketmaster, accessed December 10, 2014, http://www.ticketmaster. com/about/about-us.html.
18 "Live Nation Entertainment, Inc.," Yahoo! Finance, accessed December 10, 2014, http:// finance.yahoo.com/q/pr?s=LYV.
19 Ibid.
20 Ibid.
21 "History," Feld Entertainment, accessed March 21, 2014, https://www.feldentertain ment.com/History/.
22 It is notable that Disney continues to license its intellectual property for the less prestigious popular entertainments that are staged in stadiums, while the Broadway productions are housed under Disney Theatricals, a direct subsidiary of Disney.
23 Patrick Healy, "Like the Movie, Only Different: Hollywood's Big Bet on Hollywood Adaptations," Movies, *New York Times*, August 1, 2013, accessed June 2, 2015, http:// www.nytimes.com/2013/08/04/movies/hollywoods-big-bet-on-broadway-adapta tions.html.
24 Ibid.
25 Mazer, "The Doggie Doggie World of Professional Wrestling," 98.
26 David Savran, "The Curse of Legitimacy," in *Against Theatre: Creative Destructions on the Modernist Stage*, ed. Alan Ackerman and Martin Puchner (New York: Palgrave Macmillan, 2006), 190.
27 "Annual Report," Form 10-k, World Wrestling Federation Entertainment, Inc., *Edgar Online*, April 30, 2000, accessed October 22, 2014, http://yahoo.brand.edgar-online. com/displayfilinginfo.aspx?FilingID=1361985–1136–235098&type=sect&TabIndex= 2&companyid=7520&ppu=%252fdefault.aspx%253fcik%253d1091907.
28 James Steichen, "Are HD Performances 'Cannibalizing' the Metropolitan Opera's Live Audience?" *OUPBlog*, August 13, 2013, accessed April 3, 2014, http://blog.oup. com/2013/08/hd-broadcast-cannibalization-met-operas-live-audience/.
29 Daniel J. Wakin and Kevin Flynn, "A Metropolitan Opera High Note, as Donations Hit $182 Million," *New York Times*, October 10, 2011, accessed April 3, 2014, http://www. nytimes.com/2011/10/11/arts/music/metropolitan-operas-donations-hit-a-record-182-million.html.

Chapter 5

Wrestling's not real, it's hyperreal

Professional wrestling video games

Nicholas Ware

For many fans of professional wrestling, an oft-heard reply to revealing one's fandom is "Wrestling? You like that? You know that's fake, right?" The wrestling fan's sly reply might be something akin to, "*Hamlet*? You like that? You know that play's fake, right?" The "reality" of wrestling is both a non–issue for fans and a necessary suspension of disbelief for the drama of the genre. Pro wrestling shows are shows about sport, just as *Star Trek* is a show about the future or *Sesame Street* is a show about puppets. In the late 1990s, World Wrestling Entertainment (WWE), the world's most successful and visible professional wrestling company, began using the term "sports entertainment" to refer to its product. "Sports entertainment" acknowledges pro wrestling as sport-themed drama, not sport itself. WWE – which runs hundreds of live events in dozens of counties, produces half a dozen hours of cable television per week, sells merchandise based on their characters and brands, and maintains a streaming media service for its monthly special events and extensive back catalog of shows – had revenue of $542.6 million in 2014.[1] That figure is in real, not fake, dollars. As Oliver Lee Batman puts it, "[Pro wrestling] is first and foremost a performance. [. . .] And second, [. . .] wrestling is big business."[2]

However, the interplay of reality and fiction is at the heart of professional wrestling's narrative. The real/fake binary is important historically, and pro wrestling narratives take advantage of the questions of what is scripted and what is not scripted (what is "work" and what is "shoot"). Owing partially to the public obsession with its "fakeness," professional wrestling has mixed actual events with fictitious storylines to cater to the knowledgeable fan base and still deliver the unexpected storyline twists that fan base craves. While not all fans obsess over the "reality" of professional wrestling – whose contract is up, which wrestlers are off-screen couples, who had a DUI and might be punished by being de-emphasized on the show – the fan base that does is referred to by *Grantland* writer David Shoemaker as "meta-fans."[3] Meta-fans are not just fans of the diegetic drama of professional wrestling but fans of the business itself, and follow the meta-narrative of business deals, backstage politics, and real-world relationships that inevitably influence the pro wrestling product as presented on television. Sharon Mazer proffers that "professional wrestling is at once like life and like a lot of other things [...]: real and fake, spontaneous and rehearsed, genuinely felt and staged for effect."[4] The meta-fan seeks to enjoy both sides of each of these binaries and enjoys the construction of pro wrestling as much as constructed pro wrestling.

This dual consciousness within the fandom is what makes WWE video games a highly fascinating object of study. While the history of WWE video games – and wrestling games in general – is varied, the premiere product is the *WWE2K* series, published by 2K Sports after the previous publishers, THQ, went bankrupt. This series is published annually for the major home consoles – now the PlayStation 4 and Xbox One, as well as their predecessors – and at the heart of the game's appeal is the ability for multiple players to control wrestlers from both the past and present of WWE in simulated matches. Concepts of diegetic drama, nondiegetic professional positions, and the generic conventions of sports and fighting video games influence how these matches are played within the game. *WWE2K* represents a version of WWE that is hyperreal, a "model of a real without origin or reality."[5]

French philosopher Jean Baudrillard clarifies the idea of "hyperreal" as "sheltered from the imaginary, and from any distinction between the real and the imaginary, leaving room only for the orbital recurrence of models and for the simulated generation of differences."[6] WWE video games fit this description fully as they, through gameplay, make real the fake competition of the WWE's fictional universe, fully complicating and flattening the binary upon which professional wrestling builds stories and does business. When two players sit down for a game of *WWE2K16*, they do not simulate the reality of professional wrestlers' work. They do not meet with an agent to get the planned storyline and outcome and then discuss with each other any sequences of moves they may want to perform later during the match. In live professional wrestling, opponents are in actuality partners in a combination of stunt work, stage combat, and acrobatics. However, in WWE video games, opponents are opponents. Players control 3D representations of wrestlers and call up different strikes, grapple, and submissions with button and analog stick combinations. Pin attempts are broken up with a button press timed correctly before the three count, and the game ends when one player wins the match. Players are truly in competition with each other, only in a virtual space. "All the WWE games [...] were premised on this winner-takes-all model."[7] This model makes WWE video games both more real – the fictional competition is made real through gameplay – and more fake – the simulation is a very unrealistic representation of what wrestlers do – than WWE professional wrestling itself.

The real and the fake are part of both of the diegesis of wrestling's narrative and the mimesis, or imitation, of combat sport. Martin Puchner defines diegesis in drama as "the descriptive and narrative strategies through which modern drama tries to channel, frame, control, and even interrupt what it perceives to be the unmediated theatricality of the stage and its actors."[8] In pro wrestling performances live or on television, the diegesis presents itself through the elements of storytelling that give the simulation of a sporting event (the mimesis at the heart of pro wrestling) dramatic weight. The combat of pro wrestling does not closely resemble the rhythms or movements of boxing or mixed martial arts (MMA), its sporting cousins. The theatricality of pro wrestling is laid bare by the aesthetics of its battles. The stage is the ring, the actors the wrestlers. Entrances, backstage interviews, theme songs, costumes, and storylines frame, control, and even interrupt the battles. If WWE video games were simply playable representations of the in-ring combat, it would only give fans an opportunity to be engaged with mimetic elements of professional wrestling. However, as noted earlier, that would not be enough for meta-fans.

Meta-fans are interested not only in the in-ring fights of pro wrestling, but also in the process of putting together the show, making event cards, choosing which wrestlers will be featured, and even tweaking appearances or entrances for wrestlers. WWE games allow for meta-fans to experience this side of wrestling as well through a game mode called WWE Universe. WWE Universe gives players the power of Vince McMahon, the majority owner, CEO, and primary creative decision-maker of WWE. Meta-fans, through this mode, can decide which wrestlers are champions, set up rivalries and heel/face alignments, and set up virtual television shows (*Raw*, *Smackdown*, *Main Event*, *Superstars*, or *NXT*) or virtual pay-per-view events (including, of course, *WrestleMania*). The matches on these shows can be performed by computer AI or by one or more human players. Through skill, a human player can determine the outcome of any match, guaranteeing their favorite wrestlers overcome their rivals and creating their ideal virtual WWE. The WWE Universe mode represents the "reality" of wrestling: the event planning, the decision-making, the storyline-building. However, just as the matches themselves – virtual competitions representing physical non-competitive exhibitions – are hyperreal, so is WWE Universe mode. Virtual wrestlers from any era, such as deceased legends like André the Giant, can compete with current superstars like John Cena or any original character the player can concoct through the game's create-a-wrestler mode. Time is flattened, death is conquered, and the difficulties of running WWE events are reduced to simple menu options. Within the video game's space, real and fake do not matter. The video game refuses the binary that defines the actual WWE and produces a virtual WWE that seems close to pro wrestling, but on further examination is a simplistic and inaccurate representation.

Sharon Mazer reminds us that professional wrestling "intersects, exploits, and finally parodies the conventions of both sport and theatre."[9] Pro wrestling is theatrical, involving acting and characters, and requires the same athletic performances as legitimate sport. The WWE Universe mode intersects with real wrestling show construction, exploits fans' desires to be in control of the product as a selling point for the mode and the game, and parodies reality by creating wrestling that exists outside of the constraints of time or death with deceased wrestling legends fighting fantastic, fully fictional player creations. However, the *WWE2K* series intersects, exploits, and parodies several qualities with its closest generic relatives in the video game realm as well: sports games and fighting games, as well as its dramatic video game cousin, interactive drama. WWE adheres to all these genres because it offers a simulation of a (simulated) sports league, but one based on combat. Games based on the Ultimate Fighting Championship and other MMA leagues are the closest in gameplay to WWE and professional wrestling games, as they also offer virtual leagues, but without the additional layer of narrative drama and fiction of the WWE. Like WWE games, sports games define their brands through a simulation of its product. *Madden*, for example, defines the values, policies, and identity of the National Football League. *MLB The Show* does the same for Major League Baseball.[10] These games allow sports leagues and wrestling companies, which function both as sites of consumerism and purveyors of ideology, to shape fans' perceptions of the league both as sites where sports happen and as the governing bodies of those sports.[11] WWE Universe mode functions similarly to the general manager modes of the *Madden* NFL game or *FIFA* football (soccer) game. Enacting the duties of the highest executive office of a team, the player begins to sympathize with individuals in power whose economic benefit is far greater than those they employ. By playing a general manager in *Madden*, for example, the struggle becomes to convince "greedy" virtual players[12] to come to or stay on the player's virtual team. This occludes the labor inequalities inherent in professional sport, and the vague nature of injuries combined with the emphasis on "stat value" of virtual football players – ratings that indicate various attributes and skills – dehumanizes those players and undermines the harsh, violent reality of football and a life-threatening and life-shortening enterprise for those on the field. WWE Universe mode similarly contains none of the backstage politicking, interpersonal relationships, and contract negotiations that meta-fans obsess over as pro wrestling's meta-narrative. Injuries are flattened and occluded in ways similar to sports games as well. Wrestlers can be thrown off the top of a twenty-foot cage multiple times and show up on the next show right as rain. There are no real-life injuries that complicate WWE Universe mode, nor are there wrestlers who threaten to not sign a contract extension if they do not get a better spot on the card. While in *Madden* and other similar sports games these elements are present but muted and presented as an obstacle for the player-executive to overcome, in *WWE2K* they are simply nonexistent.

In addition to the sports genre, fighting games and interactive drama also strongly influence WWE gameplay and structure. Much of the in-ring action is akin to game series such *Street Fighter* or *Mortal Kombat*. In these types of games, two players perform martial arts moves on each other's avatars, including extra-powerful "super" and "ultra" moves, until one player's character runs out of stamina or some other end-game condition is met (such as time running out). In WWE games, two players perform wrestling maneuvers on each other's avatars, including extra-powerful "signatures" and "finishers," until one player's character is pinned or submitted or some other end-game condition is met (such as a disqualification). These two premises are clearly similar. Both genres hinge on competition, either between a player and an AI-controlled opponent or another player. However, professional wrestling games feature modes like WWE Universe that could not be approximated in fighting games, which use a tournament and not a league structure for their competitions if they have any formal narrative structure at all. Additionally, *WWE2K15* and *WWE2K16* feature MyCareer mode, which reframes the professional wrestling experience through a single character, usually one created by the player. This character works his (only his, sadly, as female wrestlers are not included in this mode) way up the ranks of WWE, ascending by winning matches and feuds with other wrestlers while getting to make narrative decisions that define his alignment and value. Will he turn on his tag team partner? Will he attack his rival from behind? How will he respond to an interview question after a tough loss? In this way, MyCareer attempts to do for the interior dramatic world of the WWE what WWE Universe does for the structural, business, let's-put-on-a-show world of the WWE, and creates a story in which the player's character is the protagonist, much like story-driven interactive drama games like *The Walking Dead* or *Life Is Strange*. Interestingly, a "match quality" system rewards the player with points to improve his or her avatar's attributes. Players are rewarded for back-and-forth action, move variety, and integration of signature moves, finishers, and high spots. This is the only aspect of MyCareer that breaks the narrative of sport. It is a crude approximation of the true job of a professional wrestler – putting on an entertaining match – and is secondary to winning. The limitations of this mode, as well as the limitations of WWE Universe mode, highlight the limitations of the WWE video games in representing the totality of the WWE experience. The hyperreal of WWE video games, even while offering dream matches that are impossible to recreate in the physical world, near-omnipotent control of the virtual WWE, cannot truly deliver the complexity or the meta-narrative that the most ardent fans desire.

It is not only the meta-narrative that fails to be fully represented in *WWE2K*'s virtual world; it is also the real history of the WWE. While *WWE2K* represents a hyperreal version of the WWE past and present, it is a version that is wholly controlled and endorsed by the company, and control of the brand, as discussed earlier, is paramount. In one specific instance, the desires of WWE and 2K to control the WWE brand created a fight over the in-game presence of fan-made versions of a real WWE wrestler. Games journalist Stephen Tolito used a combination of *WWE2K15* features – the create-a-wrestler suite and the community creations feature that allows players to download the created wrestlers from other players' games – to download several versions of deceased professional wrestler and murderer Chris Benoit.[13] In 2007, Chris Benoit, who had held the top championship in both WWE and its late 1990s rival WCW (World Championship Wrestling), strangled his wife and seven-year-old son before hanging himself with a cable from an exercise machine in his home gym.[14] Benoit missed a major pay-per-view event and, before the grisly nature of his demise had been released, was eulogized on a live episode of WWE's primary television program, *Monday Night Raw*. Once the news reached mainstream media outlets, WWE did what it had to that point done with no other wrestler: it effectively scrubbed Chris Benoit from its history. The WWE Network, WWE's pay-per-month digital streaming service, is searchable by wrestler name, and a search for Chris Benoit – a man who won championships in ECW (Extreme Championship Wrestling), WCW, and WWE, all companies whose footage is available on the WWE Network – results, as of my writing this, in a single ECW television episode from early 1995. It is likely that even that search result will be redacted at some point. Chris Benoit, who won the main event at WrestleMania XX, the company's flagship event, is a non-entity when it comes to WWE's version of their own history. WWE retrospective packages or countdown clip compilation shows do not include him. Strangely, all of his matches from WWE or WCW television and pay-per-views are available on the WWE Network, his name is simply not tagged in the search database. He shall not be named. And in the case of *WWE2K* games, he shall not be downloaded.

Stephen Tolito's experience trying to play as Benoit was not difficult to do: he searched for a fan-made Benoit character, which looked similar to Benoit and performed all his well-known moves, and found it, downloaded it, and played it.

> It's him but it's not him, right? It didn't really look like Benoit. At first, it didn't really feel like playing as him. It didn't feel like this is the guy who went on to kill his wife and kid, because it didn't feel like this is the guy. It's a couple of meta layers removed from the real person, of course, a fan creation of a man. I know this . . . or I *knew* this. I'm not Chris Benoit. I'm not wrestler Chris Benoit. I'm a fan's relatively crude rendition of what Chris Benoit the wrestler looks like. It's an artifice of an artifice.[15]

What Tolito experiences is the disassociate nature of the hyperreal WWE video game. Of course this downloadable character is not Benoit, it is simply what Baudrillard would call simulacra, a representation of reality that both magnifies and shapes the expectations of the real. It does carry the specter of Chris Benoit's crimes in it, but as simulacra, these crimes are robbed of their authenticity and depth when applied to the virtual Benoit. To play virtual Benoit is therefore a simulacra of simulation, "founded on information, the model, the cybernetic game – total operationality, hyperreality, aim of total control."[16] Tolito's guilt is built on the reflection of the real that the simulacra affords, but in this case the real has little to do with the on-screen persona of Chris Benoit, professional wrestler, which is the persona the fan creation tries to represent. Virtual fan-made Benoit is the reflection of Chris Benoit, the murderer, a persona that never existed on WWE television, only off of it. However, both personas cannot and must not be ignored. Though WWE tries to police its brand by not naming Benoit, meta-fandom remembers and needs Benoit to be part of the meta-narrative, however tragic that meta-narrative becomes with his inclusion. Due to fan demand for this meta-narrative, more direct measures are needed for WWE to write its own identity through its video games.

Chris Benoit avatars in *WWE2K15*, though numerous and available, are constantly being removed from the game's servers, along with similarly unde-sired content like Adolf Hitler or Ted Bundy wrestlers. While very few fans try to justify Hitler or Bundy, there is an outspoken contingent of fans who believe they should be able to create and share Benoit models without their content being removed, as he is a part of their understanding of WWE's history, even as WWE's official history ignores Benoit. They feel the game is more authentic with the inclusion of the excommunicated Benoit. Tolito played as Benoit, and felt differently.

> Video games have the potential to make us empathize with the characters we control. We don't become them, but we become closer to them. I got a chance to play a video game as Chris Benoit this week, and my feelings about that are no longer ambiguous. Chris Benoit is not someone I want to be closer to. Chris Benoit is not a character I want to control, not for the sake of virtual pro wrestling. If the game helped me better understand Chris Benoit's final, vicious days, I'd be more interested. But to play him as a wrestler? Count me out.[17]

Tolito uploaded the same Benoit model he had downloaded and played with. A few days later, his account was banned from any online activity through the *WWE2K15* game. Hyperreality, which lessens the impact of Benoit's crimes when reflected through his virtual image, was not enough to mitigate the need for corporate brand control. Similarly, Hulk Hogan, in mid-2015, had a taped racist rant leaked to the press. WWE removed him from their website, termi-nated their contract with him, and 2K removed his character from the then-in-production *WWE2K16* after being featured heavily in the promotion of *WWE2K15*.[18] Time will tell if fan-created Hogan models in *WWE2K16* are similarly policed.

In addition to being an example of hyperreality (and its limitations), the vir-tual world of WWE games supports Marshall McLuhan's foundational media critique, "the medium is the message," which argues that a media form, in addition to the content created within it, carries with it the message of its construction, and that construction's rules, ideologies, and conventions.[19] Pro-fessional wrestling delivers stories of physical clashes between faces and heels, rebels and corporate stooges, cocky rookies and sage veterans. However, these stories are also joined by the constant reinforcement of professional wrestling's own structure: the drama and pageantry delivered as segments of televised entertainment in front of a live audience shifting between the real and the fake but always hyperreal. Through McLuhan's theory, the narrative does not dominate the form, as it tends to in pop culture critiques and discussions of professional wrestling. Yes, by watching a single professional wrestling match we may learn of two or more characters' fates as fictional competitors. However, if we acknowledge McLuhan, by watching professional wrestling as a genre we may additionally learn its rules, its values, its expectations, and its structure as well as the rules, values, expectations, and structure of a live event presented on television or – more recently – streaming video. This supports once again Puchner's definition of diegesis as it applies to professional wrestling. In film, diegesis is simply "within the film world," but Puchner's definition allows us to acknowledge the form of pro wrestling as mediated through both live event production and video production, as part of what channels, frames, controls, and interrupts the mimesis to give the full meaning of the dramatic event. In separating his diegesis from mimesis, Puchner insists "we must distinguish between the indirect, descriptive or narrative representation of objects, persons, spaces, and events through language [. . .] and the direct presentation of such objects, persons, speeches, spaces, and events on a stage."[20] In addition to allowing for the meta-narrative to affect the narrative, Puchner's definition of diegesis allows us to fold in McLuhan's insistence that media forms are carried along with content. Combining the two furthers the argument that not only do forms carry with the content, but forms and narrative are both important elements of the content. This is already true with professional wrestling, a genre that exists in two distinct but intersecting forms: the live performance and the televised program. Many fans argue for the purity of being at a live event, that feeling the ebb and flow of the crowd's noise, the heat of the pyrotechnics, the proximity of the wrestler's movement is the truest consumption of the performance. As this performance is mimesis, perhaps it is better to frame this line of thinking away from purity but more toward Puchner's diegesis. Live, there are the fewest number of diegetic elements complicating the mimetic drama of pro wrestling, and these events carry the message of the medium of "live dramatic sports entertainment." The transmission of the live performance through television adds more layers to the diegesis through titles, commentary, backstage segments, and shifting camera angles. Additionally, the form and ideologies of televisions are laid over the live medium to complicate McLuhan's message as well. WWE video games add a third, hyperreal layer. New ways of channeling, framing, controlling, and interrupting mimesis are present. New media forms are reinforced, and the connections to sports, fighting, and interactive drama genres are made.

The *WWE2K* series sells itself as a simulation of the world of professional wrestling. However, the games are simply one layer of the simulacra of sport that is the kernel of professional wrestling as a genre, a layer that interacts and compounds not only with the layers of pro wrestling live performance and television program, but with other video game genres, the WWE's own history, and wrestling meta-narratives. While WWE games do a very poor job of presenting a playable version of *what it is to be a wrestler*, they do a very good job at highlighting the competing binaries of real/fake and fiction/meta-fiction that make professional wrestling as a genre and media form so intriguing. While the competition within WWE games is real – unlike the competition on a WWE show – the games themselves are hyperreal. For a postmodern, multimedia product like the WWE, that seems absolutely appropriate.

Notes

1 "Financials | WWE Corporate," World Wrestling Entertainment, http://corporate. wwe.com/company/financials.
2 Oliver Lee Bateman, "Why Do Developers Keep Getting Wrestling Video Games Wrong?" *Vice*, April 22, 2015, http://www.vice.com/read/why-do-developers-keep-getting-wrestling-video-games-wrong-246.
3 David Shoemaker, "WWE SummerSlam: A Theory of Trickle-Down Thuganomics," *Grantland*, August 22, 2012, http://grantland.com/features/the-ongoing-drama-cm-punk-john-cena-wwe-summerslam/.
4 Sharon Mazer, "'Real Wrestling'/'Real' Life," in *Steel Chair to the Head*, ed. Nicholas Sammond (Durham: Duke University Press, 2005), 84.
5 Jean Baudrillard, *Simulacra and Simulation*, trans. Sheila Faria Glaser (Ann Arbor: University of Michigan Press, 1994), 1.
6 Ibid., 2.
7 Bateman, "Why Do Developers Keep Getting Wrestling Video Games Wrong?"
8 Martin Puchner, *Stage Fright: Modernism, Anti-Theatricality, and Drama* (Baltimore: Johns Hopkins University Press, 2002), 349–351, Kindle.
9 Sharon Mazer, *Professional Wrestling Sport and Spectacle* (Jackson: University Press of Mississippi, 1998), 3.
10 Cory Hillman and Michael L. Butterworth, "Keeping It Real: Sports Video Game Advertising and the Fan-Consumer," in *Playing to Win: Sports, Video Games, and the Culture of Play*, ed. Robert Allen Brookey and Thomas P. Oates (Bloomington: Indiana University Press, 2015), 167.
11 Ibid., 168.
12 Ibid., 157.
13 Stephen Tolito, "I Was Chris Benoit: Playing a Video Game as a Real-Life Murderer," *Kotaku*, December 12, 2014, http://kotaku.com/i-was-chris-benoit-playing-a-video-game-as-a-real-life-1669955314.
14 Brenda Goodman, "Wrestler Killed Wife and Son, Then Himself," *New York Times*, June 27, 2007, http://www.nytimes.com/2007/06/27/us/27wrestler.html?_r=0.
15 Tolito, "I Was Chris Benoit."
16 Baudrillard, *Simulacra and Simulation*, 118.
17 Tolito, "I Was Chris Benoit."
18 "Hulk Hogan Removed from WWE 2K16 after Racism Row," *Metro*, http://metro.co.uk/2015/07/27/hulk-hogan-removed-from-wwe-2k16-after-racism-row-5314388/.
19 Marshall McLuhan, *Understanding Media: The Extensions of Man* (Cambridge, MA: MIT Press, 1964).
20 Puchner, *Stage Fright*, 393–395.

Part III

Lucha

Chapter 6

Don't leave us in the hands of criminals

The contested cultural politics of lucha libre

Heather Levi

It's June 2009, a month before congressional elections in Mexico. On the TV screen, a man walks up to a boxing ring, his face hidden behind a silver and gold wrestling mask. White boots, silver tights and a gold cape frame his bare torso. He is Místico, the most popular professional wrestler (*luchador*) in Mexico at the moment (Figure 6.1). Místico is a *técnico* (a babyface) and according to the storyline, the young, acrobatic protégé of Fray Tormenta, the famous wrestling priest.[1]

Reaching the ring, Místico vaults over the cords. He removes the golden cape with care, rolls his neck, and jogs a few steps in place. A voice-over begins.

> Many say the struggle (lucha) against drug trafficking and organized crime has never been so rough (ruda). The truth is that for years nobody had fought (habia luchado) against them.

Close up as he faces the camera, leaning one arm on the ropes and gesturing with his free hand, head tilted to one side. His naked, muscular torso glows. He continues:

> Now, the president and the PAN are entering the fight with everything they've got, and we have to support them. [The camera angle shifts, and he is seen warming up in the ring. The camera backs away further, and he is shown from above, a single figure, alone in the square.]
> That way we will defend our children and our young people, so that drugs won't reach them. This struggle (lucha) must be done for them.

He approaches the ropes (camera in close again) and jumps a few times. Finally, he is seen completing a back flip from the top rope. The camera closes in on his face and upper body once more.

> That's why I'm going to vote for the PAN.

Figure 6.1 "Now, the president and the PAN are entering the fight with everything they've got, and we have to support them." MISTICO CMLL EN COMERCIAL DEL PAN. Screenshot from YouTube.com, https://www.youtube.com/watch?v=a-nUv189UIM (accessed January 11, 2015).

And another voice intones:

Don't leave Mexico in the hands of criminals. Vote for the PAN.[2]

An observer unfamiliar with lucha libre and its intersection with Mexican political culture might wonder at the invocation of professional wrestling in this deadly serious discourse. Variously described as theatre, ritual, or "sports entertainment," pro wrestling's reputation outside of its fan base is as cartoonish, ridiculous, or corrupt – nothing with which a governing party would wish to be identified. What's more, the voice-over is that of the wrestler Místico, not the man who plays him. While politics and professional wrestling sometimes intersect in the United States, the line between reality and theatre is always clearly marked when they do.[3] Místico's endorsement of the Partido de Acción Nacional (PAN, the right-wing party that then held the presidency and both houses of congress) was different. In keeping with the conventions of lucha libre (Mexican professional wrestling), he spoke as Místico, without revealing his face or legal name. He addressed the camera as a paradox: a real person, but also a copyrighted fictional character.

Insofar as a campaign spot is a form of political theatre, it was not surprising to anyone familiar with Mexico to see a masked wrestler in that role. Since the late 1970s, leftist artists and public intellectuals have been drawn to lucha libre, and its imagery has entered the political sphere.[4] But it *was* surprising to see one soberly endorsing the PAN. By contextualizing the ad in the history of lucha libre's engagement with Mexican cultural politics, I hope to make clear why it was surprising, and what it implied for Mexico's political culture in the first decade of the twenty-first century.

Lucha libre and the social wrestler

In the late 1980s, the deployment of lucha libre themes by leftist artists and essayists led to the emergence of a type of political activist unique to Mexico, the *luchador social* (social wrestler). *Luchadores sociales* played on the double meaning of the word *luchar*, which means both "to wrestle" and "to struggle." In other words, they dressed as masked wrestlers in order to struggle for social justice. Simultaneously serious and satirical, the luchadores sociales acted as spokespeople for a variety of progressive causes: the right to housing, the rights of women, gays, street children, and animals, the defense of the environment. The best known of the social wrestlers, Superbarrio, was the primary spokesman for the Asemblea de Barrios, an influential grassroots organization of housing rights activists founded after the earthquake of 1985. A presence on the Mexican left since 1987, Superbarrio's activities ranged from leading direct actions, to standing at the side of presidential candidates Cuauhtémoc Cárdenas and Andres Manuel Lopez Obrador, to announcing his own parodic campaigns for president of Mexico (1988) and the United States (1996).[5]

The adoption of lucha libre imagery by the left made sense because of the particular context of Mexico's late twentieth-century political culture. From the end of the revolution to the start of the twenty-first century, Mexico was a multi-party electoral democracy on paper. In practice, one party, the Partido Revolucionario Institucional (PRI) maintained a monopoly on political power through tactics ranging from fraud and occasional violence to patronage and co-optation of dissenters. The PRI's claim to legitimacy rested on two principles. First, the post-revolutionary political model conceptualized the nation as the composite of corporate groups that were integrated into the state through organs of the party. To some degree, then, the party was identified with the nation, an identification strengthened by the party's deployment of national symbols.[6] Second, the PRI framed itself as the architect of Mexico's modernization through policies like the import substitution economy,[7] the expansion of public education and social services, and the cultivation (and co-optation) of arts and culture (until the mid-1980s), and neo-liberal development projects from then on.

At most levels of the system party factions would struggle for dominance in order to select candidates, who would invariably win the subsequent election. At the national level, the president, symbolically identified with the nation, held nearly unlimited power, but only for one six-year term. He couldn't run for re-election, but he had the right to select the party's next candidate. The president's final decision, sometimes referred to as the *destapa* (unveiling or unmasking) transferred the charisma of the presidency to the nominee, setting the political direction of the country for the next six years. The outcome of the general election was never in doubt; elections were not a mechanism for selecting a leader, but a ritual affirmation of decisions made at another level of the system. The destapa and the political rituals involved in the assumption of office aligned the person of the nominee/president with the legitimating discourses of sovereignty and development.[8]

In that political context, the Asemblea's adoption of Superbarrio in 1987 – first as silent icon, then as spokesman, then as presidential candidate – made sense for several reasons. First, lucha libre was closely identified with the organization's working-class base. Brought to Mexico from Texas in 1933 by the founder of the Empresa Mexicana de Lucha Libre (EMLL), pro wrestling soon adapted to local tastes. By the early 1950s, middle- and working-class fans attended the arenas and, for a short period (1952–1954) watched lucha libre on television. However, lucha libre was ordered off the air just as the social geography of Mexico City began to undergo a major shift.[9] Government investment in infrastructure expanded southward, taking the middle classes with it, leaving the city center "a combination of historical monuments and poor people's housing . . . to molder, neglected."[10] The old locations of the existing arenas now likely discouraged middle-class attendance. Without televised events, their interest waned. By the 1960s lucha libre fandom was closely identified with the culture of an urban lower class that Mexican elites viewed with contempt.

Lucha libre continued to evolve, but now in dialogue with its working-class public. In Mexico City, lucha libre was performed in venues that ranged from the 18,000-seat Arena México to neighborhood rec centers. The roles of técnico (babyface), *rudo* (heel), and referee continued to structure the in-ring dramas, but other aspects of performance changed. Wrestlers developed an acrobatic style that played to the third balcony instead of the camera or microphone. They drew their characters from a range of sources: mythological, zoological, historical, and mass-mediated.[11] The use of wrestling masks increased, which motivated the elaboration of additional rules. Masked wrestlers were obligated to keep their identities concealed, and secrecy and revelation became important tropes.[12] For fans, the mask paradoxically increased both distance from and intimacy with their heroes; it rendered the wrestlers mysterious and larger than life, but left open the possibility that they could be their friends, relatives, or neighbors.

Although middle-class Mexicans avoided the arenas, they remained familiar with lucha libre. From the 1950s through the 1980s, Mexican film studios produced dozens of low-budget action movies featuring masked wrestlers. The most famous of these was the silver-masked wrestler El Santo. El Santo was a popular and charismatic figure whose wrestling career spanned over forty years, but in addition to his work in the ring he starred in over fifty wrestling movies. In each, he played the consummate modern hero, in Anne Rubenstein's phrase "the perfect man," who provided a model of Mexican masculinity distanced from the stereotypical "macho."[13] In each movie he saved Mexico, the planet, and a female protagonist from villains ranging from gangsters to Martians to female vampires. In the lucha libre matches that punctuated the films he always wrestled as a técnico, displaying gentlemanly self-control and a modern sensibility (even though his in-ring character was fought as a rudo until 1962).[14] Proudly Mexican yet thoroughly cosmopolitan, his screen persona was equally at home in the laboratory or the ring, the mansion or the street. In the films, he deployed futuristic technology as well as wrestling skill, as he collaborated with government officials and university professors to vanquish their common foes. In the arenas, El Santo was rooted in Mexico as it was. In the movies, he held out a low-budget vision of the modern, sophisticated nation that could be. His scrupulous protection of his secret identity strengthened the identification between the two: El Santo the superhero was played by El Santo the wrestler. The man behind that mask stayed there until after he retired.[15]

Unlike live lucha libre, El Santo's films crossed class boundaries. This is not to say that they were usually taken seriously. As one viewer told me: "You'd see a cardboard box, and El Santo would say 'it's a cave,' so you would say, 'okay, it's a cave.'" Conveying wistful nostalgia for the promised future, and wry acknowledgement of the common present, El Santo the movie character exemplified what Michael Herzfeld characterizes as cultural intimacy, "the recognition of those aspects of a cultural identity that are considered a source of external embarrassment but that nevertheless provide insiders with their assurance of common sociality."[16] Superbarrio's character was partly modeled on that of El Santo. By drawing on live lucha libre, he and his creators (along with other social wrestlers) invoked and celebrated the culture of the *barrios populares.* By drawing on El Santo's films they invoked fantasies of empowerment coupled with ambivalent sentiments of national identity. But there were still further reasons to reference lucha libre in the political arena.

One policy of the PRI post-1968 was the control of dissent through the systematic co-optation of dissenters. Superbarrio, however, could not be co-opted. Since the identity of the man behind the mask was kept secret, Superbarrio (like any masked wrestler) was both a person and a fiction. Without knowing who was behind the mask, there was no knowing who to co-opt or threaten. Without a personal identity, he could represent the common interest in a way that an individual citizen could not.

Moreover, there were elements of lucha libre performance that mirrored elements of official political ritual, but inverted their values. Remember that the central ritual by which the president's legitimacy was transferred to the party's nominee was called an unmasking (destapa). To be unmasked was to be empowered. The discourse of the mask in lucha libre, however, suggested another reality. A masked wrestler is obligated to keep the mask in place when in public. If a wrestler unmasks an opponent during a match, he or she is disqualified for that round, but the unmasked wrestler is rendered powerless. He or she must leave the ring, keeping his or her face hidden, helpless until someone brings a replacement. Wrestlers can also bet their masks on the outcome of a match; the winner keeps the mask as a trophy, the loser loses both their secret identity and the right to wrestle using a mask ever again. In lucha libre masking is empowering, and unmasking a disaster. Power is found not in revelation, but in the act of concealment.

Thus, Superbarrio implicitly drew attention to a further parallel between lucha libre and twentieth-century politics: the public secret of the fixed outcome. In both lucha libre matches and in formal politics, much could be at stake. Different factions could struggle for dominance; different wrestlers maneuver for position within their promotion; decisions would be made about who would be brought into the spotlight, and who would have to wait their turn. The outcome of the match/election was predetermined, but *how* the match was played out, how much grace or force was displayed (by wrestlers, or by party members mobilizing blocs of voters or suppressing the opposition in support of the destapado) would make a difference for future matches. Between the public secret of the fixed outcome (in wrestling as in electoral politics), and the foregrounding of the relationship between secrecy and power, every match constituted a sly critique of the inner workings of the political system. Superbarrio and other social wrestlers' performance thus worked on multiple levels. With serious advocacy and with satire, they celebrated urban popular culture and mocked the state, while reminding Mexicans of their commonalities.

Television and transnational circulation

It should be clear at this point why lucha libre motifs were politicized by the populist left. A shared cultural reference for urban, working-class Mexicans, lucha libre provided a visual and gestural vocabulary that, tacking between serious and playful modes, could present a critical challenge to the authoritarian system. When the left wing of the PRI broke away in 1988 to form the Partido de la Revolución Democrática, they allied with the Asemblea and with Superbarrio, carrying lucha libre (or at least its imagery) into formal electoral politics.

But how to explain the desire of the PAN to elicit Místico's endorsement? The party ran on a neo-liberal and nationalist platform, not a populist one. In 2009 they controlled the presidency and both houses of congress; they were hardly in a position to mount a general critique of the system. I believe that the PAN's invocation of lucha libre can be traced to two developments: a gradual shift in the social meaning of lucha libre, and a transformation of the terms by which the ruling party claimed its legitimacy.

The 1990s brought two changes regarding the circulation of lucha libre, one sudden, the other gradual. In 1991, the media conglomerate Televisa came to an agreement with the Consejo Mexicano de Lucha Libre (CMLL, formerly the EMLL) to return lucha libre to the airwaves three decades after its removal. (A year later, Televisa made a second agreement with their director of public relations, Antonio Pena, forming a new wrestling league called the AAA.)[17] The return to televised broadcast had several effects. As many in the industry feared, ticket sales fell and some smaller arenas closed down. But it also broadened lucha libre's audience in Mexico both geographically and in terms of social class. Brought into the media spotlight, lucha libre's identification with particular spaces or class cultures weakened.

The second, related change arose from the transnational circulation of lucha libre. Starting in the mid-1980s, lucha libre gained greater visibility in the United States. Some luchadores were already well known in the United States before, but the cross-border circulation of lucha libre intensified over the course of the 1980s and 1990s. Wrestling masks and other images familiar to US Latino communities began crossing over into Anglo contexts through alternative comics, surf punk music, and shops specializing in punk gear. Lucha libre thus entered North American Anglo consciousness through alternative spheres of commerce, loosely associated with progressive politics, but de-contextualized and presented as edgy kitsch.

By the end of the 1990s, lucha libre had entered even wider channels of communication in the United States. CMLL and AAA wrestling could be seen on Galavision, the US cable affiliate of Televisa. El Santo movies, dubbed into English, could be online, broadening the audience for the campy, sometimes inscrutable films. Agreements between the AAA and WWE brought more luchadores to US television. In 2000, Australian animators Lili Chin and Eddie Mort pitched their idea for an animated series based on lucha libre to Warner Brothers. The series, *Mucha Lucha*, which ran from 2002 to 2005, brought lucha libre imagery to an even larger public. Finally, in 2006, Paramount Pictures released *Nacho Libre*. A light comedy (very) loosely based on the real-life wrestling priest Fray Tormenta, the film grossed over $28 million in its first weekend.[18]

The early 2000s thus introduced lucha libre to broad audiences in the United States, but in ways that foregrounded its comical aspects and de-emphasized its critical edge.[19] The bi-national traffic in wrestling went both ways: WWE wrestling, dubbed into Spanish, is now on Mexican television, and may be overtaking the CMLL and AAA in popularity.[20] *Mucha Lucha* and *Nacho Libre* were released in Mexico not long after their US debuts. However these imports, based on Mexican "originals," were understood in Mexico, the circular traffic in lucha libre helped to resignify it there, furthering its diffusion into middle-class spaces.

Examples abounded by the mid-2000s. Hijo del Santo, son of the legendary wrestler, opened an El Santo–themed cafe in the chic neighborhood of Condesa and the food court of the International Terminal of Mexico City's airport. Lucha libre imagery, long ignored by advertisers, entered new circuits of commodification. The Walmart-owned supermarket chain Bodega Aurrera's ads featured the cartoon character "Mama Lucha," who fights high prices. Blue Demon Jr. (whose father Blue Demon was nearly as iconic as El Santo) endorses Coca-Cola's Full Throttle energy drink. Perhaps, then, it should have come as no surprise when the Instituto Federal Electoral (IFE) ran a public service announcement for citizens wishing to apply for a voter's card featuring the comical masked wrestler, El Cameleón de Oro (The Golden Chameleon).[21] Here was a case of the state appropriating the ludic side of lucha libre, stripped of its critical potential.

Why the PAN? Why Místico?

By 2008, then, the meanings that lucha libre could carry had multiplied and shifted, opening space for its symbolic deployment outside of populist spaces. But how did it get from there to be invoked by the right-wing governing party, and hitched to the cause of Calderón's drug war? Part of the answer may lie in the political orientation of Místico (or that of his promoter), but it doesn't explain why the PAN was interested in Místico's endorsement. While it is true that both Místico and the PAN share a close association with the Catholic Church, I believe that Místico's campaign spot pointed to something else.

When Vicente Fox ran as the PAN candidate in 2000, he promised an end to the corruption of the PRI, transparency in government and an emphasis on law and order (while expanding the neo-liberal economic policies of his predecessors). His electoral victory failed to deliver the long-promised democratization, but it did lead to a transformation of the discursive strategy the governing party used to legitimate its rule. During the seventy-year rule of the PRI, the party alternated between relatively left wing and right wing administrations. Rather than representing (or claiming to represent) a particular political program, the party presented itself as the defender of Mexican national sovereignty (usually in relation to the United States) and as the promoter of Mexico's economic and cultural modernization. This marks a difference from the United States, where the government (whichever party is in charge) has often represented itself (and the nation) as the defender of the vulnerable good against forces of absolute evil.

In 2006 the PAN won the presidency for a second time with the candidacy of Felipe Calderón. His campaign focused less on transparency and more on law and order. He was elected by a margin of less than 1 percent. The opposition candidate never fully accepted his defeat, and his followers occupied the Zócalo and Avenida Reforma for weeks after the election calling for a recount. By September, Calderón was declared the victor and the Zócalo was cleared, but the political rituals associated with the presidential transition were all prevented or disrupted.[22] The new administration began on a terrain of uncertain legitimacy: legally certified, but symbolically unstable.

Once in office, Calderón began a concentrated campaign to break up the increasingly powerful and violent drug cartels operating in several northern and coastal states. The cartels responded with a radical escalation of violence. The crackdown on narco-trafficking coincided with increasing concern with minor crimes as well. In Mexico City the increase in police visibility was striking. On television, public service announcements encouraged citizens to surveille one another. One such announcement equated the sale of a gram of cocaine with the kidnapping of a child, the sale of pirated CDs with murder, ending with the slogan "*lo que está mal está mal*" ("what's wrong is wrong"). Another featured an elderly couple deciding to turn in their neighbor's drug-dealing son. By 2008 over 6,000 people had been killed in violence related to the drug war; the election of 2009 was, at least to some extent, a referendum on that program.

Místico's performance represented a departure from earlier incarnations of the political wrestler. Unlike the social wrestlers' street actions, Superbarrio's speeches, or the IFE's Camaleón d'Oro, Místico's campaign spot was utterly lacking in humor. Instead, he highlighted that aspect of professional wrestling that the social wrestlers drew on partly seriously, but half in jest: the struggle between good guys and bad guys, rudos and técnicos. It only made sense in light of terms through which the governing party now legitimated its rule. The drug war came to function, on a symbolic level, much as World Wars I and II, the Cold War, and the War on Terror (possibly the first war declared against an emotional state) have for the United States. Rather claiming to be the defender of national sovereignty or vehicle of modernization, the Calderón administration portrayed itself as the nation's protector in a battle against unmitigated evil. Thus the party's use of Místico: anonymous and masked, humorless and grim, alone and vulnerable against a faceless menace.

Conclusion

During the twentieth century, lucha libre functioned as a kind of theatre of resistance – an implicit critique of the inner workings of the political system. The intervention of the social wrestlers brought the implicit critique into the open, mocking the powerful while celebrating the popular culture of the urban lower class. Perhaps by hiring Místico as Místico, the PAN (or their consultants) hoped to appropriate the populist legitimacy of the social wrestlers, portraying the state as resisting the power of the cartels. That strategy had to efface the element of parody always present, if muted, in lucha libre matches and El Santo movies. At any rate, it is unlikely that the campaign spot was effective; the PAN did poorly in the elections of 2009, and lost the presidency to the PRI in 2012. The death toll in the drug war is now estimated somewhere above 120,000.[23] And El Santo is still dead.

Notes

1 Fray Tormenta (Sergio Gutierrez) is a real-life priest who debuted as a luchador in 1973 to raise funds to support his orphanage. When Místico debuted in 2004, he was presented as Fray Tormenta's protégé. His real name (Luis Ignacio Urive Alvirde) was not known to the public until 2011, when he left the CMLL for the WWE as the masked character Sin Cara (Faceless). When the CMLL assigned the Místico character to another wrestler, Fray Tormenta himself made the announcement, giving him his formal blessing in the ring. Urive Alvirde returned to Mexico in 2014 to work for the AAA as Myzteziz.

2 "Mistico CMLL en Comercial del PAN," YouTube, posted by "CMLLeLoMejor," April 24, 2009, accessed January 11, 2015, https://www.youtube.com/watch?v=a-nUv189UlM.

3 Retired wrestler Jesse Ventura was elected governor of Minnesota in 1999, but as himself, not as his character, Jesse "The Body." Hillary Clinton, Barack Obama, and John McCain all did humorous campaign spots on *Monday Night Raw* in 2008. The WWE also ran a series of matches between Hillary Clinton and Barack Obama characters, but again, it was clear that they were characters, not the then senators themselves. R.M. Schneiderman, "Better Days, and Even the Candidates, Are Coming to W.W.E," *New York Times*, April 28, 2008, accessed June 22, 2015, http://www.nytimes.com/2008/04/28/busi ness/media/28wwe.html.

4 The list includes visual artists Lourdes Grobet, Felipe Ehrenberg, Marisa Lara, Arturo Guerrero, and Sergio Arau, essayist Carlos Monsiváis, playwright Jose Buíl, and performance artists Guillermo Gomez-Peña, Coco Fusco, and others.

5 Jorge Cadena-Roa, "Strategic Framing, Emotions and Superbarrio: Mexico City's Masked Crusader," *Mobilization: An International Quarterly* 7 (2002): 201–216; Angélica Cuellar Vasquez, *La Noche Es de Ustedes, el Amanecer Es Nuestro* (Mexico City: UNAM, 1993); also see Heather Levi, *The World of Lucha Libre: Secrets, Revelations and Mexican National Identity* (Durham: Duke University Press, 2008), 127–135.

6 For example, the party's colors (red, white and green) are also the colors of the Mexican flag.

7 Import substitution industrialization is a protectionist economic policy that favors the local production of manufactured goods in place of goods produced abroad. It was the dominant policy approach in Mexico until the mid-1980s, when it was gradually jettisoned in favor of a neo-liberal free trade model of development leading to the North American Free Trade Agreement (NAFTA) in 1994.

8 This analysis is drawn from a number of works on the political culture of mid- to late-twentieth-century Mexico, notably: Claudio Lomnitz and Ilya Adler, "The Function of the Form," in *Constructing Culture and Power in Latin America*, ed. Daniel Levine (Ann Arbor: University of Michigan Press, 1993), 357–402; M.C. Needler, *Mexican Politics: The Containment of Conflict* (Westport, CT: Praeger, 1998); Peter Smith, *Labyrinths of Power: Political Recruitment in Twentieth-Century Mexico* (Princeton: Princeton University Press, 1979); Claudio Lomnitz, *Deep Mexico, Silent Mexico: An Anthropology of Nationalism* (Minneapolis: University of Minnesota Press, 2001).

9 Lucha libre was pulled off the air by the governor of Mexico City, ostensibly to protect children who might hurt themselves by imitating the wrestlers. However, the ban might have had more to do with territorial disputes between rival state agencies. (Levi, *The World of Lucha Libre*, 103–104).

10 Anne Rubenstein, "Bodies, Cities, Cinema: Pedro Infante's Death as Political Spectacle," in *Fragments of a Golden Age: The Politics of Culture in Mexico since 1940*, ed. Gilbert M. Joseph, Anne Rubenstein, and Eric Zolov (Durham: Duke University Press, 2001), 223.

11 The types of characters most popular in Mexican lucha libre differ from those in the United States, where wrestlers have tended to represent social types. Luchadores, in contrast, are more likely to chose characters based on mystical, animal, or pop culture icons, natural phenomena, or abstractions (Levi, *The World of Lucha Libre*, 65–78).

12 All wrestlers have to be licensed by a commission appointed by the state following a formal exam, but masked wrestlers have a specific license. The exam for masked wrestlers is supposed to be more rigorous than for those who don't plan to use a mask.

13 Anne Rubenstein, "El Santo: Many Versions of the Perfect Man," in *The Mexico Reader*, ed. Gilbert Joseph and Timothy J. Henderson (Durham: Duke University Press, 2003), 570–578.

14 Evan Lieberman has rightly noted that El Santo's conduct in the on-screen matches served to display qualities of gentlemanly self-control that were central to his character's appeal. Evan Lieberman, "Mask and Masculinity: Culture, Modernity, and Gender

Identity in the Mexican Lucha Libre films of El Santo," *Studies in Hispanic Cinemas* [new title: *Studies in Spanish & Latin American Cinemas*] 6 (2009): 3–17.

15 El Santo's careful protection of his secret identity was legendary, even among fellow wrestlers. He was said to wear the mask even when crossing borders, asking to be taken to a private room to remove it so that customs agents could verify his identity. He revealed his name and exposed his face to the public for the first and last time during a televised interview on January 26, 1984. He died of a heart attack ten days later, and was buried with his mask in place.

16 Michael Herzfeld, *Cultural Intimacy: Social Poetics in the Nation State* (New York: Routledge, 1997), 3.

17 Under the new arrangement, the AAA, using stars drawn away from the CMLL, would promote events in arenas outside of Mexico City, and Televisa would broadcast the matches nationally. Initially, Televisa would only broadcast AAA events, but returned to broadcasting CMLL events after the national wrestler's union (the Sindicato Nacional de Luchadores) went on strike.

18 "Nacho Libre (2006)," Internet Movie Database, accessed September 24, 2015, http://www.imdb.com/title/tt0457510/?ref_=ttfc_fc_tt.

19 Live lucha libre (professional wrestling specifically presented in the Mexican style) has also become easier to find in the United States. It has become an arena partly for the assertion of ethnic pride in areas with significant Latino populations. But it has become more available to crossover audiences, whether through the parodic appropriation of Lucha VaVoom (an L.A.-based promotion that mixes lucha libre with burlesque), or promotions like the Philadelphia-based Chikara that present Mexican style wrestling (featuring both Mexican and Anglo wrestlers) to mostly Anglo wrestling audiences.

20 Derrik J. Lang, "Clinton, Obama and McCain on WWE's Monday Night Raw," *USA Today*, April 22, 2008, accessed January 10, 2015, http://usatoday30.usatoday.com/life/television/news/2008–04–21-candidates-WWE_N.htm.

21 In it, a large man dressed in wrestling mask, cape, and tights goes the to service window in an IFE office and declares himself the Camaleón De Oro. When the young woman behind the counter asks for identification, he shows her a tattoo, declaring that everyone knows him. She explains that he needs a piece of government-issued identification like a military service card or birth certificate. He responds by offering to do a "camaleonazo," and dives to the floor with his signature move. Here is lucha libre in its comical mode, but emptied of the potentially critical elements of the live performance, as well as the heroic elements of the cinematic version. ("La Versión Completa," *YouTube video*, 1:09, posted by "La Cueva de Camaleooon," February 6, 2007, accessed September 24, 2015, https://www.youtube.com/watch?v=sOlxABydPP4.)

22 There were three public political rituals associated with the presidential transition, none of which went off normally in 2006: the outgoing president's final address to Congress on September 1, his last delivery of the Grito de Dolores from the Zócalo at midnight September 15, and the incoming president's swearing-in ceremony in front of the Senate on December 1.

23 Molly Molloy, "The Mexican Undead: Toward a New History of the 'Drug War' Killing Fields," *Small Wars Journal*, August 21, 2013, accessed June 30, 2015.

Chapter 7

Wrestling with burlesque, burlesquing lucha libre

Nina Hoechtl

A white man is standing in the center of a stage in front of the ring. He is holding a microphone in his hands. He is wearing glasses, a black tie, a white shirt,
and black suit. He is ready to start the night and so is the audience:

MAN: Lucha . . .
AUDIENCE: VaVoom!
MAN: Lucha . . .
AUDIENCE: VaaVooooom!!!
MAN: Lucha . . .
AUDIENCE: VaaaaaaaaVoooooooooooooom!!!!

He is stand-up comedian Blain Capach, who has been providing commentary
for the wrestling and burlesque bouts of Lucha VaVoom since its beginnings in
2002. It is my first time at the Mayan[1] in downtown Los Angeles, a theatre that
opened its doors in 1927 and whose design drew inspiration from the archi-
tecture and iconography of pre-Hispanic Mesoamerican cultures. I am standing among approximately 1,500 people[2] and I am not yet familiar with Lucha
VaVoom's formula. I came here after a poster in a shop window in downtown
Los Angeles had caught my attention. As a passionate fan of lucha libre (free
fighting/struggle, refers to professional wrestling in Mexico),[3] I wondered what
an event announced as *Mexican Masked Wrestling & Saucy Striptease* could be –
especially when its promotion draws so clearly on the aesthetics from film
posters of the *Cine de Luchadores*, popular films with fantastic plots, featuring
luchadores in starring roles.[4]

Since then I have been back six times, and because of that I sometimes fan-
tasize myself as a performer – my unfitness aside, how was I to perform the
attempt to dismantle the structures of domination that enable my privileges?[5]
How do they impact my reading of Lucha VaVoom and the performances of the
hula hoop burlesque dancer Karis and the *exótiqui*[6] wrestler Cassandro under
consideration? How am I to perform a disidentifactory reading practice of
exoticist modes of representation, perception, and consumption? Is there a danger of this in Lucha VaVoom? Or does Lucha VaVoom rather leave the audience

to weigh the contradictions, assess the implications, and speculate on possible agencies?

Starting with an introduction and theoretical framing of Lucha VaVoom, this article retraces the transnational beginnings of burlesque and lucha libre by paying special attention to what I term the audience's "againstogether" participation in Lucha VaVoom. Through a closer look at discussions on the practices of exoticism, I will dwell on a multitude of bodies upon which Lucha VaVoom builds. Inspired by Emma Pérez's "decolonial desires," Jossianna Arroyo's "cultural drag," and José Esteban Muñoz' strategy of "disidentification," I will finally analyze performances of Karis and Cassandro, a hula hoop burlesque dancer and a exótiqui wrestler, respectively. Does the strategy of cultural drag challenge and/or disidentify with exoticist tendencies of reducing specific and complex histories and agencies into celebratory, essentialist, consumable commodities? Might there be something enabling and agential for Karis and Cassandro by working on and against exoticist modes of representation?

At Lucha VaVoom: a multitude of bodies on stage, in the ring, and among the audience

Lucha VaVoom, with its diverse performances during intermissions – such as mariachi or rock musicians, folk, hip hop, or Mexica dancers – combines lucha libre wrestling, which is supposedly from Mexico, and burlesque, which is considered to be from the United States. However, the anthropologist Heather Levi and cultural historian Robert Clyde Allen have affirmed that both have transnational beginnings and the capacity to stage and "act out" contradictions.[7] As I have proposed elsewhere these contradictions are wrestled againstogether by the performers and the audience alike: "The audience masks itself as audience to complicitly participate in the body of the audience in which the body becomes another body, while simultaneously playing with what it means to be in a body, with others."[8] According to Lucha VaVoom co-producer Liz Fairbairn, "the audiences are so self-conscious here. They're more concerned about who's looking at them than about what they're watching."[9] In contrast to lucha libre there are no weekly events, no children are allowed, and the audience, who can at least afford $40 for a ticket, is a mix of "female and male, gay and straight, young and middle age, upwardly mobile and aspirational, Asian, Latino, African American and white."[10] Without a doubt, given the diverse audience, I easily fit in.

As with lucha libre, at approximately ten Lucha VaVoom events per year,[11] the audience, rather than being just a background dedicated to passive consumption, is consciously performing its role as audience – testing, playing, and monitoring how far they can take their emotions and desires in relation to the other spectators and the performers. At Lucha VaVoom I sometimes find myself looking askance at the performances of the bodies; sometimes wondering about some of the performers; sometimes imagining the audience's performance from

an arena in Mexico transferred to the Mayan; sometimes imagining the participation of other *luchadoris* changing the course of actions; sometimes screaming
¡*Beesoo*! ¡*Beeesooo*! (Kiisss! Kiiiiiisss!) while Cassandro wrestles without anyone
joining me; sometimes explaining to accompanying friends. After the journalist
Chris Jones had joined in the audience at Lucha VaVoom's excursion to Chicago in 2005, he states:

> You could view "Lucha VaVoom" as cultural exploitation, cultural appro-
> priation or a happy celebration of diversity. Shrewdly, it's all of these and
> none of these. Mainly, it's vicarious excitement – a desperate lunge for the
> edge in a world where there almost is no edge left.[12]

It seems to me that the space in between "all of these and none of these,"[13]
which supposedly fills the lack of edge in life to be anything else but bored, is
surrounded by, dances with, and wrestles with exoticism – an "aestheticising
process through which the cultural other is translated, relayed back through the
familiar."[14] The comparative literary theorist Dorothy Figueira and the feminist,
activist, and author bell hooks – to name but two – argue that the practice of
exoticism is an expression of different lacks in life, such as "no edge left"[15] or
boredom. Through exotic quest, according to Figueira, "one seeks . . . to invest
one's existence with greater intensity,"[16] while hooks argues that the "commodification of otherness has been so successful because it is offered as a new
delight, more intense, more satisfying than normal ways of doing and feeling."[17]
All of which Jones recognizes that Lucha VaVoom does and of which I became
increasingly wary over the course of my various visits. Here I am specifically
thinking of how sexually, gendered, ethnically/racially othered bodies are central to "multiculturalism's celebratory 'rainbow' visions."[18] The postcolonial
literature theorist Graham Huggan points out that "the faultlines within contemporary multicultural discourse [are] . . . when it intersects with, becomes
scarcely distinguishable from exoticist modes of representation."[19] Exoticism,
according to Huggan, has shifted "from a privileged mode of aesthetic perception to its contemporary status as a global mode of mass consumption."[20]
Exoticism as a mode of mass consumption effectively disguises its highly contradictory nature as a practice, which "renders people, objects and places strange
even as it domesticates them, and which effectively manufactures otherness
even as it claims to surrender to its immanent mystery."[21] By focusing on the
shift from a mode of perception to one of consumption, Huggan highlights the
role of the audience in this process.

Further reinforcing both the audience's and my own consumption and
"vicarious excitement,"[22] the Lucha VaVoom set also includes several screens,
where short edited clips from the *cine de luchadores* vast movie history are played.
Along with these clips, specially produced by the Lucha VaVoom crew in
relation to its theme nights – Valentine's Day, Cinco de Mayo (5th of May),[23]

summertime, Halloween – the audience can also see the fancy low-rider car parade, used to escort the performers to the entrance of the theatre. This saturation of the stage space by images from a variety of media emphasizes the daily habits of viewing and image consumption, at least in an average metropolitan context of today, but through its particular combination of lucha libre and burlesque – two genres where the body comprises the spectacular focus – Lucha VaVoom brings the emphasis back onto the body, for performers and the audience alike.[24] Every hold, clutch, claw and lock, every jump, flexing muscle, nipple tassel, bottom shimmy, bump and grind, every scream, applause, boo, wow, and cheer calls attention to the physicality and presence of the body and its ability through gesture to "differentiate, swerve and remark"[25] – the body as the driving force and shaker of promises and constraints. Performances, as performance studies theorist Sharon Mazer reminds us, are built upon bodies – bodies that invite to look and bodies that do the looking, mine being the latter.[26]

On Lucha VaVoom's ring and stage the bodies are mixed gender-wise, ethnically/racially, straight and queer, in size and body type. They are a celebration of the entire spectrum and everything in between and beyond. Yet they are all fit and well-trained, in charge of themselves and dressed up in dazzling costumes: dancers, wrestlers, little people, burlesque dancers (or "buxoticas" – a mix of burlesque and exotica – as they are called in Lucha VaVoom). What is at stake here is not lucha libre's and burlesque's cultural authenticity – or lack of it – but that through alluringly celebrating different bodies Lucha VaVoom might actually and unwittingly serve to mask persistent gender, sexual, ethnical/racial tensions and divert focus away from social-political issues – discrimination and unequal access, as well as gender, heterosexual, and ethnic/racial privileges, among others – that are very far from being resolved in society at large.[27]

Karis and Cassandro: disidentificatory performance practices on stage and in the ring

There is as much of a multitude of bodies as there is a diversity of performance styles contributing to Lucha VaVoom. As I now seek to elaborate, while the performances of Karis and Cassandro are disidentificatory, others are undoubtedly well executed; comedic, even hilarious, but largely perpetuating gender, heterosexuality, racial, and ethnic norms. Karis and Cassandro's performances rather exemplify what literary theorist Jossianna Arroyo has conceptualized as "cultural drag"[28] – a political utilization of drag where the feminine is used "as a vehicle for representing identity." Simultaneously, however, "it constitutes itself as the 'performance' of other cultural, sociopolitical, and subjective orders such as race, class, gender and sexuality."[29] By hula hoop burlesquing and wrestling as cultural drag, do Karis and Cassandro employ disidentificatory performance practices that are not only manifestations of "queer survival"[30] but also strive toward "decolonial desires"?[31] The feminist historian Emma Pérez describes the move into decolonial desires as the following:

> The decolonial imaginary embodies the buried desires of the unconscious, living and breathing in between that which is colonialist and that which is colonized. Within that interstitial space, desire rubs against colonial repressions to construct resistant, oppositional, transformative, diasporic subjectivities that erupt and move into decolonial desires.[32]

Consistent with Pérez, communication and performance theorists Michelle A. Holling and Bernadette Marie Calafell position the "healing of psychic trauma" at the forefront of a decolonial performance practice.[33] This practice works through and performs trauma creating a decolonialized space "in which Chicana/os' agency is possible, permitted, and enacted."[34] Elaborating more extensively on the notion of performance as a site of agency for lesbian, gay, bisexual, trans★, queer people of color, who are left out of representation in a space "colonized by the logics of white normativity and heteronormativity,"[35] performance theorist José Esteban Muñoz proposes a strategy of "disidentification"

> that works on and against dominant ideology. Instead of buckling under the pressures of dominant ideology (identification, assimilation) or attempting to break free of its inescapable sphere (counteridentification, utopianism), this "working on and against" is a strategy that tries to transform a cultural logic from within, always laboring to enact permanent structural change while at the same time valuing the importance of local or everyday struggles of resistance.[36]

Disidentification is purposely a disparate combination of approaches that "captures, collects, and brings into play various theories of fragmentation"[37] and manages to be "a hermeneutic, a process of production, and a mode of performance."[38] Most of all, though, it is not something that can be simply and effortlessly tried out or experimented with, it is rather and decisively "about cultural, material, and psychic survival" and "managing and negotiating historical trauma and systemic violence."[39] It is the "disidentificatory performance's power of critique and its vision of transformative politics"[40] that interests Muñoz and myself. In other words, for me, disidentification is the strategy of survival that comes about within a decolonial imaginary.

Karis and Cassandro's performances as cultural drag

MAN: Lucha . . .
AUDIENCE: VaaaaaaaaVoooooooooooooom!!!!
MAN: Ladies and gentlemen, would you now please welcome everyone's favorite . . . Kaaariiiis!

Karis, who has been with Lucha VaVoom since its beginnings in 2002, enters the stage in a variation of a Tehuana costume,[41] which most of the audience will consider clothing for women and identify with some of the most popular of Frida Kahlo's dresses. The only difference is Karis wears two long woven scarves – one in black with thin stripes in varied colors and the other one in pink with broader stripes in rainbow colors – loosely wrapped around the neck and shoulders and knotted just above the hips. Her flowing, long, black hair is adorned with a white, long, lace headdress crowned with flowers, and her forearms are covered with golden bracelets. This promises to be a racial/ethnic performance that seems so well considered for the night of the Cinco de Mayo celebration, however, the audience's amazement – and with it my own – increases dramatically as Karis's disidentification plays with the conventions of burlesque, drag, and racial/ethnic performances.

Born in a small town in Mexico, and relocated to Los Angeles when ze[42] was just months old, Karis had been bullied as a teenager for being gay. Ze created an anti-violence after-school group, attended prom in drag and worked as a fashion designer for stars in the music and acting industries before ze then started hooping at nineteen as an "outlet for stress."[43] Describing hir show as "a dance/hula hoop spectacle that draws its roots in my own ancestral history, contemporary influences and my background as a fashion designer"[44] makes the significance ze gives to roots evident. The understanding of roots is something that Karis also deems a pressing issue for the LGBT (criticism of the term notwithstanding)[45] community: "No one reads up on their history, like Harry Hay and his struggles with The Mattachine Society – it took a lot of work to get to where we are now. There's so much more to being gay than this pop bubble-gum couture."[46] It seems to me that Karis considers that, in most instances, the pop bubble-gum couture of exoticist modes of representation is unable to account for the specificities of sexually, gendered, ethnically/racially othered bodies, their histories and agencies. They are more often than not erotic/exotic performances that serve a purpose for commodification.

At each swing the Tehuana dress whirls up granting a glimpse of slender, trained legs, in metallic green-blue platform heel sneakers. By catapulting hula hoops around the whole body in elaborated flips, tosses, dancing moves, and body rolls, Karis removes the layers of couture and reveals an androgynous body rather than the assumed female one in tight, black, small colorful striped lederhosen, which most will identify with German-speaking regions. It is a skilled revealment of the construction of racial/ethnic and gender representations, and a teasing and disidentificatory one, which works with contradictory gender and ethnicity/race markers in order to resist and confound identification within an essentialist ethnic/racial attribution and the two-gender system.

MAN: Lucha . . .
AUDIENCE: VaaaaaaaaVooooooooooooom!!!!
MAN: Es un caballero, la reina del ring, el Liberace de lucha libre . . . (He is a gentleman, the queen of the ring, the Liberace of lucha libre . . .) ¡Casaaandroooo!

After an almost three-hour long program, the time has come for the highly anticipated last lucha match of the night: The famous exótiqui Cassandro first appears on a big screen, showing his back in a white jacket with a brocaded train. Cassandro not only alludes to, but also considers himself the "Liberace of lucha libre,"[47] and for a moment, some of the audience might think that Liberace miraculously rose from the dead to give a surprise performance. While Cassandro makes his way up the stairs from the basement, the tremendous train of his outfit falls at least eight steps behind him. The *caballero* is attired in a skin tight pink leotard with shiny silver patterns and a décolletage that plunges to his midriff. The *reina* dances his way through the theatre to the ring to the cumbia rhythm of La Sonora Dinamita's "No Te Metas con Mi Cucu" ("Don't Mess with My Butt"),[48] embedded in the audience's – as much as my own – enthusiastic applause, showing his golden-white boots adorned with big butterflies and rainbows on the tongues, and the occasional sparkle of glitter on his body.

Growing up in Juárez/El Paso with six siblings, an alcoholic father, and a co-dependent mother (they divorced when Cassandro was thirteen), he was sexually abused between the ages of six and sixteen.[49] "Someone considered me as a sex-toy and they used me whenever it pleased them. You live with that and bear the negative parts,"[50] Cassandro says openly. Today, through the choice of his entry song, I consider that Cassandro invites people to admire his butt while simultaneously making it clear to everyone not to mess with it. As the lyrics go:

Si quieres puedes mirar	You can look if you want
Lo que a ti te da la gana	whatever you want
Pero si intentas tocar	but if you try to touch
te daré una cachetada	I'll slap you

The reina is not only Lucha VaVoom's wrestling coordinator, but also undoubtedly the star of the night, relentlessly applying holds and locks, doing aerial maneuvers and even a *beso* (kiss). The last goes almost unnoticed, unlike in a lucha in Mexico where the kiss, as I have shown elsewhere, is centrally important to the lucha itself, and to the audience's participation.[51] Within the luchas' course of action and the audience's unique complicity is the beso, which is demanded, fought over, received, and consummated in the ring and beyond. I would even go so far as to consider it as part of the wrestlers' repertoire of holds, but unlike a hold, it is not directly used to defeat an opponent, but might be applied to distract and/or to provoke. Cassandro elaborates:

When an exótico feels like giving a kiss inside the ring he simply does so, as well as if the public begs for one to be given to a particular spectator. From the very moment the audience sees us stepping into the ring they are already yelling "¡beso!, ¡beso!," as they already know our ways. Many times we feel like giving a kiss to the luchadores because we are very loving characters, yet we are also quite fierce.[52]

It is important to note that in Spanish, Cassandro does not use gender neutral terms. In the last sentence he switches from the masculine gender (the endings '-o(s)' or '-e(s)') in "luchadores" to the feminine one (the ending '-a(s)') in "unas fierecitas" (fierce ones). In this sense, Cassandro cross genders or ambiguously genders the exótiquis and clarifies: "We exóticos are homosexuals, and that's how we fight. We don't experience a conflict with being men and women at the same time."[53]

At the Cinco de Mayo show Cassandro teamed up with El Bombero to wrestle against Dr. Maldad and Puma King. The latter, in a dark gold and yellow mask and outfit, flew in from Mexico City where he wrestles week after week for the oldest lucha libre enterprise, Consejo Mundial de Lucha Libre (World-wide Wrestling Council – CMLL) in Mexico. El Bombero, in his fireman's mask and tight red briefs, and the heavyweight Dr. Maldad, in a black mask and outfit with the colours – red, green, and white – of the Mexican flag, are, like Cassandro, regulars at Lucha VaVoom. The wrestlers rapidly exchange arm and leg locks, dropkicks, diving leg drops, body slams, and flips off the ropes. One moment, when Puma King is on the mat, Cassandro executes a front flip for the joy of the audience and to show his opponent who is the star of the ring and night. A bit later, however, Puma King entraps Cassandro in a maneuver that renders the latter's arms and legs into a lock behind his own butt, while pinning him down. As soon as Cassandro's shoulders touch the mat the referee Plataini-tos starts to count but as Cassandro ingeniously escapes he only gets to smash the mat twice. Now it is the turn of El Bombero and Dr. Maldad: it is an easy one for the latter, who in a turning manoeuver slams the lighter opponent, El Bombero, on his back with his lower legs raised. Suddenly, the spotlights picks Cassandro out, high on a tower of loudspeakers planning to dive. Is the Liberace of lucha libre going to do it? He does, deep into the seats, scattering the audi-ence. It must have been four meters to the floor. The audience is thrilled and wants more. Back at the ring, however, Cassandro hits a Sunset flip on Puma King while El Bombero delivers a 450 splash on Dr. Maldad, both from top ropes. The referee counts one, two, three – the match is theirs and the audience is on its feet, applauding, screaming, whistling. What a lucha!

There are two important disidentifactory strategies Cassandro demonstrates in relation to his choice of identifying with Liberace. First, Cassandro is openly gay, and second, unlike Liberace's famous flying performances over the stage and audience, while being attached to a wire, Cassandro puts his body at risk again and again, high flying cordlessly from the loudspeakers, as in the lucha described before, or from the balcony into the crowd. As a result, at the Cinco de Mayo show, Cassandro announced that he was going into retirement due to multiple injuries over the years that require yet another surgery. After a masterful and vic-torious lucha libre performance, he makes the limits of the body obvious while acknowledging his bodily vulnerability. In this sense, Cassandro does not shy away from destabilizing, working on, and against – or disidentifying from – invincibility in a field where the characters are almighty and no defeat can be final.

Karis and Cassandro's performances activate the strategy of cultural drag. According to Arroyo this strategy "deconstructs and parodies 'pure essences' of identity, while the audience plays within these 'essential' constructions by putting their own gaze in evidence."[54] By employing gender and racial/ethnical ambiguity Karis and Cassandro call attention to how gender and racial/ethnical markers play a decisive role in categorizing, judging, empathizing and/or consuming bodies. During their performances it is the audience who performs gender and ethnicity/race when they strive to identify in "this in-between space in which the body does not attain an all-encompassing significance, but it remains in that place of negotiation and agency."[55] It is the audience who, in the very process of seeing and participating – through identification, disidentification, and everything in between – might realize their own role in the performance of gender and race/ethnicity as a constant state of becoming.

Awry Lucha VaVoom: Againstogether exoticist modes of representation, perception, and consumption

Lucha VaVoom is both haunted by and resistant toward exoticist modes of representation, perception, and consumption. Lucha VaVoom, as a whole, cannot fully shake off the traces of "the logics of white normativity and heteronormativity"[56] or ensuing exoticism that its performances verge on, neither through the performing nor the looking. It takes place in between the very space of an established hierarchy of sexuality, gender, and ethnicity/race on which sexual, gender, and ethnic/racial diversity is predicated. There are complex, transnational, and often contradictory subject positions that mark Lucha VaVoom, while the exotic is always already in excess of any attempt to contain it. It might be in the space againstogether of excess and containment that lets the contradictions of Lucha VaVoom unfold themselves leaving the audience to weigh what they see and participate in.

Performances like the ones of Karis and Cassandro push Lucha VaVoom to a place where questions are posed, and not just to a place where the audience, and me along with it, are simply satisfied. They enable an interrogation of the way in which exoticist modes of representation operate as a mask. During their performances this mask moves and even temporarily slips to forge a critical and disidentificatory way of perceiving and consuming. Through exposing the exotic/erotics underlying the performative "againstogether" of performers and audience, their performances empower, as Muñoz put it, a disidentification "as a way of shuffling back and forth between reception and production."[57] Without a doubt, Karis and Cassandro play with images of the exotic; however, they work on and against mainstream's sexualization and exoticization of bodies of color.

In their performances as cultural drag, embodiment is tangible, visible, experienced, enhanced, and performed allowing the audience to join in, to put their participation in evidence. Here, while the audience glimpses a queer survival striving for decolonial desires they are simultaneously reminded to be very wary of easy and feel-good celebrations of diversity.

Notes

1 Since its opening in 1927 the theatre changed its name three times: the Mayan Theatre, the Fabulous Mayan (in the 1960s) and the Mayan (since the 1990s). At first, the Mayan Theatre was showing musical and theatre productions. In the 1940s, it was a burlesque house. By the end of the decade it screened arthouse films. From the 1950s to the early 1970s, it was used as a Mexican film venue before it became an adult porn theatre. After being solely a nightclub since 1990, the concept and setting of Lucha VaVoom, as I set out to show in my article "El Teatro Maya" (Hoechtl, 2015), links the space back to the history of the Mayan Theatre itself. My article analyzes through the notion of "cultural travestism" the processes of appropriation, exoticization, incorporation, commodification and consumption of imageries belonging to modernity/coloniality of the Mayan Theatre.

2 The Mayan Theatre had originally a seating capacity of 1,491. Since the 1990s the main floor has been terraced and no longer has fixed seating.

3 The basic framework for lucha libre as it exists today came about through the founding of the private Consejo Mundial de Lucha Libre (Worldwide Wrestling Council – CMLL), back then the Empresa Mexicana de la Lucha Libre (Mexican Wrestling Enterprise – EMLL). On September 21, 1933, lucha libre made its debut in the Arena Modelo in Mexico City. The promoter Salvador Lutteroth and his partner Francisco Ahumada first brought in wrestlers from Texas, and later on from Germany, Poland, Italy, and beyond. Lucha libre was not directly part of the state-funded, post-revolutionary cultural projects, yet it began in the context of the post-revolutionary period, when the modern relationship between popular culture and *mexicanidad* (mexicanness) was born. Lucha libre is organized by empresas, private enterprises consisting of at least one promoter and a stable of luchadoris. Today the biggest competition to CMLL http://www.cmll.com/ is Triple A (AAA; http://www.luchalibreaaa.com/), which was founded in 1992 and is owned by the television company Televisa. For more about lucha libre in Mexico, see Janina Möbius, *Und unter der Maske . . . das Volk. LUCHA LIBRE – Ein mexikanisches Volksspektakel zwischen Tradition und Moderne* (Frankfurt: Vervuert Verlag, 2004); Heather Levi, *The World of Lucha Libre. Secrets, Revelations, and Mexican National Identity* (Durham: Duke University Press, 2008); Nina Hoechtl, *If Only for the Length of a Lucha: Queer/ing, Mask/ing, Gender/ing and Gesture in Lucha Libre* (PhD diss., Goldsmiths, University of London, 2012), among others.

4 Since 1952 approximately 300 lucha libre movies – Cine de luchadores – have been produced. In them the luchadoris liberate the world from crazy scientists, monsters, aliens, vampires, mummies, and other infamous threats. For more on the Cine de luchadores see Nelson Carro, *El Cine de Luchadores* (Mexico City: Filmoteca de la UNAM, 1984); Raúl Criollo, José Xavier Nava and Rafael Avina, *¡Quiero ver sangre!: Historia ilustrada del Cine de luchadores* (Mexico City: UNAM, 2012).

5 I am a close to 40-year-old, white, abled, highly educated bio-female from a middle-class background in Austria who has been living in Mexico City the last eight years and goes regularly to lucha libre events. As the feminist writer and theorists Anne McClintock points out, it is very important to keep in mind that it makes a difference if a person – like me – who is part of a privileged group is the one displaying ambiguity or if it is one who does not belong to this group:

> The disruption of social norms is not always subversive, especially in postmodernist commodity cultures where formal fluidity, fragmentation and marketing through

diff erence are central elements. Indeed, privileged groups can, on occasion, display their privilege precisely by the extravagant display of their *right to ambiguity*. . . . In short, the staging of symbolic disorder by the privileged can merely preempt challenges by those who do not possess the power to stage ambiguity with comparable license or authority. (1995, 68–69, italics in the original)

6 The Spanish language has two genders, masculine and feminine; it has no neutral noun class. In the plural, a group of mixed gender objects will traditionally carry masculine gender. One proposed alternate spelling that allows identities that are not covered by the feminine, or masculine gender is with the ending *-is*. Replacing *-o-a* or *-e* with the letter *-i* does work as much in written Spanish as when it is pronounced. See Richard Stallman, "Un nuevo sistema fácil para conseguir neutralidad de género en la lengua castellana," 2011, accessed March 23, 2012, http://stallman.org/articles/castellano-sin-genero.html. I do not apply this alternate spelling in quotes.

Since the beginning of lucha libre in Mexico in the 1930s, men have wrestled men, and since the 1940s women and exótiquis have joined in. *Exótico* is a term used to describe the bio-male wrestlers who cross-dress and/or display mannerisms usually coded as female in the ring. The majority of exótiquis today identify as gay. The term exótico is related to the Spanish term raro, a commonly used word that roughly translates as "queer." In addition to these wrestlers, since the 1950s *minis* or "midget" wrestlers have participated. Minis mainly imitate the appearances of successful luchadoris as they wrestle. In Mexico, in a *lucha mixta*, everyone fights against everyone: women vs. men vs. minis vs. exótiquis. For more about the exotiquis, see Heather Levi, "Lean Mean Fighting Queens: Drag in the World of Mexican Professional Wrestling," *Sexualities* 1, no. 3 (1998): 275–285; Nina Hoechtl, "Lucha libre: un espacio liminal. Lis exótiquis "juntopuestas" a las categorías clasificadoras, unívocas y fija" in *La memoria y el deseo. Estudios gay y queer en México*, ed. Rodrigo Parrini (Mexico City: PUEG-UNAM, 2014), 223–251, among others.

7 Levi, *The World of Lucha Libre*, 26; Robert C. Allen, *Horrible Prettiness: Burlesque and American Culture* (Chapel Hill: University of North Carolina Press, 1991), 27.

8 Hoechtl, *If Only for the Length of a Lucha*, 113.

9 Reed Johnson, "Lucha VaVoom and Cirque Berzerk are L.A.'s Theatre of the Odd," *Los Angeles Times*, July 19, 2009, accessed April 7, 2015, http://articles.latimes.com/2009/jul/19/entertainment/ca-alternative19.

10 Ibid.

11 Besides their events at the Mayan, Lucha VaVoom has sold out 1,000-seat venues in Amsterdam, Calgary, Toronto, San Francisco, New York, Chicago, Seattle, Portland, and Philadelphia, among many other cities.

12 Chris Jones, "Lucha va va voom! Mexican Wrestling is Blended with Burlesque, Heavily Spiced with Irony," *Chicago Tribune*, May 9, 2005, accessed April 15, 2015, http://articles.chicagotribune.com/2005–05–09/features/0505090016_1_wrestling-mexican-announcers.

13 Ibid.

14 Graham Huggan, *The Postcolonial Exotic: Marketing the Margins* (London and New York: Routledge, 2001), 7.

15 Jones, "Lucha Va Va Voom!"

16 Dorothy M. Figueira, *The Exotic: A Decadent Quest* (New York: State University of New York Press, 1994), 13.

17 bell hooks, "Eating the Other," in *Black Looks: Race and Representation* (Cambridge, MA: South End Press, 1992), 21.

18 Huggan, *The Postcolonial Exotic*, 153.

19 Ibid.

20 Ibid., 13.

21 Ibid.

22 Jones, "Lucha Va Va Voom!"

23 In her article *Rethinking Cinco de Mayo*, human relation and multicultural education theorist Sudie Hofman names the ethnic stereotypes embodied in the commercial appropriation of Cinco de Mayo as it is celebrated in the United States. For more see Sudie Hofman, "Rethinking Cinco de Mayo," *Zinn Education Project*, May 5, 2012, accessed March 15, 2015, http://zinnedproject.org/2012/05/rethinking-cinco-de-mayo/.

24 In his introduction to *Steel Chair to the Head*, media studies theorist Nicholas Sammond points out that wrestling shares with burlesque "a celebration of public (hetero)sexuality and a complex and imperfect expression of gendered power relations (Allen, 1991)." Nicholas Sammond, introduction to *Steel Chair to the Head: The Pleasure and Pain of Professional Wrestling*, ed. Nicholas Sammond (Durham: Duke University Press, 2005), 3.

25 Carrie Noland, *Agency and Embodiment: Performing Gestures/Producing Culture* (Cambridge, MA: Harvard University Press, 2009), 212.

26 Sharon Mazer, "Skirting Burlesque," *Australasian Drama Studies* 63 (October 2013), 28.

27 For example, the legislation SB1070 in the state of Arizona from 2010 reflects very contemporary acts of (neo-)colonial enforcement and exclusion, as it criminalized daily interactions with undocumented immigrants, imposed severe penalties on immigrants who failed to carry immigration documentation, and mandated the police to investigate immigration status of those they thought might be in the country without authorization. For more see Ann Morse, "Arizona's Immigration Enforcements Laws," *National Conference of State Legislatures*, July 28, 2011, accessed August 8, 2015, http://www.ncsl.org/research/immigration/analysis-of-arizonas-immigration-law.aspx.

In *Queering the Color Line*, gender studies theorist Siobhan B. Somerville argues that it is not "a historical coincidence that the classification of bodies as either 'homosexual' or 'heterosexual' emerged at the same time when the United States was aggressively constructing and policing the boundary between 'black' and 'white' bodies." Siobhan B. Somerville, *Queering the Color Line: Race and the Invention of Homosexuality in American Culture* (Durham: Duke University Press, 2000), 3. In *Queering the Borderlands* the Chicana historian Emma Pérez took her premise further and argues that "it is not historical coincidence that the classification of homosexual and heterosexual appeared at the same time that the United States began aggressively policing the border between the United States and Mexico." Emma Pérez, "Queering the Borderlands: The Challenges of Excavating the Invisible and Unheard," *Frontiers: A Journal of Women Studies* 24, no. 2/3, Gender on the Borderlands (2003): 126.

28 Jossianna Arroyo, "Mirror, Mirror on the Wall: Performing Racial and Gender Identities in Javier Cardona's 'You Don't Look Like,'" in *The State of Latino Theater in the United States: Hybridity, Transculturation, and Identity*, ed. Luis A. Ramos-García (New York: Routledge, 2002). Arroyo distinguishes between the concept of "cultural drag" used in her essay "Mirror, Mirror on the Wall" and the notion of "cultural transvestism" that grounds her book *Travestismos Culturales* (2003). The cultural drag as a strategy questions class, race, gender, and sexuality, while cultural transvestism implies a mode of deception by a hegemonic writing subject that appropriates the voices of minoritarian peoples.

29 Ibid., 156.

30 José Esteban Muñoz, *Disidentifications: Queers of Color and the Performance of Politics* (Minneapolis: University of Minnesota Press, 1999).

31 Emma Pérez, *The Decolonial Imaginary: Writing Chicanas into History* (Bloomington and Indianapolis: Indiana University Press, 1999).

32 Ibid., 110.

33 Michelle A. Holling and Bernadette Marie Calafell, "Identities on Stage and Staging Identities: ChicanoBrujo Performances as Emancipatory Practices," *Text and Performance Quarterly* 27, no. 1 (January 2007): 78.

34 Ibid.

35 Muñoz, *Disidentifications*, xii.

36 Ibid., 11–12.

37 Ibid., 31.

38 Ibid., 25.

39 Ibid., 161.

40 Ibid., 189.

41 The term Tehuana refers to an indigenous woman from the town of Tehuantepec, Oaxaca, the center of Zapoteca culture.

42 In order to keep the gender ambiguity of Karis's performance in my writing I hereby use the pronouns "ze" instead of "he" or "she" and "hir" instead of "his" or "her." "Interview with . . . Kate Bornstein on Gender Outlaws," April 26, 2012, accessed December 18, 2014, http://fivebooks.com/interviews/kate-bornstein-on-gender.

43 "Karis Wilde," *Frontiers Media*, June 30, 2011, accessed March 28, 2015, https://www.frontiersmedia.com/uncategorized/2011/06/30/karis-wilde/.

44 Ibid.

45 Many persons, especially those coming of age, have different conceptions of gender and sexuality and they do not define themselves in the terms of LGBT. For more see Michael Schulman, "Generation LGBTQIA," *New York Times*, January 9, 2013, accessed August 3, 2015, http://www.nytimes.com/2013/01/10/fashion/generation-lgbtqia.html?_r=0.

46 Ibid.

47 Ibid.

48 It is important to note that in Spanish the word *cucu* is a made-up word. It is through the context of the other words that it becomes clear that it refers to the butt. In the exótiquis' fighting repertoire, the butt plays a crucial role. Whenever it touches an opponent's crotch or face, hence symbolically inviting them to anal intercourse or "salad-tossing," it makes them run away or faint, respectively.

49 Lucas Gutierrez, "Cassandro 'El Exótico': El Liberace de la lucha libre," *FriendlyLife*, September 26, 2014, accessed March 28, 2015, http://friendlylife.com/espectaculos/18076; William Finnegan, "The Man without a Mask: How the Drag Queen Cassandro Became a Star of Mexican Wrestling," *New Yorker*, September 1, 2014, accessed March 28, 2015, http://www.newyorker.com/magazine/2014/09/01/man-without-mask.

50 Lucas Gutierrez, "Cassandro 'El Exótico.'" Translation from Spanish: "Alguien me miraba como un 'sex toy' (juguete sexual), me usaban cuando querían. Vives con eso y cargas con lo negativo."

51 Hoechtl, *If Only for the Length of a Lucha*, 118–126.

52 Lola Miranda Fascinetto, *Sin Máscara Ni Cabellera: Lucha libre en México hoy* (Mexico City: Marc Ediciones, 1992), 195. Translation from Spanish:

> Cuando a un exótico le nace dar un beso arriba del ring lo da y también cuando el público lo pide para algún especador en particular. Desde el momento en que el público nos ve salir para subir al ring ya está gritando "¡beso!, ¡beso!," pues ya conoce nuestra forma de ser. Muchas veces a nosotros nos nace darle un picorete a los luchadores porque cariñoso es nuestro modo de ser, pero a la vez somos unas fierecitas también.

53 Ibid., 194. Translation from Spanish: "Los Exóticos somos homosexuals y así es el tipo de nuestra lucha. Nosotros no vivimos en conflicto de ser hombres y mujeres a la vez."

54 Arroyo, "Mirror, Mirror on the Wall," 166.

55 Jossianna Arroyo, "Sirena canta boleros: travestismo y sujetos transcaribeños en *Sirena Selena vestida de pena*," *CENTRO: Journal of the Center for Puerto Rican Studies* 15, no. 2 (2003): 42. Translation from Spanish: "un espacio intermedio en el que el cuerpo no logra una trascendencia totalizadora, sino que se queda en ese lugar de negociación y agencia."

56 Muñoz, *Disidentifications*, xii.

57 Ibid., 25.

Part IV

Gender

The impact of women's pro wrestling performances on the transformation of gender

Keiko Aiba (translated by Minata Hara)

In this chapter[1] I examine how the performance of women pro wrestlers trans-forms Japan's gender norms. In Japan, promoters have staged women-only pro wrestling matches separate from men's pro wrestling organizations. All-Japan Women's Pro Wrestling Corporation (Zenjo [All Women], for short), estab-lished in 1968 was the main promoter of these matches.[2] Three times between the 1970s and the early 1990s, Zenjo succeeded in promoting the women pro wrestlers as popular pop icons. As women wrestlers came into the spotlight, women's pro wrestling changed its image from an erotic sideshow to a sport entertainment with healthy glamour.[3]

In the late 1970s, Fuji TV made major contributions in creating a pop icon image by airing women pro wrestling cards on television. Fuji TV carefully staged each event by costuming the wrestlers in dazzling outfits and making them sing their popular hit songs.[4] For about two decades, from 1971 to 1990, singers dominated Japan's entertainment scene.[5] Thus women wrestlers who sang their original songs before their wrestling matches were regarded as enter-tainers and gained popularity not only by their wrestling but also through their songs. The emergence of the tag team "Crush Gals," which became immensely popular, was epoch-making for women's pro wrestling due to their genuinely aggressive techniques mainly borrowed from karate to "defeat the opponent" instead of "pulling the punches" like their predecessors did.[6] As their popularity grew with "real aggressive fight," high-level techniques became the new stand-ard for women pro wrestlers (Figure 8.1). On the other hand, this standard has increased injuries among women pro wrestlers, causing some serious physical damage. Even though most are staged matches, serious fights would result in occasional injury.

To examine how performances of women wrestlers transform gender norms in Japan, I interviewed twenty-five women pro wrestlers in Japan (three of whom were retired) and attended many bouts in 2004 and 2005. First names of the wrestlers in the case study section are all pseudonyms unless otherwise stated.[7]

Figure 8.1 Komando Borishoi delivers an Avalanche Backdrop Suplex on Kura-gaki Tsubasa. (© JWP).

The sex/gender system and the gender order

Like many Western countries, gender categories of "man/woman" in Japan are socially constructed in accordance with sex categories of "male/female" determined by one's physical traits. Moreover, the individual sex category is assumed to define not only one's gender category (man/woman) but also one's sexual orientation (i.e., whether one is attracted to men or women).[8] Sex, gender and sexual orientation are assumed to be a dichotomous construct comprised of only two categories[9] and have close ideological links with each other. I call this the "sex/gender system," after the work of Gayle Rubin who conceptualized this ideological triad of sex, gender and sexual orientation in 1975.

It is mandatory for all individuals in this dichotomous world to indicate which sex category one belongs to. Thus one is driven toward the typical body image of the corresponding sex category one belongs to (either masculine or feminine).[10] Although the model image one pursues is that of an ideal male or female body, it is by no means mandatory in daily life to embody this ideal, providing that others can perceive your gender expression. Thus, the body retains the ideal female (or male) image as long as the expression can be recognized as feminine (or masculine). I refer to this as the normative female body versus the normative male body.

People who are classified as male or female by the sex/gender system conduct diverse social practices that are constructed through regularly conducted social practices strongly tied to male or female categories.[11] Through these social practices people acquire either men's or women's "gender habitus." Yumiko Ehara defines gender habitus as a standard of assessment by which we assess the "human appearance, demeanor and behavior based on such aesthetic perceptions as beautiful – ugly."[12] Ehara further states that gender order consists of three components: (1) the structural traits attributed to sex category (i.e, asymmetric power distribution between the two categories); (2) regularly conducted social practices strongly tied to the two categories based on item 1; and (3) gender habitus generated by item 2.[13] Ehara contends that the gender division of labor and heterosexuality are the two constructs of the gender order. The gender order inherent in the gender division of labor defines men as *subjects* of action and women as *supporters* of the action of others. The heterosexual gender order defines men as *subjects* and women as *objects* of sexual desire. My analysis in this chapter focuses on the heterosexual gender order.

The heterosexual gender order and the ideal body

Ehara contends that the heterosexual gender order induces a perception–oriented assessment pattern to evaluate a woman's worth based on "sexual attractiveness," and encourages women to adapt to this perception–oriented scale in daily practice that regulates one's outer appearance and demeanor.[14] This means that women acquire a gender habitus, or a "psychological tendency to perceive themselves as 'objects of sexual desire.'"[15] This gender habitus is formed through the "idealized male/female images that abound in the social environment."[16]

The problem here is the fact that the body women idealize for themselves is not exactly the same as the female body image idealized by men.[17] Since my study focuses on how women wrestlers evaluate and transform their bodies, in my analysis I will use the female body image women idealize, as well as the male body image men idealize. According to some studies,[18] the feminine body idealized by men and women from the late teens and early twenties is defined as thin, with long slender legs and full breasts. On the other hand, the ideal body male students wish to have for themselves is the so-called inverted triangle, characterized by muscular build, broad shoulders and a trim waistline.[19]

Normative male and female bodies in sport

Through the study of gendered bodies in sport, I became aware of the fact that although modern competitive sport embraces body images similar to the aforementioned ideals, normative body image is constructed independently for men and for women. Since there are few studies that address this viewpoint in Japan, I would like to draw from studies conducted in the English language. First, R.W. Connell argues that, in the Western world, the ideal masculine image is constructed through sport. The social definition of a man as a person in power is "translated not only into mental body-images and fantasies, but into muscle tensions, posture, the feel and texture of the body."[20] This physical perception of masculinity easily transforms into male superiority or male dominance over women.[21] This shows that the ideal masculinity is constructed as men develop specific types of bodies through sport.[22] In contrast, the female body, which has no such muscles, is assumed to lack this kind of physical power and aggression.[23] You may notice some women in sports developing muscles and conducting aggressive performances; those features, however, are not celebrated by the media, at least in Japan, because they are not normative for women. For example, when the all-Japan women's football team won the World Cup in 2011, Japanese media flocked to feature several outstanding players on the team. Yet, as I argued in 2013, few media reports celebrated their muscles or physical strength. This shows that, at least in the Japanese sports scene, the normative male body is defined as a body with a muscular build that is strong, powerful and aggressive. On the other hand, the normative female body is considered to be non-aggressive and without rugged muscles even in sport.

Reproduction and transformation of gender norms

This section explains the criteria of how women wrestlers' performances are interpreted as reproduction or transformation of gender norms. If a woman pro wrestler has the gender habitus to regard herself as an object of sexual desire, or practices daily conduct that constructs one's own appearance or demeanor based on this habitus, she is regarded as reproducing the heterosexual gender order. This means that a woman pro wrestler who embodies an idealized female physique is reproducing the heterosexual gender order.

On the other hand, if a woman pro wrestler's gender habitus is such that she considers herself a "subject" of sexual desire, or practices daily conduct that constructs one's own appearance or demeanor based on this habitus, she is transforming the heterosexual gender order. Furthermore, the body of women wrestlers who allow the traits of the ideal *female* body and those of the ideal *male* body to coexist in themselves effectively destabilizes, and thus transforms, the dichotomous sex–gender system that defines the ideal female/male bodies as separate constructs and prohibits these traits from coexisting in a single body.

If the performance of a woman wrestler does not exhibit rugged muscles or aggression but expresses weakness, she is *reproducing* the normative female body in sports. On the other hand, if the woman wrestler represents a muscular body that is strong and aggressive, which are the traits of the normative male body, she is *transforming* the normative female body image in sports.

Performances of women pro wrestlers

In this section, I will examine the performance of women pro wrestlers captured through interviews and observations by using the criteria explained in the previous section.

"Sexy" use of the body

In her bouts, the wrestler Rumi Kazama (her actual ring name) performs such sexy poses as shaking her hips and putting up her hair. This type of performance presents herself as a sexually attractive object to the spectators, and is thus considered to reproduce the heterosexual gender order. Kazama, however, does not always perform this kind of sexy performance in the ring.

In her bouts, this kind of sexy performance comes in between very aggressive hard combat. In her performance, Kazama expresses aggression, which the normative female body in sports is by no means encouraged to perform. Thus, by showing aggressive pro wrestling, Kazama is transforming the normative female body in sports. At the same time, by making sexy moves, she reminds the spectators that her body is sexually attractive. This means Kazama practices a gender habitus constructed by the heterosexual gender order that makes her body sexually desirable, and thus reproduces the heterosexual gender order.

"Kawaii" (adorable) trait and women pro wrestlers

Masumi is another woman wrestler who has been expected to perform the role of a wrestling pop icon. According to Ichikawa (2002), an "idol" (pop icon) is defined in Japan's postwar mass culture as "a popular girl (or boy)-next-door."[24]

To be an idol, one must have a "friendly-looking face or appearance."[25] In other words, you must be *kawaii*. While the definition has changed over time, female pop stars in Japan have always been highly expected to be *kawaii*.[26] Since Masumi is idolized by her fans, she must be a *kawaii* wrestler.

How, then, can we define *kawaii*? Inuhiko Yomota argues that kawaii is the antithesis of "beauty," and states that kawaii is the opposite of what is "sacred, perfect or eternal."[27] It is "something that is forever superficial, fading and transient; secular; imperfect; immature."[28] Meanwhile, "looking at it from the other side," he defines kawaii as "familiar, easy to identify with, and having a construct of psychological proximity that makes it highly accessible."[29] Moreover, Yomota contends that this proximity and accessibility is "synonymous to a desire to dominate someone who is inferior."[30] Since Masumi was relatively small compared to other women wrestlers, she was "the little one." At the time of the interview, her career as a pro wrestler was less than five years, a period too short to be regarded as an experienced fighter. For these reasons, Masumi was regarded as a kawaii-type idol among the women wrestlers.

Are kawaii wrestlers treated as sexual objects? According to Miyadai and Ohmori, the concept of kawaii became an attribute "suitable for 'sexually mature bodies'" with the emergence of female pop icons of the late 1960s.[31] The kawaii female idols of this era have even appeared in men's magazines donning a swimsuit.[32] This means that being an idolized wrestler is congruent with becoming an sexual object. Masumi herself, however, is quite unreceptive to the treatment she receives as an idol-wrestler. On her way to a venue for a match, she prefers sportswear for the gym over "pretty outfits" that are essential for maintaining an idol wrestler image. Masumi's acts that reject the stereotyped idol-wrestler image can be considered to transform the heterosexual gender order that requires women to express their outer appearance based on the women's "psychological tendency to perceive and assess oneself as a 'sexual object.'"[33]

Another wrestler, Yuko, also states that "being *kawaii* is not enough, you must be able to express what you are," otherwise women wrestlers won't be able to have a successful career. In postwar Japan, especially since the sixties and the seventies, mass pop culture continuously produced kawaii pop icons.[34] Women's magazines targeting women readers at large trumpet how women *should* stay kawaii.[35] Some women boast how much they profit by acting kawaii in society.[36] Considering all this, being called kawaii is generally a compliment for many women, although its reception may vary by age. In women's pro wrestling, however, Yuko contends that merely being kawaii is not sufficient if you want to become a popular figure. What women wrestlers need is to establish a powerful persona through their performances and leave a strong impression in the mind of the spectators. This, in turn, means that even if a woman wrestler does not embrace the usual attribute of kawaii – which is a value most women of contemporary Japan embrace – she still has a chance to succeed in the world of women's pro wrestling. Even with large and strong female bodies that are difficult to describe as kawaii and outfits that do not embody kawaii-ness in the least, women wrestlers gain a positive reception from the spectators as long as they are highly entertaining. Here, the heterosexual gender order is transformed to such an extent that the kawaii element is reduced to just one of the many elements of personality.

"Poor little baby face . . .!"

With her performance, Masumi tries to evoke feelings of sympathy among the spectators: "look at poor little baby face all bashed up!" Sanae is also a "baby face" (the heroic, "good guy" wrestler), so it is crucial to show how much pain she suffers in order to evoke pity and win the hearts of the audience. In contrast, Yuko's and Maki's narratives show that women wrestlers who are physically larger or look more powerful become "heels" (the "bad guys") who bully the baby faces.

The baby face wrestlers Masumi and Sanae are relatively small; they are not very strong and can seldom win, while Yuko, who is tall and a heavyweight, seems to be much bigger in size.[37] Compared to Masumi and Sanae, Yuko was a wrestler with more appeal in terms of physical strength. Therefore, Masumi and Sanae reinforce the normative female body in sport, while Yuko transforms the normative female body conceptualized in sport.

The physique of Masumi, Sanae and Yuko can also be analyzed using kawaii as a parameter. One crucial element of kawaii is to be small, so the slight build of Masumi and Sanae is recognized as a kawaii physique. Similarly, kawaii is synonymous to being easily dominated,[38] which makes the kawaii body a weak body. Moreover, since kawaii bodies are regarded sexually desirable, the slight build and the helpless-looking bodies of Masumi and Sanae reproduce the heterosexual gender order. In contrast, a large-sized female body is not a kawaii body; it is not the typical, sexually desirable body men sympathize with. Under the male/female gender habitus of the heterosexual gender order, Yuko's large-sized female body is considered "ugly" or "unpleasant,"[39] so she logically ends up taking on the role of the wicked "heel" who bullies the sexually desirable baby face. Nevertheless she was one of the more popular wrestlers because the kawaii element in women's pro wrestling exists as just one of the many elements of personality and the spectators enjoyed her performances.

Let me further elucidate that Masumi's physique and performance have a complex relationship with the heterosexual gender order that encourages women to perceive themselves as a "sexual object." On one hand, the refusal of Masumi to play along with her idol-wrestler image duly transforms the heterosexual gender order that requires her to present herself as a sexual object. On the other hand, the small and helpless physique she presents in her performance suggests a sexually desirable body that reinforces the heterosexual gender order.

The wrestler's outfit versus the female body

Mika says she is conscious of her own traits as a feminine wrestler. Her costume expresses her femininity. Sanae's costume was decorated with pretty ribbons that emphasized her kawaii qualities. Both Mika and Sanae reproduce the heterosexual gender order by expressing femininity and kawaii tastes. Sawako, another wrestler, goes on to say that she wears "revealing costumes that inadvertently show the cleavage" to emphasize her womanliness. Because cleavage is a prominent feature of the ideal female body, the effort to emphasize this point in the costume is considered a clear expression of one's will to be regarded as sexually desirable. This, in turn, reproduces the existent heterosexual gender order.

Ryoko wears a costume that widely exposes her back and emphasizes the size of her breasts. Showing part of her bottom emphasizes the sexy look. These qualities depict her as someone who is sexually desirable, and reproduces the existent heterosexual order. On the other hand, Ryoko's shoulders are broad, her back bulky and her waistline firm. As I explained, broad shoulders are one of the ideal elements of the ideal male body in Japan. So, while her wide-open costume and her large breasts express the ideal female body, her X-shaped torso represents the element of the ideal male body. Ryoko's body possesses the ideal elements of both the female *and* the male body. In this sense, her body works to transform the existent heterosexual gender order. Furthermore, as Ryoko's body possesses the ideal elements of both female and male bodies, it destabilizes and thus transforms the dichotomous sex/gender system that does not allow normative male/female elements to coexist in one body and keeps them separate.

Conclusion

The typical scheme of the "poor little baby face" versus the "wicked heel" reproduces the heterosexual gender order. In the world of women's pro wrestling, however, kawaii is not the only and foremost value; rather, it exists along with the other personality traits. This value system in women's pro wrestling in Japan transforms the heterosexual gender order. Similarly, if we look at the body of the women pro wrestlers and their outfits/costumes, those who wished to express kawaii and "sexy" qualities would reproduce the heterosexual gender order. Meanwhile, those women wrestlers who simultaneously perform traits of the ideal *female* body and the ideal *male* body would transform the heterosexual gender order. The bodies of these women wrestlers destabilize and transform the dichotomous construct of the sex/gender system, which separates the construct of the ideal *female* body from the ideal *male* body and prohibits these traits from coexisting in one single body. These reproductions and transformations generate complexity in the world of women's pro wrestling.

Notes

1 This chapter is a part of chapter 6 of Keiko Aiba, *Joshi puroresura no shintai to jenda-kihanteki onnarashisa wo koete* (*Body and Gender of Women Pro-Wrestlers in Japan: Beyond "Normative" Femininity*). Tokyo: Akashi Shoten, 2013.

2 Yoshie Kamei, *Joshi puroresu minzoku shi: Monogatari no hajimari* (*Ethnography of Women Pro Wrestling: So the Story Begins*) (Tokyo: Yuzankaku, 2000), 48.

3 Ibid., 42, 50.

4 Ibid., 24.

5 Hiroshi Ogawa, "Aidoru kashu no tanjyo to henyo" ("Birth and Transformation of Idol Singers"), in *Gendai no ongaku* (*Modern Music*) (Tokyo: Tokyo Shoseki, 1991), 91.

6 Kamei, *Joshi puroresu minzoku shi*, 29.

7 For details see Keiko Aiba, "Japanese Women Professional Wrestlers and Body Image." In *Transforming Japan: How Feminism and Diversity Are Making a Difference*, ed. Kumiko Fujimura-Fanselow, New York: Feminist Press, 2011.

8 Judith Butler, *Gender Troubles* (New York: Routledge, [1990] 1999), 30; Sara Crawley, Lara J. Foley, and Constance L. Shehan, *Gendering Bodies* (Lanham, MD: Rowman & Littlefield), 16.

9 Butler, *Gender Troubles*, 30; Gayle Rubin, "The Traffic in Women: Notes on the 'Political Economy,'" in *Toward an Anthropology of Women* (New York: Monthly Review Press, 1975), 159.

10 Yumiko Ehara, *Jenda chitsujo* (*Gender Order*) (Tokyo: Keiso Shobo, 2001), 330.

11 Ibid., 116.

12 Ibid., 331.

13 Ibid., 120.

14 Ibid., 147.

15 Ibid., 151–152.

16 Ibid., 330.

17 Megumi Kanamoto, Tamio Yokozawa, and Masuo Kanamoto, "Shintai ni taisuru sougo ninshiki ni kansuru kenkyu," *Jochi Daigaku Taiiku* 32 (1999): 1–10; Kiyotada Kato, Tadaaki Yajima, and Kazumasa Seki, "Gendai nihonjin seinen no shintaibikan ni tsuite – Daigakusei no chosa kara," *Waseda daigaku taiiku kenkyu kiyo* 22 (1990): 13–20.

18 Reiko Tanaka, "Wakai jyosei no soshin dzukuri ni kansuru shakaigaku teki kosatsu: jyoshigakusei kunin no jirei wo tooshite," *Taiikugaku kenkyu* 41 (1997): 328–339.

19 Kiyotada Kato, Tadaaki Yajima, and Kazumasa Seki. "Gendai nihonjin seinen no shintaibikan ni tsuite – Daigakusei no chosa kara," *Waseda daigaku taiiku kenkyu kiyo* 22 (1990): 18; Toshiko Sugawara, "Daigakusei no shintai ishiki ni tsuite – danshi shintai ishiki no gonindo," *Toyo Daigaku Kiyo Kyoyokatei hen* (*Hokentaiku*) 1 (1991): 23–39.

20 R.W. Connell, *Gender & Power* (Stanford: Stanford University Press, 1987), 85.

21 Ibid.

22 Jennifer Hargreaves, "Where's the Virtue? Where's the Grace?," *Theory, Culture & Society* 3, no. 1 (1996): 112.

23 Ibid.

24 Koichi Ichikawa, *Ninkimono no shakai shinri shi* (*Social Psychological History of Popular People*) (Tokyo: Gakuyo Shobo, 2002).

25 Ibid., 8.

26 Shinji Miyadai, Hideki Ishihara, and Akiko Ohmori, *Zoho sabukarucha shinwa kaitai: Shojyo, ongaku, sei no henyo to genzai* (*Dismantling the Myth of Sub-Culture: Transformation and the Current Situation of Girls, Music, Manga and Sexuality and Current Situation*), rev. ed. (Tokyo: Chikuma Shobo, 2007), 392.

27 Inuhiko Yomota, *Kawaii ron* (*On Kawaii*) (Tokyo: Chikuma shobo, 2006), 76.

28 Ibid.

29   Ibid.
30   Ibid.
31   Miyadai et al., *Zoho sabukarucha shinwa kaitai*, 392.
32   Ibid., 391.
33   Ehara, *Jenda chitsujo*, 152.
34   Miyadai, Ishihara and Ohmori, *Zoho sabukarucha shinwa kaitai: Shojyo, ongaku, sei no henyo to genzai*, 392.
35   Yomota, *Kawaii ron*, 148–149.
36   Ibid., 61.
37   Yuko had already retired by 2004, so this is a mere conjecture based on magazines of the epoch.
38   Yomota, *Kawaii ron*, 76.
39   Ehara, *Jenda chitsujo*, 331.

Chapter 9

"Most women train with mostly men, so why not wrestle them?"

The performance and experience of intergender professional wrestling in Britain

Carrie Dunn

This chapter explores the performance of intergender professional wrestling in Britain. This form of "sports entertainment" is historically dominated by men, and, like many sports, has been a place where male physical dominance can be displayed. However, intergender professional wrestling – where women compete with and against men – allows women to encroach upon this male turf. Yet this is not simply a Battle of the Sexes–style set-up, where acknowledged female sporting excellence is tested against men. This scripted performance of physical power is, on the whole, created by men – the "bookers" of the show, who decide upon storylines, and the promoters, who pay the wages. This means that women's entrance into intergender professional wrestling is carefully controlled and depends not only upon the approval of these gatekeepers (a well-established concept in sports sociology),[1] but also upon how they expect their audience to react to a man fighting a woman.

I draw upon an ethnographic study in progress on the British wrestling scene, using qualitative interviews from across the wrestling circuit, as well as journalistic accounts of the industry. The chapter asks the participants about their experience of intergender wrestling; and I conclude by pointing towards some of the ambiguities around gender in professional wrestling, suggesting that media portrayals of professional wrestling expect a stronger adherence to traditional stereotypes than the participants encounter in real life.

Gender in sport and sports entertainment

As Cora Burnett[2] observes, contemporary competitive sport is assumed to be "male" and "masculine"; and with that goes the suggestion that women are marginalised. Christy Halbert[3] looks at a "real" combat sport – boxing – and shows that in displays of boxing prowess (i.e., bouts) women are largely shown only as decoration (as ring girls), and defined in terms of their relationship to men (as caregiver or supporter – whether she is mother, wife, or girlfriend). Michael Messner et al.[4] assess televised sport and sports entertainment, and they highlight that often women competing in sport or reporting on it are marginalised by the media presentation, which focuses only on the women who function as "sexy props or prizes." They specifically mention televised wrestling's use of "scantily clad women" to escort male wrestlers to the ring, and of "sexually provocative dancers" as additional performances for entertainment.

Sharon Mazer argues that in wrestling performance, whether they are decorative or combatants, women function as not–men, as points of comparison for stereotypical masculinity, saying: "What women reveal in their bodily displays and performances is that no matter how closely their actions converge on those of men, they are not and never can be men."[5] Women in professional wrestling performances do things that men do not and look like men do not. Yet as she observes, there are no differences in the way in which men and women train to become professional wrestlers; they are engaged with and display violence on the same terms. As she says: "A warrior is a warrior, regardless of gender."[6] Men and women in professional wrestling are not different because of the training they do or the moves they can do in the ring; instead, they are different because of the ways in which they perform and behave in character in the ring, and the ways in which they are perceived by their audience.

The history of women's wrestling in the UK

Much academic work on professional wrestling has focused on the representations seen within the programming of World Wrestling Entertainment (WWE); scholars such as Danielle Soulliere[7] and my own work[8] have explored how gender stereotypes are portrayed on their television shows, focusing on the types of masculinity and femininity that are put forward; and Dafna Lemish[9] argues that televised wrestling reinforces gender stereotypes. Women's wrestling in the UK, however, faces slightly different issues. Simon Garfield's popular book *The Wrestling*[10] gives a good account of how many wrestling promoters have historically thought that women's wrestling is somehow morally objectionable and overtly sexual. This parallels the analysis put forward by Messner et al.[11] that women's sports in general are often presented as an opportunity for sexual voyeurism. However, Garfield also interviews legendary wrestlers such as Mitzi Mueller and Klondyke Kate, who deny that their work was ever "sexual." They also talk about how they trained with men, and Kate is quoted as describing herself as "one of the lads."

Saraya Knight (her ring name), a veteran wrestler who has worked all over the world but has been based in the UK, now helps to run a promotion and is also a very successful trainer. She argues that part of the problem in the 1970s and 1980s was the lack of top-class female wrestlers, saying in interview:

I have seen women's wrestling dip to a point that I wrestled Klondyke Kate every day for four years because there wasn't anyone else out there to work – although I loved working Kate . . . Some of the workers out there now are breathtaking and some are even better than the boys. I wish they could have been about 10 or 15 years ago so I could have spent more time with them. With these girls in the job, the business is in good hands.

Challenging sexism in wrestling

Although as Saraya observes there are now more women going into wrestling, the industry continues to be rife with sexism. Some female wrestlers in Britain have been incredibly outspoken about this problem, criticising promoters and urging them to treat their female talent equally, and using their media platforms and social media for this.

Sarah is a particularly good example. She is a UK-based wrestler who has also worked in the United States and Japan, and has used her increasing profile to write guest columns for industry magazines highlighting sexism, making her a very interesting and significant case study. In an interview with me, she was incredibly honest about some of the sexism she had faced behind the scenes:

> It was a birthday night out and the promoter had put his coat on a seat. He went to the bar and I sat briefly down on the seat to talk to my friend. When he came back I went to get up to give him back his seat and he was like, no, it's OK if you sit there – "I'll smell your flaps off my coat later on." Exact words. I was pretty hurt and betrayed that this particular person said it . . . Looking back I think it was a joke but as I have said . . . would he have said that to a guy?

Sarah uses the benefit of hindsight to give the promoter the benefit of the doubt, but it is worth highlighting here that in British wrestling, often there will be just two women on a card with probably a dozen or so men, meaning they are hugely outnumbered; and, of course, promoters are the people who book the matches and are effectively employing the wrestlers. So it would be difficult for someone like Sarah – even though she is well established – to challenge this kind of comment. Other female wrestlers have reported similar experiences, but choose to play it down as much as possible, removing themselves from confrontation. Lucy, a wrestler who has worked mostly in the United Kingdom and the United States, agreed:

> We have been around the rude guys and the guys that don't shake your hand because they don't think you're a wrestler or they think you're after something. It was quite disheartening eight years ago when we first got into wrestling but as we've grown up we tend to focus on the positive and stay away from those people. We got into wrestling because we absolutely, wholeheartedly love wrestling; we train with guys and go through the same stuff that they go through and I guess we are lucky that some of our best friends are the boys we work with.

Intergender training

Lucy raises a key point for professional wrestling here – as in many "legitimate" combat sports, and as previously observed, the women train with the men, and are often heavily outnumbered. Marianne's experience is particularly interesting – as a teenage girl she joined a residential summer camp for wrestling training, and was the only female there. She reported:

> It was the most terrifying experience of my life. I flew away from home by myself for the first time, then I got the train down to Portsmouth, and I was the only girl. I think there was 30 of us, 29 guys and me . . . I'd have to go into the toilet and lock the door to get changed because I didn't want to get changed with the boys. I felt quite nervous because most of them had been there before, and they were like, ugh, it's a girl. I'm sure they'd had girls come and go, but they never came back. The first time I went over there, they were like she's going to be here once. At night I'd go to sleep in this room with all these guys, and just lie there, feeling really self-conscious as well, especially when you're a teenager. But it was all right. I survived it.

Obviously, in educational environments, we would expect girls and boys to have separate living accommodation for this kind of residential trip; wrestling in the UK, however, often seems to think it has laws of its own, and Marianne's experience highlights this. She was not given her own space, she had to seek out her own space; she mentions that no other girls had gone back, and perhaps that is not surprising. Here we see a real-life example of the idea that if women want to participate in male-dominated sport, they must present themselves (perform their identity) as "one of the lads," as Klondyke Kate told Simon Garfield, or at the very least gender-neutral – they have to join in with the boys and not make a fuss. Marianne does indicate that the boys reacted to her negatively because of her femaleness; to be accepted and to get through the training, she had to play that down and perform a more acceptable identity.

Intergender competition

Even though women and men train together, it is still unusual for them to face each other in the ring. WWE, the most high-profile promotion in the world, have only very occasionally featured women fighting men (for example, the highly muscular, almost androgynously presented Chyna held the Intercontinental title belt; she, Beth Phoenix and Kharma have all featured once each in the annual Royal Rumble pay-per-view, facing men). As Soulliere points out, the dominant hegemonic man in wrestling is presented as violent, aggressive, emotionally restrained, tough, risk-taking, strong, courageous, powerful, dominant, competitive and successful; more than that, he is presented in contrast with a woman, with what he is not (as Mazer also argues, as we have seen).[12] Halbert observes that the female athlete and specifically the female fighter shares these "masculine" qualities, and often thus relegates herself to the very boundaries of acceptable femininity.[13] This, I argue, represents a problem for professional wrestling, reliant on performance of stereotypes, especially with regard to gender identity. Professional wrestling very often employs an exaggerated "superhero" trope that necessitates exaggerated gender stereotypes – most often the macho, powerful strong man saving the physically weak damsel in distress. Insults are flung between male characters casting aspersions on their masculinity; beauty, femininity, heteronormative attractiveness and a boyfriend of high social status are the most highly prized qualities for female characters. The 2015 feud between Rusev and Dolph Ziggler is a fine example of this – their respective storyline girlfriends Summer Rae and Lana competed over which woman was the more physically attractive, but they rarely resorted to physical fights. Summer Rae claimed she and Ziggler had been having an affair behind Lana's back; Rusev and Ziggler's in-ring fights were framed within this sexualised wider storyline.[14]

In the UK, intergender wrestling is slightly more common than in WWE. My respondent Sarah had been part of several intergender matches, but expressed some doubts about the concept initially:

> I don't tend to like wrestling guys one on one . . . apart from some exceptions, I'm not interested in working with males one on one. Personally I feel a guy hitting a girl too much can be offensive on family shows and sends the wrong message.

Some promotions have specific intergender competitions. Tara has been one-half of her promotion's intergender tag team champions, and has also wrestled in singles matches against men. Tara herself is only just over five feet tall in her wrestling boots, which means that her matches have to be carefully structured to ensure that she looks like a threat to her opponents, whether they are male or female. She told me that she has enjoyed the opportunity to wrestle more experienced performers, both male and female, saying:

> Most women train with mostly men, so why not wrestle them? Part of what made me love people like Sara Del Rey [star of CHIKARA and other indie promotions] was how well they wrestled not just against women, but men too. Smaller women beat bigger women all the time, so why shouldn't women wrestle men if they can make it look good?

Tara was about ten years younger than the more established female wrestlers I spoke to, and she seemed surprised that intergender wrestling wasn't more popular with these women. She referred to Sarah's well-known objection to wrestling against men:

> I do understand if she wrestled a lot of men it could be seen as her just saying these women aren't good enough for me just to wrestle. At the same

time, intergender wrestling is kind of important, because you have people
like Harriet who wrestle men on a regular basis as well as women and she's
still seen as a great women's wrestler, and she's part of the bigger scene in
the UK.

Tara refers to another female wrestler here, who has often wrestled men as
well as women. Marianne was unconvinced that Harriet should be wrestling
and beating men regularly. She explains that she felt that Harriet's size meant
that any decent and coherent match would have to follow the same storyline
to be convincing – Harriet's speed and guile beating her male opponent's brute
strength – which would be repetitive and dull to watch:

> She's hard as nails, she's tough, she's really tough, I think the stuff she's done
> is great . . . [but] I personally don't believe she's going to be able to beat all
> these guys, because look at the size of her, look at the size of the guys she's
> in there with, even if they're not the biggest guys, they're packing a lot of
> muscle. She's not the biggest – she's strong, don't get me wrong, but she's
> definitely one of the smaller girls, which means she looks tiny and then of
> course it's speed versus strength, and then I think the way it always goes has
> to be like a big man/small man match, it's that same kind of dynamic . . .
> There's a case made for weight classes and stuff in certain martial arts and
> stuff, they're like, well, they're in the same weight class, why not have a guy
> and a girl go at it? Fine, but that's not how wrestling works, and that's never
> what wrestling's about.

Marianne's narrative is particularly fascinating because she stresses the point
that wrestling is based on appearance and performance – not actual physical
strength. Harriet *is* strong, but she *looks* small – and as such for the performance
of the wrestling match to be convincing, the range of narratives available to
her are limited; she is simply unable to signify someone who is a physically
strong competitor. Her performance as wrestler is constrained by her bodily
appearance.

The promoters' views

For reasons of brevity, this next section focuses on the views of one promoter.[15]
Dann has had intergender matches on his cards, but acknowledges that some
men in the business are still horrified at the idea that they might "lose to a girl."
That is not the case with all the men on the circuit, including some of the big-
ger names such as Rockstar Spud, who was signed to global promotion TNA
Impact.[16] Dann recalled:

> Now, most guys don't want to work the girls let alone put a girl over [allow
> her to win]. Spud lost what was effectively a squash match to Alpha [the

Alpha Female, one of the stars of the European women's circuit, a muscular, towering bleached blonde] because he understood his role in this play. Rockstar Spud comes out and just shits on women's wrestling the way that only Spud can do, and out comes this giant behemoth of a woman who looks like a superstar and whom the entire crowd are begging to see murder this obnoxious and arrogant wannabe rockstar – and she does! The crowd have been highly entertained, they now love Alpha even more, and Rockstar Spud is such an antagonist that it would take a long time for a crowd to tire of seeing him getting his arse handed to him after one of his verbal onslaughts.

He sees this, though, as a simple extension of how he theorises the importance of winning and losing, and invokes the metaphor of the theatre and performance:

> In short, in the casting of the night's theatre production entitled "WRES-TLING!," the role of the evening's villain – "Rockstar Spud" – was played by James Curtin, the role of the evening's hero – "Alpha Female" – was played by Jazzy Gabert. In the evening's play, Rockstar Spud lost a wrestling match to Alpha Female. James Curtin didn't lose a match and Jazzy Gabert didn't win a match – because they didn't actually wrestle!

For Dann, characters and storylines are important, and he sees his wrestlers as actors rather than athletes; their gender is irrelevant because they simply need to tell the story and engage the audience.

Audiences' reactions to intergender wrestling

Although some audiences express discomfort when seeing men and women fight, some object to seeing women fight at all, whether that is wrestling or "real" fighting. Marianne responds:

> It's a bit polarised . . . It's not just wrestling, it's MMA – people don't want to see girls hit girls. That's the mentality. It's not necessarily wrestling. On the same tangent, I would never want to be involved in a match where I was going to bleed. I don't think people want to see women bleed.

The way that the audience at a wrestling show responds to the action is crucial, as in any form of entertainment;[17] and Marianne's ideas are certainly reflected in some research. Gordon Russell et al.[18] summarise psychological research reporting that men respond negatively to seeing women fighting each other in a professional wrestling context; despite viewers knowing that this aggression is fictional, these performances raise their hostility towards the participants. Ho Keat Leng et al.[19] argue that wrestling is perceived as "violent entertainment" and more suitable for men; even though its fictionality is acknowledged, the violence inherent to it is perceived as a behaviour more appropriate for men to perform. Concurrent to this runs the idea that female wrestlers participating in and performing this type of entertainment are transgressive, not just in their behaviour but in their appearance, which is often more muscular, hence "unfeminine."

Marianne's comments there were simply a personal perspective; she did not present any evidence or mention any other people's views. However, interestingly, she also raised the issue of how best to improve women's wrestling as a whole and raise its profile in its own right, suggesting that perhaps intergender matches might not be the best way forward. She said:

> I've wrestled for promotions that have women's matches as part of their show, it's just another everyday part of the show and that's fine, they seem popular, but they are constantly seen as some kind of special attraction match, as it were, so I guess it is still kind of separate. The influx of the women's promotions I think has been really good, in that it does give us a mantle for ourselves to be like, well, look, we can put on a really good show without any guys on it . . . in some ways it does isolate women's wrestling, because it's a whole show of women, "I don't want to see it because women can't wrestle." On the other hand, some may go, see eight matches with women in it, and maybe they're more keen to see them on other shows as well, so I think it's a catch-22.

Marianne pointed out that the acceptability of intergender matches depended on the audience demographic, expectation and understanding:

> We know wrestling's a work, we know it's pre-determined, but we still want to suspend our belief . . . Extreme example, if you put AJ Lee [a very petite female WWE wrestler] and John Cena [WWE's long-time face of the company] in a ring together, you would never believe she could beat him, she just couldn't. You'd say, she's going to get her ass kicked, or he probably won't touch her, because he doesn't want to . . . If you go somewhere like ICW [Insane Championship Wrestling, a UK promotion], it's an over-18s show, they don't care, to the point where they know it's a work. She might have some bruises in the morning, but they know she's consented to this match and all that kind of stuff, but at a family show, or one where there are going to be younger people, a younger audience, that's just not cool, because for them as well they don't necessarily all know that it's a work, and they're just seeing some guy hitting some girl.

Conclusion

As I have shown in this chapter, there is a long history of women's wrestling in the UK but it has historically been relegated to a sideshow, much as women's sport is sidelined in comparison to "real" (i.e., men's), sport. In terms of wrestling training, however, women and men usually participate equally in the same sessions and schools; but this does not translate into what is seen on shows in front of an audience, with intergender matches seen only infrequently. Respondents attributed this partly to issues around the quality of female wrestlers and the need to make a staged fight look "convincing," but also around audience reception to the performance, and discomfort around seeing men's violence against women. I have argued elsewhere[20] that there seems to be a developing discomfort around seeing women fight women, even in a staged professional wrestling bout; perhaps these ambiguities around the concept of women's wrestling and intergender wrestling is additional evidence for the idea that although in "real life" women's equality of opportunity is maintained and promoted, when it comes to mediatised performance women continue to be expected to uphold traditional standards of heteronormative femininity.

Notes

1 For discussion of initiation into the traditionally male domain of football (soccer) support in England, see, for example, Anne Coddington, *One of the Lads: Women Who Follow Football* (London: HarperCollins, 1997); Patrick Murphy, John Williams and Eric Dunning (eds), *Football on Trial: Spectator Violence and Development in the Football World* (London: Routledge, 1990); Garry Robson, *"No-One Likes Us, We Don't Care": The Myth and Reality of Millwall Fandom* (Oxford: Berg, 2000); Carrie Dunn, *Female Football Fans* (Basingstoke: Palgrave Pivot, 2014).

2 Cora Burnett, "Whose Game Is It Anyway? Power, Play and Sport," *Agenda* 49 (2001): 71–78.

3 Christy Halbert, "Tough Enough and Woman Enough: Stereotypes, Discrimination and Impression Management among Women Professional Boxers," *Journal of Sport and Social Issues* 21 (1997): 7.

4 Michael Messner, M. Dunbar and D. Hunt, "The Televised Sports Manhood Formula," *Journal of Sport and Social Issues* 24 (2000): 380.

5 Sharon Mazer, *Professional Wrestling: Sport and Spectacle* (Jackson: University Press of Mississippi, 1998).

6 Ibid., 123.

7 Danielle Soulliere, "Wrestling with Masculinity: Messages about Manhood in the WWE," *Sex Roles* 55 (2006): 1–11.

8 Carrie Dunn, "Sexy, Smart and Powerful': Examining Gender and Reality in the WWE Divas' Division," *Networking Knowledge* 8 (2015): 3.

9 Dafna Lemish, "Girls Can Wrestle Too: Gender Differences in the Consumption of a Television Wrestling Series," *Sex Roles* 38 (1998): 9–10.

10 Simon Garfield, *The Wrestling* (London: Faber and Faber, 2007).

11 Michael Messner, M. Carlisle Duncan and C. Cooky, "Silence, Sports Bras, and Wrestling Porn: Women in Televised Sports News and Highlights Shows," *Journal of Sport and Social Issues* 27 (2003): 38.

12 Soulliere, "Wrestling with Masculinity."

13 Halbert, "Tough Enough and Woman Enough."

14 WWE stereotypes their female characters on their main TV show, *Monday Night Raw*, as variously "jealous" (a motivation attributed to women in various storylines) and "overemotional." They also employ a corrective line of so-called slut-shaming for female characters who interact too much with men; see, for example, the ways in which AJ Lee was described after her storylines with leading male characters including John Cena, Daniel

Bryan, CM Punk and Dolph Ziggler. I have discussed this in more detail elsewhere (Carrie Dunn, "Sexy, Smart and Powerful: Examining Gender and Reality in the WWE Divas' Division," *Networking Knowledge* 8, no. 3 [2015], http://ojs.meccsa.org.uk/index.php/netknow/article/view/378.).

15 However, other promoters spoke at length about their use of intergender matches; George told me that he booked them because of the high quality of women's wrestling in the UK and he felt that intergender matches gave the women a better opportunity to showcase their skills. He added that he wanted to "erase the line" between men and women in wrestling.

16 See Carrie Dunn, *Spandex, Screw Jobs and Cheap Pops: Inside the Business of British Professional Wrestling* (Worthing: Pitch, 2013).

17 See Broderick Chow and Eero Laine, "Audience Affirmation and the Labour of Professional Wrestling," *Performance Research: A Journal of the Performing Arts* 19, no. 2 (2014): 44–53.

18 Gordon Russell, V. Horn and M. Huddle, "Male Responses to Female Aggression," *Social Behavior and Personality* 16 (1988): 1, 51–57.

19 Ho Keat Leng, S.Y. Kang, C. Lim, J.J. Lit, N.I. Suhaimi and Y. Umar, "Only for Males: Gendered Perception of Wrestling," *Sport Management International Journal* 8 (2012): 1, 44–53.

20 Dunn, "Sexy, Smart and Powerful."

Part V

Queerness

Chapter 10

Grappling and ga(y)zing

Gender, sexuality, and performance in the WWE debuts of Goldust and Marlena

Janine Bradbury

World Wrestling Entertainment (WWE) performers have long flirted with film, even as this dialogic relationship is mediated via live theatrical performances and televised productions.[1] Wrestlers such as Dwayne "The Rock" Johnson (the highest grossing actor of 2013),[2] "Rowdy" Roddy Piper (*They Live* [1988]),[3] and Jesse "The Body" Ventura (*Predator*,[4] *The Running Man* [1987])[5] all adapted their in-ring performance skills for the big screen. Moreover, whether it is Sting's face-paint inspired by *The Crow* (1994),[6] the Legion of Doom's *Mad Max*–style "Road Warrior" monikers,[7] or Scott Hall's *Scarface* gimmick,[8] Razor Ramon, wrestlers have long brought recognisable tropes from big-screen action films into the squared circle, adding an extra element of drama to their performances, and personified popular and recognisable (and stereotyped) masculinities in the ring (the loner, the warrior, the mobster). But when performers Dustin Runnels and his then wife Terri brought the conventions of classical Hollywood glamour and cinema to the squared circle in the mid-1990s, they complicated the ways that gender norms operated in the ring.

Without a doubt, two of the most intriguing debuts, or should I say, "premieres," in WWE history were those of the "gender-bending," body-caressing, wig-wearing Hollywood star(let) Goldust (Dustin Runnels) at *In Your House 4* in October 1995 in a match versus Marty Jannetty,[9] and his "director" Marlena (Terri Runnels) several months later at the *Royal Rumble* in January 1996.[10] In this chapter, I argue that the Goldust gimmick, described by fellow WWE superstar Chris Jericho as "one of the most successful creations from Vince McMahon,"[11] and which took Runnels more than six months to master,[12] and Marlena's valet character draw heavily from the conventions of Hollywood film in ways that force a reconsideration of how gender is performed through the spectacle of televised pro wrestling.[13] Offering a queer reading of cinematic intertexts, in-ring performance, and Goldust's use of drag, I suggest that their performances both resist and uphold dominant or hegemonic models of masculinity and femininity. Moreover, when their debuts are read alongside Laura Mulvey's well-known (and oft-contested) essay on classical Hollywood, spectatorship and gender, "Visual Pleasure and Narrative Cinema" (1975),[14] it becomes clear that pro wrestling at the very beginning of the "Attitude Era" (at least in this instance) both parodies and indulges the heteronormative, masculinist gaze that Mulvey critiques in her work.[15]

Cinematic intertexts

In his debut match, Goldust – billed as hailing from Hollywood, California – is presented as a celebrity and actor. At ringside Vince McMahon, Jim Ross, and Jerry Lawler make special efforts to adapt the register of their colour commentary to compare Goldust's ring entrance to an opening night of a Hollywood film. They repeatedly describe his debut as "his premiere," and Jerry Lawler exclaims, "this is like being at the Academy Awards, McMahon! For the opening of a big movie. Look at this!"[16] As his entrance music begins, the stadium falls into pitch darkness and a golden spotlight projects a lone Hollywood star with Goldust's name on it onto the entrance ramp. As gold glitter falls from the arena ceiling, Goldust emerges and glides into the spotlight, occupying his position on the star, *as* a star, as "cameras" flash all around. In an attempt to convey Goldust's celebrity status, McMahon observes, "there are plenty of [. . .] photographers around. I don't think I've ever seen anybody with this kind of coverage," while Lawler squeals, "That's paparazzi, McMahon! You wouldn't know anything about the dozen photographers that follow big stars like Goldust around."[17] Throughout the match, the filmic references continue.

But Goldust is not your typical leading man; Runnels's "camp" performance as a smouldering starlet (replete with blonde wig and breathy dialogue) undermines the conventions of what a traditional "masculine" wrestler "should be." Originally conceived as a pastiche of the Welsh drag-glam wrestler Adrian Street,[18] in his debut Goldust channels a Marilyn Monroe or a Jayne Mansfield and performs a striptease in the middle of the ring. In a promo shown on the TitanTron before his first appearance, Goldust describes his debut as: "the Hollywood premiere that the whole world has been anticipating. Tonight [*inhales*] it will be lights, cameras, ooh, sooo much action. Mr. DeMille, I'm ready for my close-up. Remember the name [*inhales*] Goldust."[19] Borrowing the immortal closing line from Billy Wilder's Academy Award–winning film *Sunset Boulevard* (1950),[20] Goldust assumes the role of Gloria Swanson's character Norma Desmond, an unhinged former actress with delusions of grandeur. Repeated descriptions of Goldust as a "strange," "unusual," "bizarre," and obsessive film buff, "an eccentric" who gives Jerry Lawler "the jitters," and from "Hollyweird," not "Hollywood" all serve to amplify the intertextual association with Desmond.[21]

A wrestling fan familiar with classic film would recognise that Goldust's persona therefore explores the psychology of performance and acting while drawing upon *Sunset Boulevard*'s status as a "camp classic" as a way of heightening the androgyny and sexual ambiguity of Goldust himself.[22] Indeed, journalist Gregg Shapiro goes so far as to say that Swanson's immortal lines "have become part of the gay lexicon" and therefore when spoken from the mouth of Goldust, his masculinity and heterosexuality is cast into doubt.[23] I suggest that Goldust invites his audience to remember that wrestling itself is camp. As Susan Sontag suggests, camp, much like professional wrestling, is a "way of seeing the world as an aesthetic phenomenon,"[24] which holds as its central "metaphor" the notion of "life as theatre."[25] Few other industries can lay claim to a "love [. . .] of artifice and exaggeration,"[26] "stylization,"[27] "travesty, impersonation, theatricality,"[28] "glamour,"[29] and a "glorification of 'character'" than professional wrestling.[30]

If Goldust is ready for his close-up as Desmond in *Sunset Boulevard*, then in her 1996 *Royal Rumble* debut Marlena assumes the guise of Cecil B. DeMille. Accompanied by a cinema usher in full costume, Marlena sits in a director's chair at ringside and gazes at Goldust's body. Positioning herself as the director to Goldust as actor, Marlena draws upon Wilder's meta-cinematic strategies and reminds us that professional wrestling, like narrative cinema, is about storytelling, artifice, and gazing – although this time it is the male body that is seemingly object to the female subject's desires.[31] From her director's chair, Marlena implicitly controls the narrative, and rather than being a passive object she exhibits a control and command over the spectacle presented. Certainly, as Douglas Battema and Philip Sewell suggest, "female characters [typically] assume the role of manager for or manipulator of male wrestlers" and "are always on display, distracting referees or opposing wrestlers with skimpy attire."[32] In her debut, Marlena seems to adhere to this convention by distracting the referee, serving as a human shield for Goldust, and assisting in Goldust's victory. However, the implication that Marlena directs the "Hollywood" narrative here upsets Mulvey's suggestion that in film, "the man's role [is] the active one of forwarding the story, making things happen," despite the patent formal differences between televised wrestling and cinema.[33] And so, the duo nod to the motifs of classical Hollywood film (the clapperboard, the director's chair, the cigar, the spotlight, and so on) in their live performances as a way of, to borrow from Mulvey, "reflect[ing], reveal[ing] and even play[ing] on the straight, socially established interpretation of sexual difference which controls images, erotic ways of looking [or 'gazing'] and spectacle."[34] Like Goldust, the Marlena character uses cinematic intertext to challenge gender norms in the squared circle.

Experimenting with drag

In addition to alluding to camp Hollywood classics, Dustin Runnels experiments with drag and cross-dressing to resist being read as conventionally masculine. While Goldust is never implied to be a female impersonator, drag is of course a central component of the androgyny that Vince McMahon intended for this character.[35] As well as wearing a long platinum blonde wig, a feather boa and a dressing gown, in early performances, Goldust's black and gold makeup accentuates the hallmark features of the Hollywood pin-up: the brows, the eyes, the lips. Both Goldust and later Marlena are objects of erotic spectacle, with

Goldust harkening back to a more modest bygone Hollywood era, and Marlena, as the buxom valet, with voluminous blonde hair, clad in a revealing ball gown, invoking the contemporary glamour of Pamela Anderson or Jenny McCarthy (both of whom appeared at *WrestleMania XI* less than a year before Marlena's debut).[36] So even though Mulvey's reading of cinema relies upon a (now critically contested) binary of "woman as image/man as bearer of the look" or "active/male and passive/female,"[37] in the more dynamic arena of professional wrestling through which this pastiche of cinematic spectatorship is performed, Goldust solicits male spectators to gaze upon male, as well as female, bodies.[38]

Reading Goldust's use of drag also enables us to unpack what Runnels is doing with gender more broadly in his debut. Judith Butler argues that at its most subversive, drag performance, "[i]*n imitating gender,* [...] *implicitly reveals the imitative structure of gender itself – as well as its contingency.*"[39] She continues:

> In the place of the law of heterosexual coherence, we see sex and gender denaturalized by means of a performance which avows their distinctness and dramatizes the cultural mechanism of their fabricated unity.[40]

In other words, Butler suggests that drag draws attention to the artificial, constructed, and performative nature of masculinity and femininity as social categories and blurs the lines between these binary oppositions that in the popular imagination, are often perceived as dichotomous and mutually exclusive, as well as biologically encoded. Indeed, the ease with which Goldust shifts from bewigged starlet commanding the gaze of the crowd to attacking Jannetty in the opening seconds of the match undermines any readings of Goldust's effeminacy as passive and inert; instead, Runnels moves effortlessly between, within, and beyond these rigid gendered and sexual binaries. Given that Butler argues that not only drag, but gender itself is "a corporeal style, an 'act,' as it were, which is both intentional and performative, where 'performative' suggests a dramatic and contingent construction of meaning,"[41] Goldust's in-ring appearances permit a multivalent deconstruction of gendered "reality." His is a performance (wrestling) of a performance (drag) of a performance (gender) that discards and occludes a reading of essential masculinity.

Goldust's drag gimmick thus queers rigid gender and sexual binaries, signifying what Eve Kosofsky Sedgwick describes as "the open mesh of possibilities, gaps, overlaps, dissonances and resonances, lapses and excesses of meaning when the constituent elements of anyone's gender, of anyone's sexuality aren't made (or can't be made) to signify monolithically."[42] In particular, Runnels uses drag to undermine what Butler describes as "heterosexual coherence"[43] in readings of the body; or in other words, he wears wigs and make-up to encourage readings of Goldust as "gay." After all, as Esther Newton observes, "homosexuality is symbolized in American culture by transvestism,"[44] and therefore Goldust's cross-dressing operates as shorthand for the audience of his sexual desire for men. Of course, critics have long considered the squared circle a quietly

queer space that evokes supposedly emasculating same-sex desire even as heteronormative masculinity is performed and enacted. As R. Tyson Smith argues,
"pro-wrestling's show of loud disgruntled men solving their disputes through
physical violence is usually characterised as masculine,"[45] even as it simultaneously revels in more muted homosocial, and to an extent, homoerotic physical
performances involving, as Catherine Salmon and Susan Clerc put it, "nearly
naked men rolling around in the ring."[46]

By contrast, Runnel's performance dramatically ruptures this opposition
between loud, brash, and violent heteronormative masculinity and quiet queerness. In Goldust we have a man who speaks softly, but dresses gaudily, who
caresses gently, yet maintains a vicious and threatening (and occasionally "hard-
core") in-ring working style and a distinct height and weight advantage over
his opponent that in many ways allays (and perhaps even justifies) the sexually threatening elements of his performance. As Jim Ross phrases it, at 6 feet
6 inches, "He's a big man!"[47] Indeed, his debut match is a particularly brutal
one; there are two devastating clotheslines, one delivered by Jannetty on the
concrete floor outside the ring and one from Goldust inside the ring that send
each man spinning. Goldust also delivers his now signature "uppercut" slap, in
which he slides in to a kneeling position in front of his opponent, with his head
at groin height and brutally slaps his opponent's face in a fascinating move that
transforms a position of sexual submissiveness (connoting oral sex) into one of
physical domination.

Even without the hint at drag and homosexuality, Goldust's costume mitigates his claims to conventional masculinity in the eyes of the audience.
Although a display of muscular flesh is a central trope in professional wrestling,
by wearing a head-to-toe costume consisting of body paint, a body suit, and
even gloves, Goldust refuses to substantiate his masculinity through the display
of his body to the crowd. Indeed, not only is Goldust's skin concealed, but his
body is not contoured. Richard Dyer notes that historically, "the built body," a
desired characteristic of the pre–Attitude Era pro-wrestler, is "cut," "hard and
contoured, often resembling armour," and he contends that the "look of hardness: the skin stretched over pumped up muscle [which] creates a taut surface"
is a premium motif of masculinity.[48] Even in his early days, Runnels never
possessed a sculpted and "built body," and Goldust's gold lamé bodysuit draws
attention to this fact. It is close-fitting, but not skin-tight, and is effeminizing
in that it accentuates the softer parts of his body, for instance his "love handles,"
and draws attention to the possibility of homosexual intimacy by teasingly and
seductively skimming his genitals, depending on how he moves around the
ring. Goldust's attire not only undermines his position as a man, but as a white
man. Dyer argues, "many of the formal properties of the built body carry connotations of whiteness: it's ideal, hard, achieved, wealthy, hairless and tanned."[49]
While "smart" fans might recognise Runnels from his WCW days and know
that he is "white," because his skin is not on show, his whiteness remains contested until his opponent literally beats the make-up from his face.

Queer "heat"

As much as Runnels's drag-gay gimmick upsets a hegemonic model of embodied white heterosexual masculinity, it simultaneously provides the crowd with an opportunity to vociferously and vocally reject queerness. In other words, the Goldust gimmick expresses an ambivalent relationship with gender and sexual norms, undermining these norms and facilitating opportunities for them to be reinstated. In fact, as Runnels suggests in an interview with Jericho, one of the reasons he harnessed this long-held association between cross-dressing and gay culture was in order to generate heat from the crowd. In his words, even though he "didn't wanna do any of the gay stuff," the gimmick "just wasn't working" without it.[50] And so in his early performances, Runnels would not only cross-dress, but would often flirt with and sexually tease his opponents, an act that would solicit audible homophobic slurs from spectators in ringside seats.[51]

Henry Jenkins III argues that this process of casting homophobic aspersions on "effeminate" and sexually ambiguous wrestlers is one way in which the physical elements of a match liable to be perceived as homoerotic are made normative.[52] Recalling an incident he witnessed when he took his son to see a live show in the early 1990s, Jenkins remembers that when the Beverly Brothers hugged each other before a tag-team match against The Bushwhackers, "their down-under opponents [. . .] turned upon them in a flash, 'queer-baiting' and then 'gay-bashing'" the double act.[53] Jenkins argues that "[w]hat may have necessitated this homophobic spectacle was the need of both performers and spectators to control potential readings of the Bushwhackers' own physically intimate relationship."[54] A central part of Butch and Luke's routine is that they lick each other and so they are thus "constantly defined as polymorphously perverse and indiscriminatingly oral."[55] "By defining the Beverly 'Sisters' as 'faggots' outside of acceptable masculinity," Jenkins continues, "the Bushwhackers created a space where homosocial desire could be more freely expressed without danger of its calling into question their gender identity or sexual preference."[56] I wonder whether a similar dynamic is at play in Goldust's Royal Rumble contest with Razor Ramon. In the match, billed as a challenge to Razor's Latin machismo, Runnels sensually rubs his body against his opponent from behind and, to reinstate his sexual dominance, Razor repeatedly gets Goldust into a bent-over submissive position and slaps the back of his head. As Jenkins observes, "wrestlers 'share things,' but they are not allowed to get 'too close,'"[57] and even as both men draw attention to the prevalent homoerotic aspects of the sport to the crowd, Razor's "homosexual threat" is legitimised via the audience's "gay-bashing" of Goldust.[58]

The scorching heat directed at Goldust for being "gay" is additionally regulated (although not altogether extinguished) by Marlena's presence. While Marlena may command a phallic symbol of her own throughout her debut in the form of a cigar (the tip of which she seductively sucks, presciently eroticising a central motif of the Monica Lewinsky scandal some years later [1998]), she still

basically "plays to and signifies male desire" and phantasy.[59] Despite performing as a character who directs the action, Marlena's early role as a silent manager (who only whispers to the men around her) is not altogether subversive.
As Battema and Sewell rightly argue, in WWF wrestling, "[t]he use of female
figures to incite voyeuristic activity is obvious, and even explicitly acknowledged by wrestlers proclaiming the need for what they term 'eye candy' during
matches."[60] As such, "their presence underpins a misogynist version of heterosexual masculinity and sexuality concerned with defending its entitlements
from competing versions of masculinity and sexuality,"[61] including those represented by the Goldust character. And yet, even though she is "eye candy,"
Terri Runnels's director gimmick subtly and radically introduces the notion of
a "female gaze" into the pro wrestling arena, one that Salmon and Clerc imply
has hitherto been supressed to assuage the "danger to the straight male viewers
and performers in allowing the camera to linger in ways that might be read
as gay and that, coincidentally, would please straight female viewers."[62] They
suggest that "given the implicitly straight male look of the camera [. . .] female
fans have had to develop their own strategies for obtaining pleasure from visual
media."[63] I would add that Marlena is a vehicle and a symbol for this subversive
process, deriving sexual pleasure from gazing at Goldust from the best seat in
the house.

Like Goldust, then, Marlena's interaction with gender norms is complex
and paradoxical, radically undermining misogynist expectations of women in
wrestling while continuously reifying them. Given Mulvey's suggestion that
"the male figure cannot bear the burden of sexual objectification"[64] and that
"[m]an is reluctant to gaze at his exhibitionist like"[65] perhaps it is more appropriate to consider Marlena a mediator of the gaze, who channels this from the
predominantly male audience and casts it upon the men in squared-circle, a
figure who mitigates and moderates the male audience's consumption of Goldust's body as erotic spectacle. In this sense, Marlena personifies Luce Irigaray's
argument that "[w]oman exists only as an occasion for mediation, transaction,
transition, transference, between man and his fellow man, indeed between man
and himself."[66]

For a "smart" fan, Marlena also assuages Goldust's "deviant" behaviour
because we know that this is a real life couple, a fact that on an unreconstructed
level mitigates Goldust's claims to gay identity. I would suggest McMahon –
recognising the increasing fluidity of kayfabe in the proto–Attitude Era – knew
that some fans would recognise Marlena as the mother of Goldust's child
and that this would temper some of the more adverse responses to Runnell's
experimental character. So when she joins her husband in the WWE, fans are
thus (either wittingly or unwittingly) paradoxically presented with the ultimate symbol of heterosexual coherence (husband and wife, father and mother),
as well as the ultimate corruption of that symbol (a polymorphously sexual
husband and a wife who calls the shots). Marlena's presence, then, is a central
component of the ambivalent message this duo offers.

Moreover, even as Runnel's gimmick controversially capitalises on and draws its energy from garnering homophobic heat from the crowd and resists emulating the white built body, in Goldust's debut match Jannetty fails to cap, control, or contain Goldust's homoerotic "threat."[67] Indeed, it could well be argued that there is a certain sexual gratification in seeing Goldust emerge triumphant, his sagging and crumpled golden form recovering and erecting into vertical splendour, resembling a real-life Oscar award. Goldust's inhaling is conveyed as a process of gradual climax that sees him suck air into and up his body, traced by his caressing hands into a position of rigidity punctuated by a satisfying exhalation of air, which mimics ejaculation. As outlandish as this reading may seem, Roland Barthes also hints that the male wrestler's body constitutes a phallic symbol:

> The flaccidity of tall white bodies which collapse with one blow or crash into the ropes with arms flailing, the inertia of massive wrestlers rebounding pitiably off all the surfaces of the ring, nothing can signify more clearly and more passionately the exemplary abasement of the vanquished.[68]

In a sense then, in the course of the match, Goldust challenges and undermines the recognisable conventions of white masculinity before reifying them through performed violence. In being beaten, Goldust's whiteness is exposed, made manifest, and substantiated, and in his recovery, Goldust (as symbolic phallus) emerges triumphant. In this sense, the violence in the ring permits, to borrow a phrase from Richard Slotkin, a quintessentially American process of regeneration of both whiteness and masculinity through violence.[69]

To conclude, Goldust and Marlena engage in a deeply ambivalent and hugely playful exploration of gender roles, sexual power, and performativity inspired by Hollywood cinema and enacted through the unique spectacle of pro wrestling. Their gimmicks represent a complex challenge to heteronormative models of masculinity and femininity, simultaneously queering and reinstating what it means to "be a man" or a valet in (and around) the squared circle. Moreover, this process works symbiotically once Marlena joins Goldust at ringside. Whenever – with his love of the feminine, with his striptease, his flirtation, and his queerness – Goldust undermines the "misogynist version of heterosexual masculinity and sexuality"[70] that characterises sports entertainment, Marlena – as eye-candy, as silent wife, as unquestioning mother – is there to reinstate it. Vice versa, whenever Marlena transgresses her subordinate position, by calling (suggestively, if not vocally) the shots, or by gazing longingly at the male form, Goldust reassures the crowd that the man is still in charge, pummelling his opponent into submission, even as he forces the spectator to grapple with ga(y)zing.

Notes

1   Indeed, capitalising on the natural synergy between these two performance-based arts, in 2002 Vince McMahon's company launched WWE Studios in Los Angeles, described by Vice President Andrew Whittaker as "a natural extension of the entertainment

business we're already in." See Barney Ronay, "How Wrestling Is Taking Over the Movies," *Guardian*, September 2, 2010, http://www.theguardian.com/film/2010/sep/02/wrestling-movies.

2 Ben Child, "Dwayne 'The Rock' Johnson Named Highest Grossing Actor of 2013," *Guardian*, December 18, 2013, http://www.theguardian.com/film/2013/dec/18/dwayne-the-rock-johnson-highest-grossing-actor-2013.

3 *They Live*, directed by John Carpenter (1988; London: Momentum, 2002), DVD.

4 *Predator*, directed by John McTiernan (1987; London: Twentieth Century Fox, 2003). DVD.

5 *The Running Man*, directed by Paul Michael Glaser (1987; London: Universal, 2010), DVD.

6 *The Crow*, directed by Alex Proyas (1994; London: EIV, 2003), DVD.

7 *Mad Max*, directed by George Miller (1979; Burbank: Warner Home Video, 2006), DVD.

8 *Scarface*, directed by Brian de Palma (1983; London: Universal, 2004), DVD.

9 "Goldust's WWE Debut," *YouTube video*, 16:18, posted by "WWE," September 30, 2013, 16:18, https://www.youtube.com/watch?v=3j9KFh_5cDs.

10 "Royal Rumble 1996," *WWE Network video*, 120:49, originally aired January 20, 1996, http://www.wwe.com/wwenetwork.

11 Goldust and Stardust, interview by Chris Jericho, *Talk is Jericho*, podcast audio, August 6, 2014, http://podcastone.com/pg/jsp/program/episode.jsp?programID=593&pid=426708.

12 "The Man Behind the Paint: Inside the Bizarre Career of Goldust," by James Wortman, WWE. com, October 20, 2013, http://www.wwe.com/inside/goldust-rhodes-retrospective-interview-26157145.

13 It is important to note that in any given wrestling match the narrative is crafted by the wrestlers/performers in the ring, by the referee, the timekeeper, and the ring announcer, and is shaped by the interactions between these performers and their live audience in the arena. It may then be filmed and televised. This televised image is sometimes transmitted live (as Goldust's premiere originally was on pay-per-view), sometimes pre-recorded and offered in edited form, and sometimes streamed live and edited later for subsequent screenings. The action is complemented by a series of metanarrative devices, such as vignettes and backstage interviews screened on the TitanTron, and finally of course is framed by the commentators – whom a televisual audience at home can hear, but the live crowd cannot. Rather than implying a conflation of theatre, television, and film here, I am close-reading televised performances, which are the product of theatrical performance, which in this specific case offers a pastiche of Hollywood cinema.

14 Laura Mulvey, "Visual Pleasure and Narrative Cinema," in *Film Theory and Criticism: Introductory Readings*, ed. Leo Braudy and Marshall Cohen (New York: Oxford University Press, 1999), 833–844.

15 For very useful reflections of how we might use Mulvey's work to explore the live spectator's response to Goldust and Marlena (as opposed to the televisual audience), see Susan Bennett, *Theatre Audiences: A Theory of Production and Reception* (London: Routledge, 1997), 74–85, and Jill Dolan's discussion in *The Feminist Spectator as Critic* (Ann Arbor: University of Michigan Press, 1991), 45–51.

16 "Goldust's WWE Debut," *YouTube video*.

17 Ibid.

18 Goldust and Stardust, interview by Chris Jericho, podcast audio.

19 "Goldust's WWE Debut," *YouTube video*.

20 *Sunset Boulevard*, directed by Billy Wilder (1950; London: Paramount, 2003), DVD.

21 "Goldust's WWE Debut," *YouTube video*.

22 Gregg Shapiro, "'Sunset Boulevard' Still a Camp Classic," *Wisconsin Gazette*, February 21, 2013, http://www.wisconsingazette.com/dvds/sunset-boulevard-still-a-camp-classic.html.

23 Ibid.

24 Susan Sontag, "Notes on Camp," in *Against Interpretation and Other Essays* (London: Penguin, 2009), 277.

25 Ibid., 280.
26 Ibid., 275.
27 Ibid., 277.
28 Ibid., 280.
29 Ibid., 284.
30 Ibid., 285.
31 For more on metacinema, see William Siska's article "Metacinema: A Modern Necessity," *Literature Film Quarterly* 7, no. 4 (1979): 285–290, and Linda Hutcheon's discussion in *The Politics of Postmodernism* (London: Routledge, 2002), 102.
32 Douglas Battema and Philip Sewell, "Trading in Masculinity: Muscles, Money, and Market Discourse in the WWF," in *Steel Chair to the Head*, ed. Nicholas Sammond (Durham: Duke University Press, 2005), 269.
33 Mulvey, "Visual Pleasure," 838.
34 Ibid., 833.
35 Goldust and Stardust, interview by Chris Jericho, podcast audio.
36 "WrestleMania XI," *WWE Network Video*, 120:25, originally aired April 2, 1995, http://www.wwe.com/wwenetwork. Despite the subversive potential of the Marlena character, it would have been more exciting, I think, had Terri Runnels herself debuted in drag, paying more overt homage to her namesake Marlene Dietrich, who wore a tuxedo in *Morocco*, directed by Josef von Sternberg (1930; London: Universal, 2008), DVD.
37 Mulvey, "Visual Pleasure," 837.
38 That both Goldust and Marlena share and assume the position of sexual objects for the male spectator can be seen most clearly in their risqué photo-shoot for March/April 1997 edition of *WWF* magazine, in which both Dustin and Terri pose nude. See "10 Baddest WWE Magazine Covers," WWE.com, accessed January 13, 2016, http://www.wwe.com/inside/magazine/10baddest.
39 Judith Butler, *Gender Trouble* (London: Routledge, 2010), 187–188.
40 Ibid.
41 Ibid., 190.
42 Eve Kosofsky Sedgwick, "Queer and Now," in *Tendencies* (Durham: Duke University Press, 1994), 8.
43 Butler, *Gender Trouble*, 175.
44 Esther Newton, *Mother Camp: Female Impersonators in America* (Chicago: University of Chicago Press, 1979), 3.
45 R. Tyson Smith, *Fighting for Recognition: Identity, Masculinity, and the Act of Violence in Professional Wrestling* (Durham: Duke University Press, 2014), 93.
46 Catherine Salmon and Susan Clerc, "'Ladies Love Wrestling, Too': Female Wrestling Fans Online," in *Steel Chair to the Head*, ed. Nicholas Sammond (Durham: Duke University Press, 2005), 168.
47 "Goldust's WWE Debut," *YouTube video*.
48 Richard Dyer, *White* (London: Routledge, 1997), 152.
49 Ibid., 150.
50 Goldust and Stardust, interview by Chris Jericho, podcast audio.
51 Ibid.
52 Henry Jenkins III, "'Never Trust a Snake': WWF Wrestling as Masculine Melodrama," in *Steel Chair to the Head*, ed. Nicholas Sammond (Durham: Duke University Press, 2005), 55.
53 Ibid.
54 Ibid., 55–56.
55 Ibid., 56.
56 Ibid.
57 Jenkins, "Never Trust a Snake," 55.

58 Ibid.
59 Mulvey, "Visual Pleasure," 837.
60 Battema and Sewell, "Trading in Masculinity," 269.
61 Ibid.
62 Salmon and Clerc, "Ladies Love Wrestling, Too," 170.
63 Ibid.
64 Mulvey, "Visual Pleasure," 838.
65 Ibid.
66 Luce Irigaray, *This Sex Which Is Not One* (Ithaca: Cornell University Press, 1985), 193.
67 See Smith, *Fighting for Recognition*, 186n13. Smith contends that if anything, "the entertainment itself flirts with" gay innuendo; in the 1950s, "Pat Patterson played a flamboyant, arguably gay character" (Patterson is now openly gay) and "[i]n the early 2000s the WWE crafted story lines around two gay wrestlers named Billy and Chuck."
68 Roland Barthes, "The World of Wrestling," in *Steel Chair to the Head*, ed. Nicholas Sammond (Durham: Duke University Press, 2005), 28.
69 Richard Slotkin, *Regeneration through Violence: The Mythology of the American Frontier, 1600–1860* (Norman: University of Oklahoma Press, 1973).
70 Battema and Sewell, "Trading in Masculinity," 269.

Chapter 11

"King of the ring, and queen of it too"

The exotic masculinity of Adrian Street

Stephen Greer

Born in 1940 into a family of coal miners in Brynmawr, a small town in the south of Wales, and rising to become one of wrestling's 1980s superstars, Adrian Street's life and career is a project of self-staging spanning more than half a century. Featured in Jeremy Deller's film and installation for the São Paulo Biennial, *So Many Ways to Hurt You, The Life and Times of Adrian Street* (2010), Street appears in his most iconic form in silver trunks, brightly coloured tights, knee-high boots, elaborate eye make-up and long bleached blonde hair.[1] At the centre of the exhibit is an image of Street in full regalia standing next to his father at the mouth of the mineshaft where he once worked at a young man – where he had been mocked for his ambitions and vowed never to return when he left for London at the age of sixteen. Lips slightly pouted, he is staring into the lens of the camera with an expression of confidence and, perhaps, contempt for his surroundings. He is the flamboyant king of the ring "and queen of it too," television's glamour boy, the Exotic Adrian Street.[2]

In this chapter, I explore the emergence and evolution of Street's professional persona as a form of improvisational and oftentimes pragmatic performance that responded to the rapid disaffiliation of the historic, symbolic association of masculinity with "hard work" and physical strength, and the emergence of alternative masculinities in the midst of broader social change in attitudes towards sexuality and gender. If Street's career offers a pocket history of the development of professional wrestling – in particular, the rise of televised wrestling following the late 1960s and 1970s – it also traces a shift in the UK following World War II from an economy centred on manufacturing and mineral industries towards one dominated by services and entertainment. More than anything else, Street's story is one of an ambitious, *entrepreneurial* masculinity that capitalised on the possibilities of the male working body made public. In emphasizing the work of the corporeal body, this masculinity is distinct from the culture of risk-taking that emerged from the male-oriented space of the city and financial markets during the 1980s.

Wrestler turned ethnographic researcher Laurence deGaris suggests that matches must be

> constructed in dialogue (or maybe colloquy) between or among wrestlers and the crowd. [. . .] The wrestlers are never in total control of the

crowd – though they are frequently the manipulators or at least the facilitators. In effect, the crowd tells the wrestlers the story it wants to hear.[3]

Street's exoticism, I suggest, demonstrates the central role of hegemonic tropes of gender in such collaborative exchange – not only working to determine which wrestlers will be characterised as "blue-eye" good guys or villainous "heels," but also structuring a broader cultural economy of immaterial labour in which the production of intangible goods of entertainment and culture might nonetheless involve determinedly corporeal bodies, exposed to risk.[4] That is to say, we can understand hegemonic gender as a field of cultural meaning that determines which bodies count as working bodies at all, and then proceeds to allocate particular forms of labour in relation to a wider system of judgment about "natural" abilities and the "appropriateness" of different kinds of work.

By risk, I do not only mean the possibility of pain and injury but the unpredictable forms of recognition that might be invoked in and through public display. Though Street's professional career as a wrestler was defined by consciously provocative practices of self-styling intended to make his fans love and hate him, it first emerged through a process of self-discovery inflected by misrecognition. As I will explore in this chapter, Street's initial construction of exoticism through tropes of effeminacy came about as a response to chance discovery – or, more precisely, as a face-saving response to a hostile crowd. In briefly tracing the emergence of Street's exotic persona, a project described and continued through the pages of his self-published, multi-volume autobiography – *My Pink Gas Mask* (2012), *I Only Laugh When It Hurts* (2012), *So Many Ways To Hurt You* (2012), *Sadist in Sequins* (2012), *Imagine What I Could Do To You* (2013) and *Violence Is Golden* (2015) – I also acknowledge the wrestling ring as a space in which masculinity is imagined and re-imagined, often in response to broader social and historical narratives.[5] That space is at once highly theatrical, marked by identifiable characters and "gimmicks," and involved in the materialization of authentically "real" male bodies and identities. I use the word "real" with some caution here, not in dispute of blood and sweat but in acknowledgment of professional wrestling's refusal to conduct itself as either a wholly factual sport or a merely theatrical fiction – existing instead as a skilled spectacle involving the sensibilities of both. Roland Barthes's brief (but often cited) essay on wrestling suggests that "there is no more a problem of truth in wrestling than in the theatre."[6] For his own part, Street's response to the related question of whether professional wrestling is real or fixed is "yes."[7] In turn, my sense of "materialize" invokes Judith Butler's account of the production of gender *as* gender through the reiteration of culturally intelligible acts: the material acts, that is, which give rise to the "authentic" materiality of gender itself.[8]

Street's desire to become a professional wrestler – and a famous one at that – begins at an early age. As a teenager he travels with his brother to see British "Mr. Universe" Reg Park compete in a physique contest in Cardiff, joins a gym in the neighbouring town of Ebbw Vale and becomes a voracious reader of bodybuilding and wrestling magazines, where he encounters the stars of

American professional wrestling: "super athletes, the colourful, brash characters of the modern day Gladiators, Don Leo Jonathan, Gene Stanley, "Nature-
Boy" Buddy Rogers and Dr Jerry Graham."[9] Hating formal education slightly
more than the prospect of working in the mine, Street leaves school at the
age of fifteen to work alongside his father but loathes the colliery and the
future that it foreshadows. Like his older brother before him, he finds the work
"dirty, unhealthy, poorly paid and dangerous,"[10] and while the mine is a space
of masculine labour shaped by strength and toughness – where men might
earn respect by "doing a hard job well and being known for it"[11] – Street finds
little solidarity and is mocked for his ambitions. With few possessions and less
money, Street leaves for London at the age of sixteen and introduces himself at
the offices of Dale Martin's Wrestling Promotions, where he is told to return
when he is bigger, older and has become an amateur champion. Street joins a
local gym and begins to compete in club and interclub matches, but struggles
to support himself.

When another wrestler suggests that he might earn money posing for "muscle magazines," Street is flattered by the prospect of appearing in publications
that he had voraciously consumed since childhood. Posing for Bill Jones (working under the pseudonym "Mark") is "the easiest money" that Street has ever
earned: "5 pounds for half an hour of doing what I like best – showing off."[12]
While appealing to Street's vanity, physique photography was also pragmatic –
granting publicity in service of the pursuit of his wrestling career and providing
a form of self-determined income outside of the precarious economy determined by promoter interests (and, as Street narrates, promoter grudges). The
income from modelling allows Street to invest in his professional self-image
by purchasing increasingly elaborate costumes: again and again, Street's autobiography recounts his return to the camera whenever he needs to acquire a
new "look" to support the next step of his career. Billed for his first professional match as the "Welterweight Champion of Wales" (a title invented by the
promoter) under the name Kid Tarzan Jonathan (in homage to the American
wrestler Don Leo Jonathan), Street realizes he needs to make a strong first
impression. In logic that repeats across his self-narrative, Street narrates the
prospect of professional advancement in terms of the public image that he
might create for himself: "What would Kid Tarzan Jonathan wear, and more
to the point, how would he pay for it?"[13] After returning to Jones for another
lucrative posing session, Street meets another photographer, John Graham –
who demands a longer shoot but pays less. Graham's explanation for the different rates – recounted by Street seemingly without innuendo – is that he relies
upon photography to earn a living whereas Jones is a wealthy man who enjoys
physique photography as a "hobby." While the (homo)erotic nature of Jones's
pastime remains unspoken, the possibility of Street's body as the object of male
desire becomes explicit when a third photographer, "Lon of London," makes
a clumsily aggressive pass and gropes at Street's groin. Returning to challenge
Graham, Street is confronted with the existence of men who desire male bodies:

"Surely Adrian, you must have realized that Gary and I are homosexuals? [. . .] I'm queer Adrian, but you'll never have to worry – you're not my type!"[14]

While Street's youthful naivety may reflect his sheltered rural upbringing and the relative absence of a public gay culture during the 1950s, it also draws attention to the precarious economy through which a body might take on value through public display, and the unreliability of gender as a cipher for sexuality. That economy is one in which a body's value involves its exposure to the uncertain gaze of another. To enter into the public sphere is to experience *misrecognition*, in the sense of accepting terms for social legibility that are not wholly one's own because they are held in common with others. As I will discuss, in Street's serendipitous claim on tropes of effeminacy it may involve having one's chosen gender identity mistaken for another. Despite its significance to identity, sexuality is not something that we can reliably, conventionally "see" in the same way that we might presume to identify gender or ethnicity.[15] Though the imagery of physique magazines may appear manifestly homoerotic to a contemporary gaze – in part, perhaps, because its muscled and largely hairless bodies have become the dominant aesthetic of so much gay male porn – we might yet recognise the ways in which a focus on a particular kind of masculine male body allowed the circulation of same-sex desire and, at the very same time, its plausible denial. The homoerotic does not stand in opposition to the homosocial (or, indeed, to heterosexual desire) but circulates within it. While the *Reg Park Journal* – subtitled "20th century health and physical culture for men and women" – regularly featured male and female models on the same cover, the parallel imprint *Man's World & Reg Park Journal* tended towards almost exclusively male models, promising both "brilliant physique photography" and the "secrets of virile manhood" while still emphasizing training advice for practical bodybuilding. A third journal titled *Man's World* shared a number of the same models but eschewed an emphasis on training to entice the gaze of the reader by offering "wonderful art studies," "magnificent art plates" and "thrilling physique photos."[16]

As it developed, Street's capitalization of his self-image required a discursive balancing act where rendering his body public involved risking control over its meaning and circulation. Economic and promotional logics are balanced against an awareness of his own desire to be taken seriously as a wrestler; while Street enjoys the validation of appearing in magazines, he still wants more money. However, Street draws the line at posing for manifestly erotic "full frontal" nude photographs:

> As far as I was concerned, physique photography was about displaying an athletic, muscular body as a result of hard training, with heavy weights, and not cheapening it by posing as a "Private Collector's" naughty fantasy.[17]

The problem is that the masculine body built through hard and heavy labour in the gym is precisely the body that qualifies as fantasy. The idealised, muscular body produced within homosocial spaces does not foreclose desire but is its object. Chris Haywood and Máirtín Mac an Ghaill suggest that "masculinities [. . .] are produced through the work in which bodies are involved; masculinities are made through work *by* the body and what the body does. Harsh work becomes the symbol of masculinity."[18] But as Deller's framing of Street at the historical tipping point between old and new economies might suggest, Street's work required both manual labour – physically demanding "hard training" – as well as an understanding of the logic of a post-industrial economy in which a body might produce value by staging itself as spectacle. In this, the emphasis on the *display* of bodies within physique magazines for appreciation of one kind or another might be understood as a precursor to the logic of a contemporary "fetishization of muscles and muscularity in young men at precisely the moment that fewer traditionally male manual jobs exist."[19]

Yet Street's performance offers a more complex – and less deterministic – account of the development of male muscularity by describing the ease with which the logic of one kind of masculine display might be implicated in another. Acknowledging the constitutive role of a live audience in such interplay can also help us better understand how one of the instigating scenes of Street's exotic persona was one of misapprehension rather than affirmative recognition. In a story repeated across various documentaries and interviews, Street describes realising self-confidence, physical strength and technical skill are not enough to distinguish him from other wrestlers in the eyes of promoters or the general public. Eager for advancement and with his debut professional match versus "Gentleman" Geoff Moran fast approaching, Street turns to his childhood idol, World Heavyweight Champion Buddy "Nature Boy" Rogers, for inspiration. In Street's own words,

> I did have the ability and the attitude, but what Buddy Rogers had in spades that I lacked was "THE LOOK!" [. . .] So what was I going to do to stand out from all the great wrestlers of Britain? That one was easy – get my own "LOOK."[20]

Modelling himself after Rogers – bleaching his hair blonde and acquiring a new baby-blue outfit with velvet jacket and matching trunks and boots – Street undergoes a "complete metamorphosis" to resemble "a magnificent blue Butterfly after it had emerged from a boring, dull Chrysalis."[21] Yet rather than adulation Street is met with ridicule and mockery, receiving catcalls and insults from a crowd that read his carefully constructed image of self-desire as effeminate and, through the misogynistic logic of homophobia, as *queer.*

> when I walked out I thought everyone would say, "Oh wow, doesn't he look good, what a great body and outfit." Instead it was, "Woooo Mary!" and the men were all saying, "Can I see you later?" in these high voices with their wrists bent.[22]

Though the moment is "mortifying," Street narrates the appropriation of the audience's reaction: his impersonation of Rogers's "manly strut" evaporates in favour of a "graceful skip to the ring and all around it." Mocked by his opponent with the "queer gesture" of a "limp wrist wave," Street counters "with a blown kiss from pouting lips, and fluttering eyelashes. Then I approached him with my arms wide open as though I intended to embrace him." The action shifts the audience's mockery away from Street: "The audience screamed with delight [. . .] But now it was my opponent's discomfort they laughed at instead of my own."[23] In this moment, Street's improvisation is successful not merely because it spares him from public humiliation but because it allows him to reassert a connection with the crowd. If the blush of shame is foremost one of social isolation, then the route out involves a form of "interpersonal manoeuvre" that, in plainer language, requires re-staging one's relationship to others so that you are no longer alone.[24] Though adulation and admiration might be preferable and the reaction of the audience members is mixed – some cheering, some amused, some booing – Street has their undivided attention.

Once discovered, the performance of effeminacy became a tactic for using the audience to derail his opponents: an artifice with practical consequence. Faced by the charging figure of "Iron Joe" Murphy, whose physicality is "stiff, awkward and full-force" and fighting style was to make holds and throws "as tight and as painful as he could make them," Street shrieks and leaps out of range "in a way that must have resembled Little Miss Muffet recoiling from the Spider."[25] The audience laughs, and Murphy falls on his face. The politics of such scenes in which Street began to "play the poof" – to use Street's own terms – are complex, and not readily resolved either as queerly disruptive of gender norms or merely engaged in the reproduction of misogynist and homophobic attitudes. Though Street's confident performance of effeminacy might be read to challenge gender norms by presenting "a 'nancy boy' who was tougher than he had any right to be, a confusing spanner in the works of masculinity,"[26] it nonetheless traded on stereotypical tropes of gay male identity and – most clearly in a later signature move in which Street applied makeup to his pinned opponent – exploited a perceived shamefulness of being anything other than conventionally masculine. As suggested earlier, Street's persona also involved the re-circuiting of such shame as a site of shared enjoyment in the spectacle of the male body, a pleasure that was both narcissistic (allowing Street to gaze at himself through the prism of the audience) and allowed audiences to draw voyeuristic satisfaction from the display *and* regulation of Street's transgressive masculinity.

Street's tactical manipulation of his audience and opponents' response to the spectre of male effeminacy might also be read within a broader history of professional wrestlers whose performative departures from conventional masculinity structured their consciously antagonistic relationships with the crowd. That history directs our attention away from the portrayal of effeminacy as an end in itself to acknowledge a wider dynamic between masculine self-confidence and unmanly self-regard required of the professional wrestler working in the age of publicity. Though there are shades of wrestler and ex-ballet *danseur* Ricki Starr's routine in TV footage of Street's ring physicality – skipping and prancing around his opponent to mock him while simultaneously evading pins and holds – the logic of Street's persona owes more to his idol Buddy Rogers, and in a manner beyond the imitation of Rogers's appearance.[27] Tagged as "Nature Boy" by promoter Jack Pfefer, Rogers adopted his distinctive bleached blonde hair in the early 1950s to become the prototype of the cocky, sneering and arrogant heel whose pride in his appearance exceeded the acceptable terms of masculine confidence. Though Rogers's bombastic self-promotion was matched by physical ability – in the words of the commentator for his 1961 match with Haystack Calhoun offered, "Buddy's a strutter and generally has reasons to strut" – his persona remained troublesome for its presentation of a self-aware male desirability.[28] Such grudging respect for a wrestler's skill despite his un-masculine self-regard also characterises the underlying dramaturgical logic of Street's longer-term relationship with his audience, in which his performance of gender skirted social opprobrium.

Interviewed for a BBC documentary on the golden age of wrestling, fan and wrestling historian Anglo Italian recalled: "He was a great wrestler, a great athlete and fans really couldn't understand why a man like this was parading around the ring in the way in which he did."[29] Unlike 1980s American wrestler "Adorable" Adrian Adonis, who loosely imitated Street's gimmick by bleaching his hair and adopting pink clothes and effeminate gestures to "come out" as a gay stylist, Street played on the uncertainty of what his exoticism might ultimately mean – not least by incorporating his wife Linda (herself a wrestler) into his act as a ringside valet tasked with carrying his makeup and combing his hair.[30] Though Street may have flaunted the prohibition of femininity required of normative masculinity – what sociologist Robert Brannon describes as the "no sissy stuff" rule – he was also able to enact and embody other dominant tropes of male identity: the "sturdy oak" of toughness, confidence and self-sufficiency, and the "give 'em hell" aura of aggression, daring and violence.[31]

While Nicholas Sammond has argued that as workers, wrestlers "simultaneously reveal the production of their personae, their embodiment of characters of their own making, and their ultimate *lack of control* over the conditions of that making over the disposition of products of their labour,"[32] Street's construction of flamboyant exoticism suggests a more complex negotiation of agency – one in which "playing the poof" capitalised on the transgression of normative masculinities produced (and perhaps even required) by the discursive frame of wrestling itself. Street's practice of self-fashioning, in other words, evolved alongside his ability to manipulate wrestling's meta-theatrical processes: he learnt to wrestle as he learnt to perform the wrestler he would become. In the wrestling ring, the masculine capital of muscularity is produced twice over: in working hard and, at the same time, in being *seen* to work hard. If nothing else, Street's persona was calculated to make sure his audiences were paying attention to his labour, in desire or loathing. If one thread of contemporary masculinity can be characterised by the demand of young men to work on and discipline their bodies while simultaneously "disavowing any (inappropriate) interest in their own appearance,"[33] Street's self-styling was gleefully sincere in its embrace of displays of vanity and narcissism as the means to establishing his persona as a distinctly public artefact.

Though oriented on his public, Street's gender play was also grounded in a genuine affirmation of personal value: the man that he had made of himself.[34] When Street returned for his portrait in "full regalia" at the mouth of the mine where he had worked as a young man, it did not involve any ironic display – a camp effeminacy in quotation marks – but rather asserted the glamorous life he had been able to achieve for himself, a success evidenced by the literal and lavish materiality of his costuming. While Michael Hardt and Antonio Negri's account of the affective labour involved in the circulation of services, culture and knowledge describes an economy of ultimately intangible products,[35] Street's appearance – and the embodied labour that allowed him to construct it – might prompt further recognition of how immaterial goods have a material existence, and are indeed dependent upon materiality. Finally, if the image of Street at the mineshaft encapsulates the "uneasy transition from being a centre of heavy industry to a producer of entertainment and services"[36] in postwar Britain, it may only be because the deep roots of that unease can be traced to the status of the male body itself as a source of new and potentially "exotic" value beyond the masculinities that had gone before.

Notes

1 See "So Many Ways to Hurt You, the Life and Times of Adrian Street, 2010," Jeremy Deller, accessed June 1, 2015, http://www.jeremydeller.org/SoManyWays/SoMany WaysToHurtYou_Video.php.

2 This phrase – and the title of this chapter – is taken from Street's song "Sweet Trans-vestite with a Broken Nose," released on the self-published album *Shake, Wrestle 'n' Roll* (1986).

3 Laurence deGaris, "The 'Logic' of Professional Wrestling," in *Steel Chair to the Head: The Pleasure and Pain of Professional Wrestling*, ed. Nicholas Sammond (Durham: Duke University Press, 2005), 206.

4 A "blue eye" is the British equivalent of a "babyface" or "face" in North American wrestling. On the logic of immaterial labour, see Michael Hardt and Antonio Negri, *Commonwealth* (Cambridge, MA: Belknap Press of Harvard University Press, 2009).

5 See, for example, Jeffrey J. Mondak's discussion of jingoistic tropes of nationalism and ethnicity in American wrestling during the 1930s, '50s and '80s. "The Politics of Professional Wrestling," *Journal of Popular Culture* 23, no. 2 (1989).

6 Roland Barthes, "The World of Wrestling," *Mythologies*, trans. Annette Lavers (London: Vintage Books, 2009), 7.

7 Adrian Street, *So Many Ways to Hurt You* (Createspace Independent, 2012), 4–5.

8 See Judith Butler, *Gender Trouble: Feminism and the Subversion of Identity* (New York: Routledge, 1990).

9 Adrian Street, *My Pink Gas Mask* (Createspace Independent, 2012), 159.

10 Ibid., 102.

11 Paul Willis, *Learning to Labor: How Working Class Kids Get Working C. s Jobs* (Farnborough: Saxon Press, 1977), 52.

12 Adrian Street, *I Only Laugh When It Hurts* (Createspace Independent, 2012), 80.

13 Ibid., 84.

14 Ibid., 162.

15 See Jill Dolan, *Theatre & Sexuality* (Basingstoke: Palgrave Macmillan, 2010).

16 For a broad selection of bodybuilding, physique and strength magazines from the 1940s onwards, see the collector's site Vintage Muscle Mags (accessed June 18, 2015, http://vintagemusclemags.com/).

17 Street, *I Only Laugh When It Hurts*, 262.

18 Chris Haywood and Máirtín Mac an Ghaill, *Men and Masculinities: Theory, Research and Social Practice* (Buckingham: Open University Press, 2003), 29–30.

19 Rosalind Gill, Karen Henwood and Carl McLean, "Body Projects and the Regulation of Normative Masculinity," *Body & Society* 11, no. 1 (2005): 40.

20 Street, *I Only Laugh When It Hurts*, 152–153.

21 Ibid., 155.

22 Street quoted in Simon Garfield, *The Wrestling* (London: Faber and Faber, 2007).

23 Street, *I Only Laugh When It Hurts*, 157.

24 Donald Nathanson, foreword to *Queer Attachments: The Cultural Politics of Shame*, by Sally Munt (Farnham: Ashgate, 2008), xiv–xv.

25 Street, *So Many Ways To Hurt You*, 130.

26 Leon Hunt, *British Low Culture: From Safari Suits to Sexploitation* (London and New York: Routledge, 1998), 90.

27 For discussion of Ricki Starr, see Laura Katz Rizzo's chapter in this volume.

28 "Haystack Calhoun vs. Buddy Rogers," *YouTube and Chicago Film Archives*, accessed June 3, 2015, https://www.youtube.com/watch?v=zcP6KizyhXc.

29 "When Wrestling Was Golden: Grapples, Grunts and Grannies," *Timeshift*, directed by Linda Sands, *BBC4*, December 13, 2012.

30 In sharp contrast to Street's refusal of the gimmick of an explicit gay identity, the rumour persists that Adonis's persona was imposed by promoter Vince McMahon as a punishment for gaining weight. See, for example, R.D. Reynolds, *Wrestlecrap: The Very Worst of Professional Wrestling* (Toronto: ECW Press, 2003), 39–41.

31 Robert Brannon, "The Male Sex Role – And What It's Done for Us Lately," in *The Forty-Nine Percent Majority*, ed. Robert Brannon and Deborah David (Reading, MA: Addison-Wesley, 1976), 1–40.

32 Nicholas Sammond, *Steel Chair to the Head: The Pleasure and Pain of Professional Wrestling* (Durham: Duke University Press, 2005), 5. Emphasis added.

33 Gill, Henwood and McLean, "Body Projects and the Regulation of Normative Masculinity," 38.

34 In this respect, the sincerity of Street's self-fashioning runs counter to Philip Auslander's account of the glam aesthetic – from which Street borrowed, and influenced in return – as foregrounding the constructedness of gender identity. See Philip Auslander, *Performing Glam Rock: Gender & Theatricality in Popular Music* (Ann Arbor: University of Michigan Press, 2006).

35 Hardt and Negri, *Commonwealth*, 132.

36 Jeremy Deller, *Jeremy Deller: Joy in People* (London: Hayward Gallery, 2012), 176.

Chapter 12

"Gold-dust"

Ricki Starr's ironic performances of the queer commodity in popular entertainment

Laura Katz Rizzo

Introduction

It is May 7th, 1959, in Toronto, Canada. Ricki Starr, the ballet dancing wrestler, a man with dark hair and movie-star features, enters the squared circle of the wrestling ring at the Maple Leaf Gardens with a nimble leap. Clad in scant white briefs and ballet slippers, he slithers under the ropes and prances to the turnbuckle where he carefully places himself into ballet's first position. He begins a pre-match warm up with traditional elements of the classical ballet barre. Through the smoke-filled arena, the crowd begins to laugh with audible surprise.[1] His effeminate delicacy and graceful agility flabbergast and fascinate the crowd, and they wait with bated breath to see what will happen next. When his opponent enters the ring, the crowd is further impressed by Starr's bravery and lightheartedness in the face of difficulty. Lawrence Meade wrote:

> I stood on my chair at ringside to watch Ricki Starr come tripping down the aisle like a Nijinsky-with-biceps. I was amazed . . . at the small size. In a business where his opponents rarely weigh less than 220 and tower well over 6 feet, it doesn't seem possible that Starr could hold up under so terrific a disadvantage night after night.[2]

Despite his diminutive size, Ricki fearlessly propels the match forward with a slap to his adversary's rump. His silly antics, his classical ballet training and his genuinely likeable persona coalesce into magnetic performances. Ricki Starr is an onstage/in-ring persona. The character is a genteel man of the social upper crust, who simultaneously mocks his own gentility and reliance upon etiquette with unabashedly comic flair. The man behind this character is the ballet student and amateur wrestler Bernard Hermann, a Jewish boy from St. Louis working to make it in the performing arts. Expertly facilitating an exciting performance by drawing upon on his natural talents, as well as his rigorous training as an athlete and dancer, Bernard Hermann brought Ricki Starr to life. Throughout the field and in the popular media, Starr became a crowd favorite; a credit to Bernard Hermann's skills as a performer and as an intelligent and capable "shooter."[3]

Comedy, grace, style and impressive physical virtuosity all characterized Hermann's performances of Ricki Starr, and were drawn from sources in the theatre and the sports arena, the dance studio and the gymnasium. As stated in 1959 by the *Chicago Tribune*, Hermann was a "nimble footed wrestler with a penchant for ballet dancing."[4] The theatrical, performative and spectacular aspects of Ricki Starr's career in professional wrestling bear analysis through the lens of cultural and performance studies. In viewing Ricki Starr's in-ring performances through this lens I reveal not only the subtexts and cultural structures evident in these choreographies of combat and comedy, but I also connect popular cultural practices to historical cultural practices, and a legacy drawn from an aristocratic, political and formal aesthetic dance form. This chapter, then, imagines Ricki Starr's wrestling matches as performance pieces subject to the context of the post–World War II entertainment industry in the United States, the site where these performances were envisioned, produced, circulated and received.

Using evidence drawn from Bernard Herman's embodiment of his in-ring character, Ricki Starr,[5] I claim that North American professional wrestling in 1950s celebrated a fluid masculinity, one that embraced a multifaceted understanding of gender. Choreographies in the wrestling ring were in fact theorizations of gender, and Bernard Hermann's choreography of Ricki Starr represented masculinity as not only measurable in physical strength and violence, but also in style, finesse, intelligence, beauty and power,[6] acting as a "a powerful form of resistance to reinforcements of dominant gender normativity."[7]

Graceful masculinity

The voice-over man in a video from the Gala de Catch a Beauvais, a match that took place in France on March 2, 1965,[8] booms,

> Eccentric and provocative, Ricki Starr . . . is a real wrestler. His style is his reputation . . . Tonight Starr requested a "heel" much bigger than himself . . . His opponent is Robert Gastel! Ricki appeared in dance shoes and ballet tights, making ballet "points" before a stunned Gastel. The public who had come to see wrestling, whistled and hooted at this hullabaloo. Then Starr began his pirouettes, dodging Gastel lunges like a cat, urging the referee to do his job while taking a leap back, etc. . . . The audience began to laugh. Gastel irritated at being ridiculed, increased his attack. Suddenly, the dancer/clown became a marvelous wrestler, and his victory was greeted by a thunder of applause.[9]

Due to the exaggerated stagecraft employed in professional wrestling, the practice relies upon hyperbolic representations of masculine and feminine, strong and weak, fair or unfair, real or pretend. The genre therefore diverges from normative or hegemonic representations of identity. Characters like Ricki Starr evidence the reality that such queer representations not only existed, but thrived in the United States throughout the 1950s. Complex and nuanced (queer) performances of masculinity are now familiar within the genre,[10] and emerge from the forward-thinking Bernard Hermann and his enactment of Ricki Starr.

Early influences and context

Born in St. Louis in 1931, Bernard Hermann grew up wrestling at the Young Men's Hebrew Association (YMHA) in St. Louis, following in the footsteps of his father, who was a boxer and wrestler.[11] At the age of fifteen, while pursuing boxing, the young Bernard Hermann sparred in Stillman's Gym in New York, but after fighting a few rounds with boxers like Rocky Graziano, he eventually returned to the Midwest. He realized he was undersized and receiving neither notoriety nor financial reward for the hard knocks he took. Much later, in a 1957 interview, he spoke of his time as a boxer. In an interview, he was quoted as saying that boxers, "prostitute their brains and bodies for peanuts."[12]

While his Soldan-Blewitt High School didn't have a wrestling team, Hermann made a mark at the club level representing the St. Louis YMHA at 165 pounds in the 1949 Amateur Athletic Union nationals, and in 1951 he competed again, winning five of six matches at 175 pounds. With his boxing and mat wrestling skills in place, Hermann developed a sudden passion for dance, and began studying ballet at the St. Louis Lalla Bauman School of Dance. His classmates there were artists like Don Emmons and Dennis Lamonte, who went on to become a significant figure in Broadway musical theatre and an influential force inside the New York City Ballet.

Despite some frustration pursuing a dance career at home, Hermann eventually followed his classmates and left St. Louis in 1953, with a plan to establish himself as part of the entertainment industry, or "showbiz."[13] After spending time working undercards for poor pay, he decided to begin integrating the moves he learned with Lalla Bauman into his matches. The stage for this choreographic evolution was the thriving wrestling scene in Amarillo and the West Texas region during the 1950s.[14] Dory Detton and Sled Allen promoted the matches in Amarillo and Lubbock, respectively. While there, Hermann wrestled along with the likes of Wayne Martin, Frankie Murdoch, Bob Cummings, Tony Morelli, Ivan Kalmikoff, Roy Shire, The Great Bolo, Nick Roberts and Iron Mike DiBiase.[15]

In 1954, when Hermann first performed the Starr character, he donned purple ballet slippers and a matching leotard, and slunk along the ropes like a cat rubbing its back against a wall. He told the Los Angeles Times, "Bingo! I've been mixing ballet and wrestling all my life, but it wasn't until I put them together in the ring that I became a success."[16] He spoke about the experience, saying:

> I first did it in Amarillo, Texas, and I don't mind telling you that I had qualms about it . . . My crowd was made up of oil workers and cowboys . . . and, to tell the truth, a few began to hoot me. But the majority

of the people liked it. They began shouting, "Let Ricki alone, let Ricki dance!" Before the evening was over, those who had come to scoff were applauding.[17]

Hermann's success in Texas brought him to the attention of Vincent K. McMahon, who signed him to a four-year contract on behalf of Capitol Wrestling, the forerunner of the WWE. From Washington, DC, he moved to New York, where he developed a close relationship with the promoter Jack Pfefer, who booked Starr around the country between 1957 and 1962. On tour, Starr went from arena to arena, tossing miniature ballet slippers to fans screaming in awe. He won over even the most scathing critics, and consistently received reviews like this one written by Dan Parker, "an uncommonly gifted buffoon who is a combination of Nijinsky, [vaudevillian] Jimmy Savo and Jimmie Londos . . . There's nothing offensive about his routine."[18]

Despite his celebrity, Hermann/Starr was a man of mystery; an erudite intellectual who eschewed materialistic life, lived in a trailer, read Thoreau's *Walden*, listened to classical music and drank fine wines.[19] His identity and career were shrouded by paradox and contradiction.[20] In the 1960s, Hermann spent increasingly more time in Europe, and would spend the majority of the sixties and seventies, the last fifteen years of his career, in the UK.[21] From then onward he dropped from public view, becoming a reclusive "spiritualist." Reporters, fellow wrestlers and friends alike repeatedly reached out, trying to contact Hermann until 2015, when his son reported that he had died at home.[22]

Starr's hybrid performances circulated within popular culture, and relied upon choreography to communicate the narrative of Starr's progress through the ranks of professional wrestling. However, his choreography *also* communicated complicated entanglements between three particular binary constructs that both Starr's work and this chapter point to as imagined categories or definitions. Rather than understanding these concepts – art/sport, masculine/feminine and highbrow/lowbrow entertainment – as oppositional and binary opposites, Bernard Hermann's performances of Ricki Starr physicalized the lack of any real divide between the aforementioned categories. Within his choreography, masculinity is not the opposite of femininity, but is instead a diverse range of characteristics along a spectrum ranging from graceful to strong. When Starr/Hermann flaunted a queer masculinity in the wrestling ring, he also exposed the distinctions between masculine and feminine as truly constructed presumptions.

Performance as labor

Starr's performances therefore accomplished two types of work: they garnered economic and social success for Hermann, who brought fresh excitement to sports entertainment, and also created a model of potentially liberatory performance practice for both artists of the time and contemporary artists, promoters and scholars. Much recent scholarship has pointed to the homogeneity, commodification and superficiality of both ballet and wrestling, as well as other performing arts and mediated/popular entertainment.[23] Many writers have argued "that ballet (and wrestling) is a conservative form, backward looking in representations and understandings of gender and race."[24] Even a superficial reading of ballet, the 200-year-old genre, immediately exposes dated racist, misogynist and imperialistic aspects resulting from the aristocratic legacy of its emergence. However, arguments that a problematic legacy is killing the art form's relevance, as well as driving away potential new audiences, have much in common with those of the conservative social commentators and censors who make the cursory and over-determined assumption that wrestling is "a fascist spectacle of male power, depicting a world where might makes right and moral authority is exercised through brute force."[25] This analysis is based upon an external view or "reading" of performance as text. However, the lived experiences of performers and spectators often diverge and contradict what is expressed in a narrative interpretation of performance, one that does not account for the power of kinesthesia. Starr's performances brought forth powerful physical responses from spectators and opponents. Through Starr, Hermann brought ballet and the male ballet dancer icon (as a sex symbol) to the American public, challenging predominant expectations, prevailing understandings and perceptions of sport, the performing arts and masculinity.

Starr's in-ring identity was one that easily united ballet and wrestling, masculinity and femininity, art and sport. In 1959, Meade wrote:

> Starr lives two lives so earnestly and completely that it is like two individuals sharing a single body. The one you know, the swaggering, dancing, swisheroo who convulses millions of fans with masterful bumps, and who stays in character after he leaves the ring . . . and the businessman who calculates every move and word before he makes it.[26]

Using camp and parody, devices shrewdly borrowed from silent film and Broadway shows, Starr garnered financial and popular success while also diminishing threatening, unfamiliar or dangerous aspects of his queer[27] persona. Starr was funny, but his performances did more than simply elicit laughs.

He brought audience awareness to the peculiar nature of wrestling and the bizarre, overstated, hyperbolic characters in the ring. Starr's campy performances exposed the construction of identity both inside and outside of the wrestling ring. Judith Butler gives parody, or camp, a critical force and the power to transgress normative practices. She writes:

> Although the gender meanings taken up in . . . parodic styles are clearly part of the hegemonic, misogynist culture, they are nevertheless denaturalized and mobilized through their parodic recontextualization . . . In other words, parody allows us to see the discursive, constructed and performative nature of gender.[28]

From this perspective, audience laughter and vocal support of Starr's act reflect social acceptance and even help with heckling normative masculinity.[29] Sociologist Anthony Giddens promotes a concept of self-identity very useful in this situation.

His ideas around the formation of the psyche acknowledge the creative, reflexive and perhaps even performative project of articulating the self. For Giddens, forming self-identity is a lifetime endeavor in which people continuously shift, change and rewrite themselves.[30] A premise of this chapter is the idea of identity as reflexive. Bernard Hermann's creation of Ricki Starr was, then, the creation of an alternate self through performance, with Hermann as producer, choreographer and director.[31] He crafted a narrative that allowed his fans to connect with Starr's persona, his struggles, his humanity, his outsider identity and his underdog position. His matches offered spectators an opportunity for emotional connection, and the momentary pleasure of losing an egocentric perspective on the world, offering them absorption or projection into unfolding action between in-ring, larger-than-life, melodramatic characters.

Starr and his fans as collaborative constellation

Spectatorship theory holds that the fans are subjects who become sympathetic to the in-ring action through the overt construction of the performance event. Spectators and performers together co-create emotionally charged experiences.[32] This co-creation is a transformational experience of shared emotions by promoters, performers and spectators, and as such, is both a populist and inclusionary process. In this relationship between consumer and consumed, spectator and viewer, the audience relates to and uses their influence to shape the narrative spectacle unfolding in the ring.[33] Starr and his fans produced, much like the traditions from which they drew, queer performance practice, or one that exceeded the boundaries of a normative sexuality and/or gender.

Ballet, for, example, has been studied as a queer practice.

> In the Enlightenment Era, manliness was increasingly defined in terms of strength and functionality. Gracefulness came to be seen more as a womanly attribute, and ballet survived the Enlightenment in part because it could orient itself more emphatically around the female dancer.[34]

Stonely goes as far as to state, "the spectacle of ballet – even in the form of the ballerina – is always in part homoerotic."[35]

Referring to the homoerotics of wrestling, Patrice Oppliger states, "gay characters usually have a redeeming masculine side." She teases out this understanding of queer masculinity by describing an effeminate yet violent persona. She gives examples from recent wrestling history:

> The Headbangers tag team wore sheer skirts over boxer shorts and sports bras over their shirts ... revealing both masculine and feminine characteristics ... homosexual characters have to be strong enough to pose the threat

of overpowering another male . . . promoters have consistently manipulated audience reactions over the years, first Dustin Rhodes (Goldust) was straight, then gay, then eccentric, and now he is a good guy in a gold one piece jumpsuit.[36]

Pairing the feminine with violence, the gentle and the brutal, produces a relationship that resonates with both the wrestling and ballet communities of performers and spectators. Both Prince Seigfried, for example, the bird-hunting lover of the white/black swan Odile/Odette in *Swan Lake*, and Ricki Starr were physically powerful, beautiful characters with the capability to uphold or humiliate. These princes, characters on display who took part in a larger narrative paradigm, entertain the crowd and engage their audience through not only intimidation, but also Apollonian beauty of form, balance, symmetry and the male human body that exists in classical ballet.[37]

Kayfabe and self-referential critique: person versus persona

Starr was ambiguous in his gender, occupation and social status. The unsettling nature of his character made him all that more fascinating. As stated by the Zebra Kid, "Give Ricki Starr my fondest, sexiest wishes. He's so cute, I wouldn't know if I should wrestle him or fu – him."[38] In 1940s and 1950s North America, wrestling, much like Starr, was an amalgam of influences. It was closely related to film, television, vaudeville, burlesque, ballet, Broadway and the follies. Trained dance practitioners who needed to earn a living had no choice but to cobble together an income in all of these venues.[39] It was in this context, that of the general world of "showbiz," and the flourishing imaginations of Americans, that Starr's fame skyrocketed, and he took on New York City. Promoter Willie Gilzenberg said upon his arrival, "Ricki Starr is the biggest thing to hit New York in years. . . . he would sell out again and again. And, what a performer, when he wishes to be."[40]

Traditionally, wrestling was viewed as a sport, and a level of secrecy, known as kayfabe, surrounded the practice with regard to the wrestlers and their personalities and lives out of the ring.[41] For this reason, wrestlers were not recognized as socially ubiquitous celebrities, as they are now. However, as television began to broadcast wrestling, it became both sports and entertainment for the thousands of viewers, many who watched it without prior knowledge of wrestling rules and protocol. Starr, however, was one of the first performers who used wrestling as a platform for social celebrity.

> You could almost imagine Ricky, on some opera-house stage holding aloft a seven-stone-swan-necked ballerina instead of a fifteen-stone massively muscled Pole. At the end of the spin Starr doesn't so much dump his now dazed opponent as gently lay him out like a considerate undertaker. The crowd are silent for a moment. Then they lift the roof off.[42]

Starr's performances were brave popular celebrations of a socially isolated character. In the wrestling world, he portrayed a ballet dancer, small, effete and silly. Hermann led the world to believe that outside the ring too, that he was a bisexual, small Jewish man. He relied upon the popular myth of the artist as genius to compensate for his disadvantages. Although lacking in brawn, he used his slightly addled but clever mind to overpower his opponents. His classical learning, his taste in wine, his practice of a two-century-old theatrical tradition based upon manners and courtly etiquette of ballet as an exclusive, aristocratic, and feminized genre were elements of his complex persona and hybrid performance.

As he gained notoriety, Hermann appeared (as Ricki Starr playing another role) on the *Mr. Ed* show episodes "The Wrestler" (January 1962) and "The Bashful Clipper" (October 1962), playing roles in which he both performed ballet and wrestling and played the part of sex symbol within the narrative of each episode.[43] Hermann understood the cultural capital his ballet training carried, and worked an artistic and intellectual dimension into his performances as Starr. In his hybridization of ballet and wrestling Hermann managed to raise popular recognition and support of both wrestling and ballet during the years after World War II. His charismatic portrayal of paradoxical gender identity and social position capitalized on the novelty of his sexually ambiguous character.

In wrestling, spectators are more than neutral recipients of performance. As stated by Henry Jenkins III in 1997,

> Wrestling is a form of masculine melodrama which, like its nineteenth century precedents, lends its voice to the voiceless and champions the powerless. Wrestling allows a sanctioned space of male emotional release and offers utopian visions of the possibility of trust and intimacy within male friendship. It celebrates and encourages working class resistance to economic injustice and political abuse.[44]

Live professional wrestling is a performance in which creative power lies in between the performers and the fans. Although Jenkins's argument overlooks many of the ways in which wrestling reinforces imbalanced power structures, his perspective does bring to light the often overlooked desires and agency of both performers and spectators in determining the identity of characters, the narrative or plot progression of a match and the meaning of performances.

Fans and their heroes shape one another's identity in a mutually reflexive venture. As Giddens has stated, "Self-identity has continuity — It cannot easily be completely changed at will — but that continuity is a product of an individual's reflexive beliefs about his or her own life story."[45] Hermann's "Starr" persona, therefore, represents not only his own contradictory desires but also the cravings and fantasies of his many fans.[46] To a large degree, this chapter merely emphasizes how popular reception of Starr reflects a social embrace of difference. Bernard Hermann's employment of queerness promoted tolerance while valorizing difference — and earning him a handsome living.

Ricki Starr challenged the choreographic tropes by which combat typically unfolded between two men in the ring. The faux seriousness of typical wrestling matches and the absolute maintenance of kayfabe was mediated by Starr's pairing of comedy and camp performance with violent acts.[47] Starr, while a respectable wrestler, portrayed a non-threatening masculinity to both men and women. As stated by A.J. Petten,

> the characters and characterization in ... wrestling are materialized devices for the spectator/user interface. They operate within ... not only the narrative space of wrestling but also the figurative abstractions of popular culture, which wrestling propounds via its characters. . . . They are material manifestations of factions common to or within Western (primarily Anglo-American) popular media culture.[48]

Starr was a masculine sex symbol, celebrity athlete and effeminate intellectual. An extended excerpt from a 1959 *Sunday Herald* piece sheds light on this "learned," aspect of Starr's character, one that forefronts Starr's lack of interest in women, highbrow taste in books, his philosophical nature, as well as his sensuality and toughness.

> SO RICKI, who will be back here Wednesday night, went to Purdue U. and studied ballet dancing, but then discovered (and I'm glad) that he was wasting his time in the Ballet Russe de Monte Carlo. . . . Hasn't even got a wife or a girl friend to grab these lovely take-homes. No, only a trailer. This is packed full, he told me, with books and records.[49]

Through the willing participation of Hermann, his fans, his promoters and the media, Hermann indeed became Starr; inside and outside of the ring. Hermann and his fans cooperatively created a transgressive character who was loved and eagerly awaited at performances around the country.[50] Hermann/Starr worked within a cultural economy that enforced and produced gendered behaviors and representations. He creatively marketed aspects of both ballet and wrestling that were also queer practices, enacted through ritualized, repetitive and performative acts. Although sports were typically male endeavors at this time, in many cases as effort to bring some masculinity back into the lives of soldiers returned from war to a suburban, "air conditioned-nightmare,"[51] Starr truly stretched the acceptable range of behavior for men in public competition.[52]

Gendered performance

Ballet is widely seen in popular North American culture as a distinctly female realm. As stated by the ballet historian Jennifer Fischer, "Boys and men who do ballet must be either exceptionally brave or foolhardy, or both ... because of the art form's strong associations with a super-feminized world of women and the consequent amount of abuse men often take for not choosing a more conventional occupation."[53] However, Hermann's work was possible because the genres of both ballet and wrestling practice already diverge from traditional representations of hegemonic masculinity. In both practices, men are objectified and perform symbolic and spectacular displays that embrace flamboyant persona and identities. As Susan Bordo has pointed out, "it's feminine to be on display,"[54] and as John Berger has famously summarized, "men act and woman appear."[55]

Hermann's performances of Starr engaged subversive politics while concurrently attracting him a large fan base. He was both queer and popular, and in fact his queerness was part of the way his character was produced and marketed as a titillating commodity by the entertainment industry. Ballet became a symbol of Starr's good taste, allowing him to portray the elegance and grace of a dancer and emphasizing his persona as worlds away from those of the clumsy behemoths he faced in the ring. His strategic representations of "the outsider" capitalized on his training in a refined and uncommon performance art. As both outsider and underdog, Hermann charmed many men, women and families who had been beaten down physically, economically, emotionally and spiritually by the Fascist ugliness of World War II. The outsider and underdog in this context became icons of mass appeal.[56]

The exclusions of the underdog from many meta-narratives surrounding the cultural entertainment and theatrical worlds of the post–World War II era, require a new attention to practice-based and performer-focused history. Ricki Starr's work while worthy of the archive for its own entertainment sake also leads to deeper understanding of the construction, re-production, circulation and reception of both hegemonic and subordinated gender roles.[57] Through self-exploitation that relied on his rigorously trained physical body, Hermann's larger-than-life performances memorialized the ambiguity and constructed nature of identity. He used physical labor and the construction of an attractive character as commodity within the popular entertainment industry to touch his fans, and in doing so they together participated in ironic, unexpected and creative performance that transgressed normative divisions between art/sport, masculine/feminine and highbrow/lowbrow entertainment.

Notes

1 YouTube video found at: https://www.youtube.com/watch?v=UFdpXCGCaa4. Details of match found at: http://wrestlingdata.com/index.php?befehl=bios&wrestler= 2615& bild=1&details=7&kampfland=5&jahr=1959.
2 Meade, Lawrence. "Ricki Starr Gets His Kicks for Victory." *Chicago Daily Tribune*, October 24, 1959, A4.
3 A "shooter" is an industry term for a wrestler who can not only perform, but also legitimately fight with competence and expertise.
4 Meade, "Ricki Starr Gets His Kicks for Victory."
5 Starr's birth name.

6 This statement is actually a question, or the source of inquiry from which my research emerges. The chapter, as it follows, will clarify and peer beneath the surface of such a loaded, coded, subjective remark.

7 Taken from Shane Aaron Miller, "Making the Boys Cry: The Performative Dimensions of Fluid Gender," *Text and Performance Quarterly* 30, no. 2 (April 2010), 4.

8 This match is from his time in Europe, where he spent his entire post-1960 career.

9 Rickystarr.blogspot.com/search?updated-min=2009–01–01T00:00:00–08:00&updated-max=2010–01–01T00:00:00–08:00&max-results=2.

10 E.g., Adam Rose, Fandango, Goldust, Stardust.

11 Steve Johnson, Obituary of Starr, http://slam.canoe.com/Slam/Wrestling/2014/10/01/21978411.html.

12 http://newwrestlecrap.proboards.com/thread/22061/greats-golden-era-ricki-starr#ixzz3G2QKpmt7.

13 Tape recorded interview with Don Emmons at his apartment in NYC, October 2015.

14 http://www.kayfabememories.com/Regions/amarillo/amarillointro-2.htm.

15 http://www.wrestlingheritage.co.uk/starrdomrevisited.htm.

16 As stated in *Wrestling World*, April 1964, "A Look at the Nation's Top 50 Wrestlers," by Stephen Tischler "Ricki Starr has been one of the most dynamic wrestlers in the last 10 years. Ricki combines his skill as a dancer and wrestler to become one of the most hilarious and well-liked grapplers of all time. Starr has already begun a career in singing and dancing. Don't let those qualifications fool you though, Ricki can mix with the toughest and has beaten the toughest in Texas and California recently."

17 Phil Berger, "Ricki Starr, 'I Consider Wrestling an Art,'" *Wrestling World Magazine* (December 1965), 46–48.

18 Steve Johnson, personal notes, shared with author during private interview at Johnson's office, Alexandria, VA, October 2015.

19 http://www.wrestlingforum.com/classic-wrestling/1428745-ricki-starr-passes-age-83-rip.html

20 This can be seen in the following write ups: John Lyons, Advocate Sports Editor, "Cowboy Helps Ricki Starr Win," *Victoria Advocate* (December 3, 1953), "Ricki Starr Turned From Ballet to Mat," *Reading Eagle* (February 27, 1957), "Glamor Approach Versus Rough Guys On Mat Card Here Saturday," *Lexington Dispatch* (November 16, 1956).

21 Alan Warde, "Cultural Capital and the Place of Sport," *Cultural Trends* 15, no. 2/3 (June/September 2006), 107–122.

22 *PWTorch.com*. "NEWS: British Star Ricki Starr Dies at 83, WWE Issues Statement."

23 A summary of such opinions can be seen in a recent article by Alten stating, "Adair and Klein both took the subordination of women as their starting-point. Women were conceptualized as victims of patriarchal relationships in the world of dance and their representation on stage was regarded usually as oppressive. At the same time, both authors tried to show that women have played a very important part in the development of dance and that their role should be described and acknowledged. At the end of her book, Adair turned to the new generation of dancers who, often inspired by feminism, question the ideal of the dancer's body and the dancer's look in their choreographies," *European Journal of Women's Studies*, 4, 1997: 197–215.

24 This industry is to a large degree shaped by its complex funding legacy, that allowed its growth and development, but also tied artistic institutions to governmental and private institutions, therefore including the restrictive and pre-determined control of artists by institutional boards of trustees and 501(c)(3) administrators.

25 Henry Jenkins III, "'Never Trust a Snake,' WWF Wrestling as Masculine Melodrama," in *Steel Chair to the Head*, ed. Nicholas Sammond (Duke University Press, 2006), 64.

26 Meade, "Ricki Starr Gets His Kicks for Victory."

27 As Eve Sedgwick has stated, "'queer' may refer to the open mesh of possibilities, gaps, overlaps, dissonances and resonances, lapses and excesses of meaning when the constituents of anyone's sexuality aren't made (or can't be made) to signify monolithically . . . 'queer' seems to hinge . . . more . . . on a person's performative acts of experimental self-perception and filiation."

28 Judith Butler, *Gender Trouble: Feminism and the Subversion of Identity* (New York: Routledge, 1993).

29 "Hegemonic masculinity," As summarized in "Wrestling With Manhood," is considered the cultural ideal or normative definition of manhood in North American society, and is primarily reflective of White, heterosexual, middle class men (Connell, 1987; Dworkin & Wachs, 2000; Kimmel, 1990, 1999).

30 Anthony Giddens, *Modernity and Self-Identity: Self and Society in the Late Modern Age* (Cambridge: Polity Press, 1991), and Scott Lash, "Reflexive Modernization: The Aesthetic Dimension," *Theory, Culture & Society* 10, no. 1 (February 1993): 1–23.

31 Danielle M. Soulliere, "Wrestling with Masculinity: Messages about Manhood in the WWE," *Sex Roles* 55 (2006): 1–11.

32 Belidson Dias and Susan Sinkinson, "Film Spectatorship between Queer Theory and Feminism: Transcultural Readings," *International Journal of Education through Art* 1, no. 2.; Rebecca A. Adelman and Wendy Kozol, "Discordant Effects: Ambivalence, Banality, and the Ethics of Spectatorship," *Theory & Event* 17, no. 3 (2014).

33 Tony McKibbin, "The Well-Being of Friendship: Frances Ha," *Experimental Conversations* 13 (Winter 2014).

34 Peter Stonley, *A Queer History of the Ballet* (London and New York: Routledge, 2007), 10.

35 Ibid., 14.

36 A. Oppliger Patrice, *Wrestling and Hypermasculinity* (Jefferson, NC and London: McFarland, 2003), 116.

37 http://www.wrestlinginc.com/wi/news/2014/1001/582557/wrestling-legend-ricki-starr-passes-away/.

38 George Bollas, the Zebra Kid, wrote to Starr's manager Jack Pfefer in October 1959, Sports Collection at Notre Dame.

39 Adrienne L. McLean text, *Dying Swans and Madmen: Ballet, the Body, and Narrative Cinema.*

40 Johnson, "Starr obituary." http://slam.canoe.com/Slam/Wrestling/2014/10/01/2197841.html.

41 Also known as kayfabe: http://grantland.com/features/grantland-dictionary-pro-wrestling-edition/.

42 http://blogs.canoe.ca/gregoliver/wrestling/the-elusive-ricki-starr/ The elusive Ricki Starr, Steven Johnson, January 12, 2013.

43 http://www.imdb.com/title/tt0649876/, http://www.imdb.com/title/tt0649863/.

44 Henry Jenkins III, "'Never Trust a Snake,' WWF Wrestling as Masculine Melodrama," in *Steel Chair to the Head*, ed. Nicholas Sammond (Duke University Press, 2006), 64.

45 David Gauntlett, *Media, Gender and Identity: An Introduction* (London and New York: Routledge, 2002). (Extracts available at www.theory.org.uk).

46 Aida Hozic, *Hollyworld: Space, Power, and Fantasy in the American Economy* (Ithaca: Cornell University Press, 2001).

47 Phil Berger, "Ricki Starr, 'I Consider Wrestling an Art,'" in *Wrestling World Magazine*, December 1965, 46–48.

48

Wrestling has a medley of generic character types including "rednecks," "punk-rockers," "playboys," "pimps," "goths," "gangstas," "playas," "stoners," "Republicans," "Frenchmen," "Latinos," "bikers," and the list goes on. Now, this being the more contemporary profile of the character types in wrestling. This is not uncommon to other film and television practices in the history of audio-visual media. One just has to survey the many variations of typage found throughout both film and television history. Rather than traversing the ways in which wrestling characters are indicative of other traditional media characters and methods of characterization I want to discuss how characterization has been deployed in new media forms in comparison to wrestling. (Aaron J. Petten, "The Narrative Structuring and Interactive Narrative Logic of Televised Professional Wrestling," *New Review of Film and Television Studies* 8, no. 4 (2010): 446)

49 Ethel Beck, "Hey Lady! Catch Ricki Starr!" *Kansas City Sunday Herald* (August 16, 1959).
50 Petten, "The Narrative Structuring and Interactive Narrative Logic of Televised Professional Wrestling," 436–447.
51 Henry Miller, *Air Conditioned Nightmare* (New York: New Directions, 1945).
52 Dworkin and Wachs, 2000; Messner, 1992, 2000; Sabo and Panepinto, 1990.
53 Jennifer Fisher, *Nutcracker Nation* (New Haven, CT: Yale University Press, 2007), 45.
54 Susan Bordo, *Unbearable Weight, Feminism, Western Culture and the Body* (Berkeley and Los Angeles: University of California Press, 1993), 173, and John Berger, *Ways of Seeing* (London: British Broadcasting Corporation and Penguin Books, 1972), 47.
55 Niall Richardson, "The Queer Activity of Extreme Male BodyBuilding: Gender Dissidence, Autoeroticism and Hysteria," *Social Semiotics* 14, no. 1 (2004): 57.
56 Hollywood, California program, July 21, 1958 "Tricky Ricki Starr Owes Mat Skill to Ballet."
57 Lisa Edwards, "Postmodernism, Queer Theory and Moral Judgment in Sport: Some Critical Reflections," *International Review for the Sociology of Sport* 44 (December 2009): 331–344.

Part VI

Bodies

Chapter 13

Muscle memory

Re-enacting the *fin-de-siècle* strongman in pro wrestling

Broderick Chow

Wrestling fan Roland Barthes writes that the "basic sign" in wrestling is the wrestler's physique, "which like a seed, contains the whole fight."[1] He illustrates this with a vivid description of the grotesque, corpulent physique of the *salaud* (bastard) Thauvin, "a fifty-year-old with an obese and sagging body."[2] Thauvin is not only fat but literally nausea-inducing: his ugliness is "wholly gathered into a particularly repulsive quality of matter: the pallid collapse of dead flesh."[3] His hideous body exemplifies Barthes's thesis: that professional wrestling is akin to the play of good and evil in the medieval theatre, and, among other signs, it is the body that signifies these ancient archetypes.

What do bodies have to do with professional wrestling, a form of theatre that is basically fake fighting? In one sense, everything, and yet nothing at all. The body is wrestling's medium: it performs the stunts, sweats, and bleeds. At the same time, the body in wrestling is merely a sign, its corporeality subsumed to a regime of representation. Pro wrestling thus exemplifies Martin Puchner's description of the trouble with theatre, positioned between the "performing and the mimetic arts":

> As a performing art like music or ballet, the theatre depends on the artistry of live human performers on stage. As a mimetic art like painting or cinema, however, it must utilize these human performers as signifying material in the service of a mimetic project.[4]

Bodies – fragile, leaky, complex – make for troubling signifiers. The wrestler's body is both sign and flesh. Therefore, the corporeality of the wrestler's body is not entirely harnessed to a regime of representation, and thus, while doing signifying work, bodies are also sites in and through which signs and meanings are contested. Thauvin's body signifies because it easily fits into a visceral, emotive framework in which corpulent bodies are considered degenerate; he is fat, ergo he is a heel. However, is this the sole nature of Thauvin's corporeality? Could his body contest wrestling's constellation of signs while simultaneously exemplifying it? What also of the perfected, superhuman physiques of modern wrestling's "body guys," whose muscles traverse the line between heel and face, and who are the subject of this chapter?[5] Functioning as both "gimmick" (character) and object of desire, these bodies illustrate precisely the tension between the signifier and the fleshy signifying material. I suggest that what makes the muscular physique in wrestling so complex is that its excess of muscle, just like Thauvin's excess of a different kind, marks a form of labour in excess of wrestling's system of representation.

Today, the hypermuscular ideal is dominant in the wrestling industry, a trend accompanied by many well-publicised stories of the abuse of anabolic steroids and other performance-enhancing drugs. In light of wrestling's often brutal labour practices it could be argued the hypermuscular ideal makes crudely visible the commodification and consumption of the wrestler's labour. But the built body is not (or not only) a modern commercial imperative. It is a complex articulation of politics, economics, sex, and masculine identity that, in the frame of pro wrestling's acknowledged fakery, is opened up for scrutiny and deconstruction.

We can see this when we look to wrestling's origins in the physical culture movement of the late nineteenth and early twentieth centuries. In this paper, I propose an "erotohistoriography" of pro wrestling's built bodies. The concept of erotohistoriography is derived from Elizabeth Freeman's work on "queer temporalities," which is concerned with the way in which the normative use and regulation of time (for example, work and wage-labour, commemoration and holidays, the life-course of heterosexual kinship and patriarchy) binds, constrains, and ultimately constitutes subjects. She calls this process "chrononormativity," the temporal regulation of bodies towards (re)productivity.[6] On the other hand, existing out of step with this temporal regulation can be thought of as a kind of "queer time," which "generates a discontinuous history of its own."[7] Erotohistoriography is a historiography of queer time, oriented towards the sensate and affective moments of history. It is "a politics of unpredictable, deeply embodied pleasures that counters the logic of development."[8] Physical culture is a prime example of a highly sensate cultural moment, a movement and popular media apparatus of theatre, film, photography, and magazine that promoted building the body through exercise, which has been largely interpreted in relation to nationalism, industrialisation, and militarization through the body.[9] But while large amounts of physical culture print media have been preserved, including training pamphlets, magazines, and postcards, this visual and textual archive cannot preserve the embodied practice of physical culture – in other words, its corporeal, affective dimension. Thinking of physical culture in terms of performance, that is, through the body, inserts an erotic dimension into our understanding of the built body, not an erotics of reproductive sexuality but rather one of enjoyment, encounter, and "a commitment to bodily potentiality neither capitalism nor heterosexuality can fully contain."[10] As I will argue, we might read the self-making of early physical culturists as a way of queering structures of work, kinship, and productivity. When we are reminded of the origins of wrestling in physical culture, we might argue that today's body guy flexes the memory of the *fin-de-siècle* strongman, a "queer" remembrance that helps challenge the idea of the built body as an ideological apparatus, reframing it as site in which politics, economics, social trends, and history were and are "worked out." By uncoupling the body's muscular development from athletic performance, I will argue that the open theatricality of contemporary wrestling actualizes the queer potentiality of physical culture, twisting our normative categories and relations between bodies, economy, and work.

Physical culture and the wrestling body

As professional wrestling's primary medium, at a basic level the bodies of wrestlers enact a fictional drama of violent conflict. Often, these dramas reflect actual social struggles. The French sociologist Christophe Lamoureux explains: "*À certains égards, le mimodrame du catch ritualise, en situations fictives, la scène sociale de ces affrontments, brutalité et cruauté comprises*" ("In some sense, the imitative drama of professional wrestling ritualises, in fictive situations, the social scene of such confrontations, in all of their brutality and cruelty").[11] In other words, the physical struggles of wrestlers are analogous to social struggles, explaining wrestling's popular, almost ritual appearance, since, in the conflict in the ring, "*le groupe populaire pourra s'y reconnaître*" ("the people will be able to recognize itself in it").[12] The body of the wrestler is thus intended as a point of identification for its audience. But today's body guy wrestlers make strange audience avatars; superhumanly built and hardly resembling the majority of the audience – physically, at least. If the purpose of pro wrestling is the physicalization of social struggle, why would so many wrestlers, to put it plainly, be quite so jacked? Why *these* bodies, so excessive to wrestling's dramatic function?

In wrestling, a "good body" ensures continued bookings and shows. Even for new trainees there is an ongoing emphasis to work on their bodies and "look."[13] In this way, an economic imperative is channelled into the physique through the disciplinary practice of bodybuilding. Fans are not unaware of this physical imperative, as demonstrated by online forums where "smart" fans congregate (take for example these thread titles: "Who had the most impressive physique in WWE history?"; "Thoughts on wrestler's physiques"; "Wrestler's Body/Physique Changes"; "WWE.com: WWE's Top 25 Hottest Bodies in History").[14] What is interesting, however, is that fan discussion is less centred on how wrestler bodies communicate gimmicks (that is, the representational labour of the body) and more focused on the "good" aesthetic of the body. This is echoed by the way wrestlers use modern physical culture media for self-promotion, highlighting the importance of hard work and persistence in building superhuman physiques. John Cena, for example, has appeared on the cover of *Men's Fitness* at least three times and *Muscle and Fitness* once. The magazines feature a "modified" version of his training programme accompanied by a short article or interview, celebrating Cena as an icon of fitness and strength. In one interview, the wrestler is asked about his catchphrase – "Hustle, Loyalty,

Respect" – which Cena clarifies is more of a "moral code": "Work your ass off. Be loyal to those who are loyal to you. And respect everyone, even your enemies and competition."[15]

These two paratheatrical phenomena – the discussion of built bodies by fans and the promotion of muscle-building by wrestlers – connects contemporary wrestling to the physical culture movement that originated over a century earlier. In particular, the moral codes of hard work and determination espoused by wrestlers echoes the philosophy of physical culture, which connected the hard work of the body to a moral outlook and way of living. Wrestling was a key part of the spectacles of physical culture, and it was in these spectacles that the modern form of professional wrestling was developed. Physical culture grew out of earlier practices that associated moral development and citizenship with physical/muscular development and the body beautiful, such as the *Turnverein* (gymnastics) movement in Germany or Muscular Christianity in Britain. But the showmanship and entrepreneurial spirit of the physical culturists meant it could only have arisen in the transition from the Victorian era to modernity.[16] While feats of strength were a popular spectacle in nineteenth-century music halls, it was the German Eugen Sandow, whose "perfectly developed" body managed to combine strength with aesthetics, who catalysed physical culture as a movement. Through a variety of media, physical culture soon encouraged ordinary men in Europe and the United States to take up programmes of muscle building. According to Michael Anton Budd, this was the "genesis of a modern male body image as a participatory process."[17] Budd suggests that because popular culture and political reform converged in physical culture, it was a powerful ideological tool, which shaped a modern masculinity fit for work, war, and fatherhood, a suggestion echoed by other historians and cultural critics.[18] Modern echoes of this apparatus are apparent in Cena's deconstruction of "Hustle, Loyalty, Respect" in *Men's Fitness*, which echoes the American ideology of the hard-working, self-made man.

While histories of the movement suggest a direct line from the physical culturists to Cena's patriotic and conservative pronouncements, we can look to individual moments in the archives to provide a counterargument, paying attention to the pleasures and encounters of actual bodies. To illustrate this point, I want to focus on the life and career of a man who might be John Cena's *debut-de-siècle* double, George Hackenschmidt (see Figure 13.1). Born in Estonia in 1877, Hackenschmidt more than any other physical culturist gained fame as a wrestler. While evidence of whether his matches were predetermined – against such global superstars as Ahmed Madrali or Frank Gotch – their spectacular and well-attended nature made the matches clear precursors of modern pro wrestling. In addition to wrestling, Hackenschmidt authored several books in which he espoused a philosophy of physical culture. In his training manuals, he employs similar platitudes to those found in modern media. But these writings, I suggest, are often in uneasy tension with his career as a showman. In other words, the theatricality of physical culture complicates the idea that was

Figure 13.1 Cabinet card depicting Hackenschmidt posed. Courtesy of Plymouth City Council Library Services.

simply a tool for ideological interpellation, as it reveals a disavowed fascination with the male body as object of desire, and in doing so pointing the way to historical moments of affective intensity, relation, and encounter of bodies that do not (and cannot) be preserved by the archive.[19]

Take, for instance, the status of the *bare* body in physical culture. On the one hand, physical culture's scientific framing permitted the objectification of the male body, both by spectators who admired its development and by its owner. On the other hand, Hackenschmidt's preoccupation with nudity in his writing displays a sensuality that goes beyond the scientific discourse: "If at all possible, expose the naked body to the sun. Man is a creature of light and air, and I should therefore recommend little or no clothing when training."[20] In his autobiography, he also describes weight training in the nude with his first mentor Dr. Von Krajewski, after bathing together, a passage that is striking in its unembarrassed homoeroticism (a point to which I will later return).[21] Wrestling gave the bare male body something to *do*. Like weightlifting, the spectacle of wrestling was and is an athletic feat to demonstrate the development and function of the body. While there is no evidence to suggest that Hackenschmidt's matches, nor those of other wrestlers in the period, were "worked" in the sense pro wrestling matches are today, there is certainly evidence to suggest audiences did not view wrestling as they did other sports but rather as a "drama of the [built] male body."[22] As John Rickard shows, audiences were mainly going into see a demonstration of physical development.[23] According to Rickard, Hackenschmidt's tour of the Antipodes was advertised as "The Greatest and Most Magnificent Exhibition of Physical Development Ever Witnessed in the Southern Hemisphere," featuring his famous "POSES PLASTIQUES" (*tableaux vivant* in minimal clothing).[24] When the tour came to Melbourne, Hackenschmidt chose for his opponent Clarence Weber, a twenty-two-year-old local who operated a "physical culture college" and was known for his looks and body: "a nicely developed, well-built young man."[25] Later in Weber's career, a local newspaper described the moment he stripped to his wrestling trunks in the ring: "a hum of admiration for his magnificent physique arose."[26] Clearly, the built body as an object of admiration or even desire in these early wrestling scenarios is central to the form. As Rickard writes, through wrestling "the interest in the male physique, on the part of both men and women, could be asserted without embarrassment."[27]

Do modern body guys simply (re)stage this turn-of-the-century moment when the male body became an object of desire? And if so, are the monopolistic tendencies of modern corporate wrestling simply capturing and monetizing this queer history? In the final section of this chapter, I will explore the ways in which the built body, while embodying its own domination, might also resist the same structures in which it was produced, through modern wrestling's open, participatory theatricality.

A queer sort of labour: the "gimmick" of the body

Principally, it was McMahon's WWE that transformed the muscular ideal in wrestling into a powerful disciplinary practice far from the philosophies of McFadden, Hackenschmidt, or Sandow. Oliver Lee Bateman writes that McMahon's own experience in bodybuilding led to "huge, tight, and extremely vascular bodies" becoming *the* look of wrestling.[28] As McMahon's control over

wrestling in the United States grew, the diversity of bodies seen in WWE promotions decreased. In fact, from 1990 to 1992 McMahon attempted to launch
a bodybuilding competition to compete with the International Federation of
Bodybuilders, borrowing spectacle from the WWE (lights, sounds, choreographed scenarios) to sex up the typical mandatory "posing routines" (the programme was short-lived and ran until 1992). During this period, McMahon
was also caught up in the trial of George Zahorian, accused of distributing steroids and other performance enhancing drugs, when it became public knowledge that a number of wrestlers were under orders to take the drugs. Anabolic
steroids have been implicated in the deaths of a number of wrestlers, including
fan favourite Eddie Guerrero, and Chris Benoit, who murdered his wife and
son before taking his own life. These and similar events led to changes in the
WWE's tolerance of drugs, including the introduction of "wellness tests." Yet
even excluding anabolic steroids, the physical and mental costs of overtraining
and dieting remain. The built body in wrestling seems to demonstrate the way
that, under capitalism, the body has become an "accumulation strategy," in that
it generates surplus value by being shaped as variable capital.[29] The violence
done to wrestlers' built bodies, in the notably precarious labour economy of
wrestling where workers perform without health insurance or long-term guar-
antees of employment, adds literal injury to the insult. In light of such facts,
why should we want to recuperate a body type that is just an extension of the
promoter's exploitation of male bodies for entertainment?

However, the economic explanation cannot entirely account for the nature
of the built body. After all, the economic or social incentives of an admit-
tedly marginal practice like wrestling are so minimal as to render the purely
economic reading null. Instead, we might consider the built body as a body
that *exceeds* its economic or social positioning, as a purely "theatrical" element
within wrestling that repeats and remembers a queer potentiality that was first
articulated in the physical culture movement. The economic and ideological
reading of the physical culture movement is, in a similar way, unable to account
for the intensely affective, sensate moments of actual bodily practice that are
its very substance. If it was a normative labour of self-making, it was always in
danger of slipping into its opposite, a queer sort of unproductive and useless
labour, a tendency evident when we look at wrestling today.

I use the descriptor "queer" in a qualified way. Reading either wrestling
or physical culture as homoerotic or subtextually gay-coded is both obvious
and of limited interest. Rather, it is instructive to think about queer as a *critical*
position against the "normative," considering queer not as an identity category,
but as a verb (derived, as Niall Richardson writes, from the Latin "*torquere*; to
twist").[30] In this way, the complex erotics of wrestling – comprised of the bare
body, muscle, fake conflict, and real pain – queer the superficial normativity of
its representations through the vehicle of the excessive, built body. The muscular development worn by wrestling's body guys corresponds to *le spectacle exces-
sif* noted by Barthes. This term, usually translated as "the spectacle of excess"

is more accurately rendered "excessive spectacle," and suggests a theatricality beyond wrestling's formal requirements. The wrestler's built body is thus a *theatrical body*, which manages to provoke the same kind of discomfort and irritation as bad theatre, more specifically, theatre that is *trying too hard*. Muscles that exceed function appear to be obviously *performing*. They seem "gimmicky."

Writing on the "logic of the gimmick," Sianne Ngai notes that gimmicky art irritates and disturbs because it reveals a labour relation: "there is an undeniable transparency about how an aspect of [a gimmicky work] was produced and why. [. . .] what [the gimmick] does to achieve its effect seems at once too easy and also excessively laborious."[31] Although Ngai is not speaking about wrestling, her analysis would also apply to a wrestling "gimmick" in the sense of a character a worker portrays. The built body, as part of a quite obviously constructed and performative persona, seems to try too little – consider the denigration of wrestlers as mere "body guys" – and work too hard for the audience's attention. But it also works too hard in the sense that built bodies wear evidence of thousands of hours of labour in the flesh. More importantly, the gimmick also suggests a sense of agency in its overtly displayed theatrical labour, challenging the idea that the built body is merely flesh made "accumulation strategy."

In Hackenschmidt's autobiography we find a seed of this tendency. At seventeen, Hackenschmidt tells us, he was an exceptionally strong but otherwise normal youth working as an apprentice blacksmith in Dorpat, the kind of boy who enjoyed sports of all kinds. This is until he meets the wealthy bachelor Dr. Vladislav von Krajewski, who becomes his mentor, "as he wished to have me trained as a professional athlete and wrestler."[32] After little deliberation, Hackenschmidt abandons his apprenticeship and goes to live with the Doctor in St. Petersburg. The description of the Doctor's mansion is worth quoting in full:

> One room in his house was hung with portraits of all the best-known strong men and wrestlers, and he delighted in inviting them to his house, in which all foreign artists found hospitable welcome every month. Dr Von Krajewski was the organiser of a private club of men of fashion who came to him weekly and worked hard with weights and dumbbells, and practiced wrestling [. . .] All the professional strong men and wrestlers who appeared at the St Petersburg theatres visited Dr Von Krajewski and gave exhibitions of their art. While so doing, they were all carefully examined, measured, and weighed.[33]

The passage is highly homoerotic, but without explicit sexuality, the literal content of the scene contains its own erotic charge, an affective, physical intensity.[34] As Niall Richardson argues, the practice of bodybuilding, without touching upon its explicitly sexual connotations, might be read as "a queer activity with the potential of challenging the hegemonic sex–gender–sexuality continuum," as the bodybuilder invests in their own muscles/body parts as erotic objects.[35]

Away from the public, Von Krajewski stages exhibitions that make the built male body open for appreciation and specular consumption. The private nature of the training facility and the "exhibitions of [the strongman's] art" removes physical culture from an economy of purposeful and productive labour. The only aim of the labour of the private club of men of fashion is the development of the body, which must be constantly maintained, often to the detriment of other goals. Hackenschmidt, of course, gives up a steady course of remunerated labour for the path of becoming a "professional body," and this decision has its consequences: a training regime with no room for work nor study and numerous injuries.[36] At the very same time that physical culture was shaping healthy bodies for productive and reproductive labour, it also enabled practices that ran counter to productive norms.

Conclusion: queer potentialities and wrestling's theatricality

In an article titled "Male Bodies and the Lies We Tell about Them," Oliver Lee Bateman discusses the gimmick of Dino Bravo, "a skilled middle-of-the-card wrestler from the 1970s" who bulked up and got ripped in order to salvage his career in the eighties (given the timing, some steroids might have been involved).[37] His new gimmick, the "World's Strongest Man," of course, draws a direct parallel to the strongmen who originated the contemporary theatrics of wrestling. At the first Royal Rumble in 1987, Bravo bench-pressed "715 pounds." Of course, as Bateman notes, he didn't (the world record is 722 pounds). The plates are fakes; like everything else, it's a work.

For Bateman, this matters. It is "utter bullshit, but it is also extremely revealing bullshit." Bravo's fake bench press is a demonstration of the illusions and façades of hardness that men more generally perform and put on. I want to supplement Bateman's suggestion by noting that in contemporary pro wrestling's acknowledged theatricality, this challenge to masculine norms is perhaps the point. Theatricality actualizes the queer potentiality of the built body, for the worked nature of wrestling separates strength and athletic ability from muscle. While pro wrestling is a hugely athletic form, wrestling *itself* does not produce the sculpted bodies of wrestling's most famous body guys. Furthermore, fans are generally aware that the hard "look" of the body is a cover for the soft and pliant nature of the movement with an opponent. Unlike other descendants of the physical culture tradition such as strongman (a demonstration of functional strength) and bodybuilding (an aesthetic exhibition of muscular development), professional wrestling is not sport, but it is not *not* sport, it is not theatre, but it is not *not* theatre. It is a theatricalization of an athletic contest. This means that the bodily development of the wrestlers is a kind of surplus or excessive labour that is *both* exploitation and not.

On the one hand, in wrestling's particularly exploitative labour economy working on the body is surplus labour in the Marxian sense: contributing to the profits of the owners of the means of production while not adding to the remuneration of the worker. Being a "body guy" is expensive and not directly remunerated. As wrestler Tyler Reks says: "Could you imagine trying to eat out five times a day? As a body guy, you have to maintain your physique and that means eating five times a day. Spending all your money trying to maintain that? Good luck."[38] On the other hand, the superhero body can be read as a labour for the self *in spite of* the openly acknowledged exploitation of the industry. It theatricalizes, and then contests, in a literal fight, the physical ideology of the self-made man, creating the spectacle of the worker who is still able to devote his time to creating a larger-than-life version of himself. The ritualized theatrical event of pro wrestling provides the space for this labour to be appreciated. Therefore, pro wrestling might be celebrated as a subversively queer practice, not (or not *only*) in its homoerotic content, but for the way it points to a bodily potentiality outside the temporal regulation of wage labour and the possibility of intense affective encounters between men and male bodies, even in the presentation of physical violence.

Notes

1 Roland Barthes, *Mythologies*, trans. Annette Lavers (New York: Hill and Wang, 1972), 17.
2 Ibid.
3 Ibid.
4 Martin Puchner, *Stage Fright: Modernism, Anti-Theatricality and Drama* (Baltimore: Johns Hopkins University Press, 2011), p. 5.
5 In wrestling's argot, a body guy is a wrestler known more for his muscular development than his skills as a worker.
6 Elizabeth Freeman, *Time Binds: Queer Temporalities, Queer Histories* (Durham and London: Duke University Press, 2010), 3.
7 Ibid., xi.
8 Elizabeth Freeman, "Time Binds, or, Erotohistoriography," *Social Text* 23, nos. 3–4 (Fall–Winter 2005), 57–68, 59.
9 See Ina Zweininger-Bargielowska, "Building a British Superman: Physical Culture in Interwar Britain," *Journal of Contemporary History* 41, no. 4 (2006): 595–610, and Joan Tumblety, *Remaking the Male Body: Masculinity and the Uses of Physical Culture in Interwar and Vichy France* (Oxford: Oxford University Press, 2012).
10 Freeman, *Time Binds*, 19.
11 Christophe Lamoureux, *La Grand Parade du Catch* (Toulouse: Presses Universitaires du Mirail, 1993), 25 (my translation).
12 Ibid.
13 Broderick D.V. Chow, "*Work* and *Shoot*: Professional Wrestling and Embodied Politics," *TDR: The Drama Review* 58, no. 2 (2014): 72–86, 82.
14 It is interesting to note that in both the forum thread and the original WWE.com article this thread references, male and female bodies are discussed with equal enthusiasm by male commentators, with little to no recuperative homophobia (i.e., "no homo," "I'm not gay, but . . .") offered as a corrective.
15 James Demedeiros, "Welcome to John Cena's World," *Men's Fitness*, accessed July 15, 2015, http://www.mensfitness.com/life/entertainment/welcome-to-john-cenas-world.
16 John D. Fair, *Mr. America: The Tragic History of a Bodybuilding Icon* (Austin: University of Texas Press, 2015), 20–22.

17 Michael Anton Budd, *The Sculpture Machine: Physical Culture and Body Politics in the Age of Empire* (New York: New York University Press, 1997), 56.

18 See Ina Zweininger-Bargielowska, *Managing the Body: Beauty, Health and Fitness in Britain, 1880–1939* (Oxford: Oxford University Press, 2010).

19 Broderick Chow, "A Professional Body: Remembering, Repeating, and Working Out Masculinities in *Fin-de-Siècle* Physical Culture," *Performance Research* 20, no. 5 (2015): 30–41.

20 George Hackenschmidt, *The Way to Live in Health and Physical Fitness* (London: Athletic, 1911), 35.

21 Ibid., 116.

22 Ibid., 136.

23 John Rickard, "'The Spectacle of Excess': The Emergence of Modern Professional Wrestling in the United States and Australia," *Journal of Popular Culture* 33, no. 1 (1999): 129–137, 130).

24 Ibid.; Nicole Anae, "Poses Plastiques: The Art and Style of 'Statuary' in Victorian Visual Theatre," *Australasian Drama Studies* 52 (2008): 112–130.

25 *Sporting Judge*, November 12, 1904, quoted in Rickard, "The Spectacle of Excess," 132.

26 Rickard, "The Spectacle of Excess," 132.

27 Ibid., p. 135.

28 Oliver Lee Bateman, "Capitalism, Violence and Male Bodies: The Strange Saga of Vince McMahon," Good Men Project, posted October 25, 2013, accessed July 15, 2015, http://goodmenproject.com/featured-content/capitalism-violence-and-male-bodies-the-strange-saga-of-vince-mcmahon/.

29 David Harvey, *Spaces of Hope* (Edinburgh: Edinburgh University Press, 2000), 102–103.

30 Niall Richardson, "The Queer Activity of Extreme Male Bodybuilding: Gender Dissidence, Auto-Eroticism, and Hysteria," *Social Semiotics* 14, no. 1 (2004): 49–65 (p. 50).

31 Sianne Ngai, "Theory of the Gimmick," *Wissenschaftskolleg zu Berlin*, accessed July 6, 2015, http://www.wiko-berlin.de/en/fellows/fellowfinder/detail/2014-ngai-sianne/.

32 Hackenschmidt, *The Way to Live in Health and Physical Fitness*, 108.

33 Ibid., 109.

34 We might note the resemblance to the story of Olympic wrestlers Mark and David Schultz, who were invited to live and train with other wrestlers at the Foxcatcher Farm by billionaire John E. du Pont, documented in Bennett Miller's 2014 film *Foxcatcher.* Similarly, while the film (and true story) is ambiguous on the subject of sexuality, the *Foxcatcher* story demonstrates moments of affective affinity that trouble notions of productive labour.

35 Richardson, "The Queer Activity of Extreme Male Bodybuilding," 63.

36 Chow, "A Professional Body."

37 Oliver Lee Bateman, "Male Bodies and the Lies We Tell About Them: The Making and Faking of Professional Wrestling," Good Men Project, May 3, 2013, accessed January 15, 2016, http://goodmenproject.com/featured-content/male-bodies-and-the-lies-we-tell-about-them-the-making-and-faking-of-professional-wrestling/.

38 Keith Harris, "Tyler Reks: 'WWE Wrestlers Break Their Bodies to Barely Pay Their Bills,'" *Cageside Seats*, posted December 17, 2014, accessed July 15, 2015, http://www.cagesideseats.com/wwe/2014/12/17/7412959/tyler-reks-wwe-wrestlers-break-their-bodies-to-barely-pay-their-bills.

Chapter 14

The hard sell

The performance of pain in professional wrestling

Jamie Lewis Hadley

I have only intentionally bled in a wrestling match once. After having my face smashed into a title belt, I roll out of the ring and, using a small blade the referee hands to me, perform a small cut in my hairline. When I notice drops of blood hitting the floor, I try to stand and another wrestler tries to pick me up. As soon as I get to my feet, one of the bad guys tries to grab me. The ref pulls him away and, without the support of another body to hold me up, I collapse again to the floor. In this chapter I want to unpack why I believe these two responses to injury – bleeding and being knocked out – are some of the crucial tools the professional wrestler uses to realistically present a body in pain.

I have worked within the professional wrestling business for over twelve years and occupied multiple roles, including performer, teacher, promoter, writer and television producer. In this chapter I have deliberately chosen to valorize the knowledge and experiences of professional wrestlers, as well as my own observations. My methodology has included interviewing members of the wrestling and medical community, watching recent and archival professional wrestling and mixed martial arts (MMA) matches and listening to wrestlers' podcasts. A considerable part of this chapter will focus on my observations on the increasingly apparent changes in the choreographic fighting style that is performed within the largest and most recognizable wrestling company in the world, World Wrestling Entertainment (WWE, formally World Wrestling Federation). Here I will explore a post-2008 landscape where blood is banned and has forced wrestlers to employ radical new strategies with which to communicate pain to their audience. After a brief discussion of the influence of MMA on WWE, I explore three particular gestures of pain (the chop, blood and the knockout) before examining the ways that these performances circulate.

My study on pain begins with an attempt to understand what physical pain means and how the body responds and copes with the stimulus of pain as an automatic, biological response that informs the way we react to pain. As a species, we all experience pain in unique ways; our ability to manage, control and articulate pain can be unique to a culture, group or individual. However, the body's biological response to pain might be considered universal. When injured, biological responses, behaviours and actions are employed to "locate and identify the stimulus"[1] followed by a period of bodily responses dependent on the cause of pain. Paul Ingraham supports this idea, stating that pain is a "motivator . . . It exists to get us to act."[2] In reality, to act after injury might be to get out of immediate danger, call for help, or as Wall states, "carry out active movements to explore the site of the stimulus and to collect all the sensory data possible to identify the nature of the stimulus."[3] There are also studies that suggest that clutching at a body part that is in pain reduces the level of pain experienced.[4] In understanding this biological response to pain, we can begin to examine the way in which professional wrestlers exploit this idea to communicate and to share the experience of pain with the audience.

Selling is a term used in the professional wrestling industry and, at its most basic level, means reacting to moves and strikes in a particular way so as to give the impression of being injured or in pain. Selling is the key communicative tool with which wrestlers attempt to evidence pain to the audience. Professional wrestlers sell moves through a series of learned gestures. I argue these gestures come from a set of biological responses to pain that wrestlers mimic in order to externalize pain from what is usually an interior, personal event. Grabbing or clutching injured body parts is a key component of the wrestlers' gestural pallet. Within the narrative of the match, wrestlers will often work on (attack/injure) an individual body part (leg, neck, head, arm and so on), and this will inform the progression of the match. The way a wrestler clutches at these components directly correlates with how the body would respond if legitimately injured, therefore performing a response to pain that might be recognizable as authentic by the audience. Because the success of the wrestling match relies so heavily on the accurate and convincing performance of pain, it is perhaps one of the most interesting areas to investigate when critically exploring the field of professional wrestling and performance.

WWE and MMA

If professional wrestling operates in the realm of artificiality, then MMA could be considered its legitimate counterpart. The rise in popularity in the sport, particularly due to its shared target audience with professional wrestling, has had an impact on the way that pain is performed and viewed. MMA increasingly operates in the realm of the theatrical: promo interviews, weigh-ins, entrance music and dramatic lighting all contribute toward a visual presentation not dissimilar to WWE. However, when fighting begins in MMA, almost all of the theatricality of the bodies is eliminated, leaving two bodies intentionally inflicting legitimate pain (and frequently injury) on the other. When analyzing and contrasting footage recorded at live events, it becomes clear there has been a paradigm shift in the movement vocabulary performed by some WWE performers, which has major implications for the performance of pain by professional wrestlers. Mixed martial arts, according to one of the world's largest MMA companies, Ultimate Fighting Championships (UFC), is an "unarmed combat involving the use . . . of a combination of techniques from different disciplines of the martial arts, including, without limitation, grappling, submission holds, kicking and striking."[5] These fights are held in cages and follow a number of strict rules. The rise in MMA's popularity is apparent when discovering the enormity of UFC's profits. Andrew Binner traced the history of the company's success and highlights that "by 2006 the UFC had already broken the pay-per-view industry's all-time records for a single year of business, generating over $200m in revenue, surpassing WWE and boxing."[6] Considering that MMA shares a large audience demographic with WWE, especially among eighteen- to thirty-four-year-old males, how can WWE, an artificial combat sport, compete with a legitimate one such as MMA?

The rise in popularity of MMA has forced WWE wrestlers to change their movement vocabulary. Grahame Herbert, the WWE and UFC journalist for *WhatCulture*, observes this shift using the main events from WrestleMania XXX as examples:

> Part of the reality era is more realistic matches. There's still the odd gimmick or weapon being involved, but more and more, we are seeing straight-up wrestling matches. The action of these tend to be more of an MMA inspired style, further adding to the realism of the product. Daniel Bryan and Triple H's WrestleMania 30 match summed this up, there were kicks, submission holds and further hard hitting moves that had an edge of reality. Later on in the night we witnessed Brock Lesnar and Undertaker contest a similarly MMA inspired contest of holds and hits.[7]

From this observation it is clear that the MMA style of fighting – based around throws, strikes and submissions – has permeated the physicality performed by the professional wrestler. Other examples where this style is evident is with wrestlers such as The Big Show and Roman Reigns, who now use elaborate punches as their finishing moves. In presenting a style that is more believable, and associated with legitimate combat, this new fighting choreography presents the appearance of pain in a much more authentic way.

Wrestling has and always will be scrutinized by audiences for, among many other things, the slipperiness of its artificiality. In his essay "Pain in the Act: The Meanings of Pain among Professional Wrestlers," R. Tyson Smith argues that because of this unavoidable reading "pain authenticates the consequences of the performance for fan and participants alike."[8] Pain is, like professional wrestling, equally as slippery to authenticate. In her extensive study on pain, Elaine Scarry argues "whatever pain achieves, it achieves in part through its unshareability."[9] Because pain is a subjective, personal experience, it becomes almost impossible to accurately communicate. However, there are visible signals wrestlers employ that expose the experience of pain. These are both authentic, by which I mean how the body actually responds to injury, and the re-enactment of these biological responses. Smith explains how professional wrestlers manage pain in reference to its meaning among other wrestlers and how wrestlers perform pain convincingly to their audience. He argues:

> [Wrestlers] understand non–debilitating pain as a testament to authenticity and realness. Performers frequently flaunt their painful marks and bruises in a sado–masochistic fashion. Visible indications of pain like limping, bruises, bleeding, scars and red marks are commonly flaunted, legitimating the realness of hurt.[10]

These visible signifiers of injury are not always caused by accidents in the ring.

Chops, blood and knockouts

Wrestlers often deliberately inflict this "non–debilitating" pain on each other's bodies. An example of this is using a move called a "chop." A chop is performed in almost every wrestling match and involves a palm slap to the chest, using considerable force in order to achieve a loud "slap" sound. The force with which the chop is executed often ruptures blood vessels under the skin, causing the chest to redden, swell and bruise incredibly quickly. Here, pain is externalized in the flesh; the visible marks left on the surface of the skin after the move are exposed not only for the live audience but, with the help of high definition television cameras, the audience watching at home. Although these wounds only last a few days, their temporality allows these authentic markers of pain to continue due to their visibility backstage and at other wrestling events. During my training I was told that this is a move that can be performed close to a live audience for maximum effect. When I was a heel, I would often remove a spectator from their chair and replace them with my opponent. After telling the audience to "shh" I would chop the guy hard across the chest and sweat from his chest would spray onto nearby spectators. By reducing the distance between the performer and the audience, the strike's authenticity, and the resulting wound, is unavoidable. Television cameras also mimic this effect by zooming in on areas of swelling.

Blood plays a crucial part in the performance of pain in professional wrestling. In the examples of biological responses listed earlier, blood is visible only under the surface of the skin through redness and bruising. Blood that escapes the body, appearing on the surface of the skin, the mat and on costumes is a frequent signifier of pain. It is no longer a secret that the main way a wrestler produces blood is by blading, an act that involves using a small blade to perform a cut in the forehead or eyebrow. As Chow and Laine correctly point out, "the blood that wrestlers euphemistically call 'getting colour' may be the result of self-injury, but is certainly a real wound."[11] When analyzing bleeding in wrestling, Thomas Hackett argues, "If you are bleeding, who cares whether you're operating in the realm of fantasy or reality? You are still bleeding."[12] As a wrestler, bleeding is a visceral experience. It is more than just the feeling of the blood coming down your face, but also the recognizable metal taste along with the sensation of the liquid thickening as it coagulates on your skin. These factors contribute to making it easier to *feel* like you're in pain – allowing for a much more authentic performance. Blood is absolutely an effective way to present a body in pain due to its unavoidable relationship to a wound.

Although blading has been common practice throughout wrestling history, the WWE has recently completely banned wrestlers from self-induced bleeding. Since 2008, the content of WWE television and their live events has radically changed. In an attempt to expand its audience demographic and to please advertisers, investors and other corporate partners, the WWE has been presenting television that is suitable for supervised children. "In recognition of WWE's family-friendly programming," begins the policy on the WWE website, "its network partners (USA Network, Syfy, NBC and WGN America) rate WWE's weekly individual programs as PG."[13] One of the key features of this shift has been the explicit banning of blood in wrestling matches. This is not exclusive to blading. Matches are also stopped when wrestlers are busted open "the hard way" – for example, being injured from a misjudged punch – so that wounds can be treated and blood can be washed away. In such moments, referees throw on white gloves and EMTs (emergency medical technicians) rush into the ring to assess the injury. WWE superstar Chris Jericho recently spoke out about this on his podcast "Talk Is Jericho." Jericho describes a time when he accidently cut his chin open during a match on television and states there was:

> A couple of drops of blood on the mat, and suddenly referee Mike Dekota is putting on rubber gloves . . . Talk about killing the flow of your match! And this is a real thing – you have to stop and you are basically doing this wrestling match and show and then something real happens and you get cut open it's like "ok guys the show is done" cause somebody really got hurt so now we're going to stop everything and get you fixed up.[14]

It seems that this visible interruption of the match is incredibly frustrating for the wrestler. Although these actions might be standard procedure in other venues and sporting events, over many decades bleeding in professional wrestling has become part of its visual vocabulary. Now, almost completely removed, the reaction to blood might become uncanny. However, for the purposes of my argument, I believe this sterile reaction to bleeding might offer a new way of authenticating pain to the audience. This prescribed response to a wound and bleeding – including the stopping of the match, a medical professional closing the wound and stopping the blood – heightens the audience's awareness to the fact legitimate injury has occurred. Indeed, such actions authenticate the performance of pain in a way that blading might not.

Another head-related injury, the "knockout," similarly walks a fine line between theatricality and injury. A knockout, or cerebral concussion, generally occurs when the body receives trauma (impact) to the head. This impact causes the brain to bounce off the side of the skull. In response to this movement, the brain can shut down to protect itself, causing the body to collapse uncontrollably. From watching recent WWE footage, it is clear some wrestlers are mimicking this as part of their selling style. An example of how the aforementioned ideas conflate would be to analyze CM Punk's finishing move, the "Go-To-Sleep." This move involves lifting his opponent onto his shoulders, elevating them up into the air and then using a knee strike to the face to "knock them out." Upon watching many wrestlers receive this move, it becomes clear that they are authentically re-performing how the body would respond when receiving a strike to the head; their legs collapse and face falls into the mat. I believe this combination of MMA influenced moves and authentic re-enactments of, in this instance, a knockout, performed by many professional wrestlers, offers a signaling system that helps communicate the presence of pain in the match. The idea of "the knockout" is particularly important in this discussion, as it exemplifies both the paradigm shift in professional wrestlers' physicality and re-enacting authentic biological processes in order to convincingly perform pain to the audience.

I believe there is often an overlooked performer in the professional wrestling match who supports the wrestler perform pain through their own physicality: the referee. Within the plot of the wrestling match, the role of the referee is to ensure the match is fair and safe. However, in reality, he is in constant communication with the wrestlers; for example, passing messages between wrestlers and giving them the remaining time limit. At times, the referee's physicality supports that of the wrestlers' by responding to the actions in (and often outside) the ring. For example, when a wrestler hits a big move or gets hit with a foreign object (steel chair, ladder, or sledgehammer) he might clutch his head in shock, tighten his body, or even perform a simple facial wince. This hypothesis was confirmed when I questioned senior referee Brian Hebner (son of legendary WWF/E referee Earl Hebner). Brian formally worked for WWE and now works for the second largest televised professional wrestling company in North America, TNA Impact Wrestling. When I asked him about his supporting role in the match, he stated:

> I play off the wrestlers emotions as if it were real! So if they're sad, mad, frustrated, excited, hurt ... ETC. that's how I treat it! And I do react on big moves and surprising wins and what not! But most of the time these are real emotions!![15]

Here, the idea of pain is presented in a much more theatrical way, by the referee using facial and other physical gestures to respond as if the actions in the ring are real. This highlights interplay between the performance of the wrestler and the referee's performance as a secondary role, particularly when both parties are attempting to communicate pain to the audience.

Conclusion: selling outside the ring

WWE is currently in what is considered the "Reality Era." This has been embodied by producing reality TV shows such as *Total Divas*, the launch of the WWE Network, wrestlers having official WWE Facebook pages and, as mentioned earlier, a shift in the choreographic fighting style in order for the presentation to look more believable. Twitter has also been heavily utilized on television as a way to involve audiences watching at home by encouraging hashtagging and audience feedback. WWE wrestlers, Mark Serrels playfully states, use Twitter in a number of unique ways: "The wrestler Mick Foley tweets about his charity work, The Rock promotes his movies, Rowdy Roddy Piper tweets clumsily – a bit like your dad."[16] Upon surveying the Twitter feeds of a number of top WWE wrestlers – including John Cena, Sheamus and Dolph Ziggler (Figure 14.1) – it has become apparent that performers utilize this technology and means of communication in another way and one that is important for my investigation.

Figure 14.1 Dolph Ziggler (@HEELZiggler). Screen shot of Twitter post from May 18, 2015, https://twitter.com/heelziggler/status/6003330637390 27457 (accessed May 20, 2015).

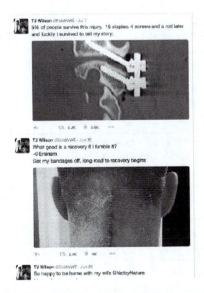

Figure 14.2 Tyson Kidd (@KiddWWE). Screen shot of Twitter posts from June 30 and July 7, 2015, https://twitter.com/KiddWWE/media (accessed September 23, 2015).

Wrestlers create their own visual documentation that legitimates their pain through a pictorial narrative often supported by a personal comment. For example, posting pictures of wounds being treated backstage, pictures of wounds after surgery and recovery processes such as physiotherapy sessions. An excellent recent example of this would be Tyson Kidd (Figure 14.2) who broke his neck and posted a number of graphic pictures on Twitter including a massive surgical scar and an X-ray of the screws put into his spine. This visual narrative is a unique way the wrestler continues to perform pain away from the professional wrestling event. In these pictures, the biology of the body performing pain is often apparent and highlighted through a considered photographic framing. Much like during the live event, bruising, swelling and wounds are flaunted as markers of endurance and signifiers of pain.

The majority of professional wrestling fans are aware that the product they are consuming is predetermined. To convincingly present the idea of authentic pain – despite this knowledge – is perhaps the hardest sell in the business. Professional wrestlers achieve this by continually evolving the presentation of their bodies, endure legitimate pain, exploit new technologies and mimic legitimate fighting sports to help us believe that the pain that they're experiencing is real. It's not an easy job, but I'm sold.

Notes

1 Patrick Wall, *Pain: The Science of Suffering* (London: Phoenix, 1999), 59.
2 Paul Ingraham, "Pain is Weird," PainScience.com, accessed June 12, 2015, https://www. painscience.com/articles/pain-is-weird.php.
3 Wall, *Pain*, 60.
4 Marjolein Kammers, Frédérique de Vignemont and Patrick Haggard. "Cooling the Thermal Grill Illusion through Self-Touch," *Current Biology* 20 (2010): 1819–1822, http://dx.doi.org/10.1016/j.cub.2010.08.038.
5 "UFC Rules and Regulations," UFC.com, accessed April 23, 2015, http://www.ufc.com/discover/sport/rules-and-regulations#1.
6 Andrew Binner, "The Rise of Mixed Martial Arts," *Aljazeera.com*, accessed June 10, 2015, http://www.aljazeera.com/sport/othersports/2014/04/rise-mixed-martial-arts-201441094427103582.html.
7 Grahame Herbert, "10 Things WWE Mean by the 'Reality Era.'" WhatCulture.com, accessed April 20, 2015, http://whatculture.com/wwe/10-things-wwe-mean-reality-era.php.
8 R. Tyson Smith, "Pain in the Act: The Meanings of Pain among Professional Wrestlers," *Qualitative Sociology* 31, no. 2 (2008): 129–148.
9 Elaine Scarry, *The Body in Pain: The Making and Unmaking of the World* (Oxford: Oxford University Press, 1985), 4.
10 Smith, "Pain in the Act," 141.
11 Broderick Chow and Eero Laine, "Audience Affirmation and the Labour of Professional Wrestling," *Performance Research: A Journal of the Performing Arts* 19, no. 2 (2014): 47.
12 Thomas Hackett, *Slaphappy: Pride, Prejudice, and Professional Wrestling* (New York: Harper-Collins, 2006), 70.
13 "WWE Parents Overview," WWE.com, accessed May 2, 2015, http://corporate.wwe.com/parents/overview.jsp.
14 Chris Jericho, "Talk is Jericho EP74 Matt and Jeff – The Hardy Boyz Pt 1," podcast audio, PodcastOne, September 17, 2014, http://podcastone.com/pg/jsp/program/episode.jsp?programID=593&pid=442593.
15 Brian Hebner, email message to author, June 5, 2015.
16 Mark Serrels, "How Do Pro Wrestlers Use Twitter?," accessed June 1, 2015, http://www.gizmodo.com.au. http://www.gizmodo.com.au/2011/10/how-do-pro-wrestlers-use-twitter/.

Part VII

Race

Chapter 15

"Tell them it's what their grandfathers got"

Racial violence in southern professional wrestling

Charles Hughes

In Louisiana in the early 1980s, the creative leadership of Mid–South Wrestling came up with a plan to boost ticket sales for an upcoming match between two black heroes and their villainous white opponents. While taping Mid–South's television show, white booker Bill Dundee told the Midnight Express to whip the black wrestlers in the middle of the ring. The team's manager Jim Cornette remembered one more instruction. "Tell them it's what their grandfathers got and it's what [they're going to get]."[1]

Watts's bluntness is shocking, but the instructions themselves reflect the broader importance of racial violence as a narrative and performative tactic in southern professional wrestling.[2] Particularly since the civil rights era in the 1950s and 1960s, black and white wrestlers have met in contests designed to engage the region's tumultuous racial history. Black heroes fought against mistreatment from white villains, while black heels triggered deeper racial anxieties rooted in the specific historical experiences of the American South. Although numerous scholars and journalists have considered how wrestling performances both reify and defy racial stereotype, fewer have framed these performances within the historical contexts of the American South.[3] Still, by contextualizing these performances in their historical milieu, it is possible to better understand both their characteristics and impacts.

Portrayals of African-Americans had been a staple of wrestling characterization since the form emerged in the late 1800s. Wrestling's emergence coincided with the height of blackface minstrelsy, which provided a template for both the exaggerated caricatures and historical resonances of wrestling performance. As scholars like Eric Lott and David Roediger have demonstrated, minstrelsy performances articulated a specific set of racial anxieties in the United States after the Civil War.[4] As African-Americans asserted new political and social rights, the idealized slave South and cartoonish stereotypes offered in blackface performances – where African-Americans ranged from uncontrollable savages to leering buffoons – allowed white audiences a chance to affirm blacks as unfit for modern society.

Early black wrestlers were similarly framed in language that foregrounded their supposedly natural physicality, connection to the primitive, and origins in slavery.[5] One writer suggested that the

> happy-go-lucky Negro of the slave-worked plantations in the United States made rich, natural material for fistic pioneering . . . Life in this country polished him, made him ready for the machine age to come. But underneath there was the tribal battler of the Congo, of Somaliland, and he took to fighting with a natural avidity and a native eagerness.[6]

This rhetoric shaped the career of the most notable early black wrestler, Viro "Black Sam" Small. Born a slave in Virginia, Small moved north, wrestled at carnivals and vaudeville shows, and faced primarily white opponents. Unlike the songs and comedy of the minstrel shows, Small's matches were *physical* battles and thus an even more provocative avatar for ongoing conflicts. In 1892, one white opponent became so enraged after losing to Small that he shot the black wrestler after a match.[7] Small's roots as a former slave, his promotion as a "tribal battler," and his clashes with whites both inside and outside the ring defined his career and helped to establish wrestling's significance on the rapidly changing terrain of American racial culture.

Viro Small made his name against white opponents, but most black wrestlers did not compete against whites in wrestling's early days. Particularly as wrestling expanded into a group of regional promotions, many of these "territories" – particularly, but not exclusively, in southern states – largely avoided pitting black wrestlers against white combatants. Beyond the general restrictions of Jim Crow segregation, many promoters claimed to fear the race riots that might occur if African-American wrestlers gained the upper hand against white opponents. The predetermined storylines allowed for little deviation, of course, but black wrestlers could gain a legitimate advantage if the match veered into a real (or "shoot") fight. Additionally, regardless of the outcome, the image of blacks fighting whites in pursuit of championships and adulation challenged the legal and social codes that enforced white supremacy. This segregation of matches – effective in some territories into the 1960s – limited the professional opportunities of black wrestlers and relegated them to a novelty status on many wrestling cards.[8]

For similar reasons, prominent African-American competitors usually performed as babyfaces.[9] Heroes like "Sailor" Art Thomas – who served in World War II – offered a safe and smiling image of black heroism that affirmed the goodness of postwar American culture without spotlighting its racial disparities. Thomas wrestled throughout the South, where he formed teams with other black wrestlers, faced off against foreign heels like Baron von Raschke in a recapitulation of wartime conflict, and even challenged for the world title in the early 1960s.[10] Art Thomas never won that title, and his character never addressed questions of civil rights, but the significance of Thomas and other heroes

should not be minimized in the aftermath of minstrelsy's demeaning charac-
terizations and in an era when positive representations of African-Americans
still remained rare.

The most popular of these babyfaces (and Art Thomas's one-time tag-team
partner) was Houston Harris, who wrestled as Bobo Brazil. Despite his exotic
name and jungle-print attire, Brazil was billed as being from Michigan and
became a huge star in the 1950s and 1960s, particularly in cities with high black
populations like Detroit and Washington, DC. In fact, it was in the nation's
capital (a literal and figurative border between North and South) that Brazil
took part in one of the era's most provocative race-based angles.[11] In 1965,
during a period of national upheaval and local riots, Brazil feuded with a white
heel named "Cowboy" Bill Watts. In televised interviews, Watts likened Brazil
to the livestock on his Oklahoma ranch. "That's what I'm gonna do to Bobo,"
he called saying. "Gouge him and gouge him, and then after I barbecue him all
he's going to be good for is shining my shoes and carrying my bags and that's
his station in life." Beyond the association with lynching, which often involved
torture and was even referred to as a "barbecue" by some participants, Watts's
claim that Brazil was only fit to serve white men created massive resentment
among Brazil's black fans in this tumultuous time.[12] Watts remembered being
pelted with urine-filled buckets during the sold-out match and having to run
from the building after the contest was completed. But, despite the controversy, wrestling promoters saw an opportunity in the controversy. "And guess
what they did?" Watts jokingly added. "[They] brought [the match] back" for a
return contest, hoping that the feverish emotions would correspond to higher
ticket sales.[13]

Indeed, despite their earlier fears, race-based contests became increasingly
appealing to southern-based wrestling companies that sought to exploit the
tensions of the civil rights era while also capitalizing on the increasing popularity of wrestling on television. But, as in Washington DC, pro wrestling's color
line was not simply a matter of in-ring performance. In areas of the country still
governed by laws mandating racial segregation in public spaces, black wrestlers
and fans faced separate seating, hotels, and other accommodations. When they
challenged those boundaries, they provoked an even more ambivalent response.

In Memphis, Tennessee, the white wrestler Sputnik Monroe embodied these
intersecting challenges by defying the color line both in real life and inside
the ring. In the late 1950s, so many black fans showed up to root for Monroe
that they overran the segregated balcony, leading Monroe to demand that the
promoters open up the floor to African-Americans. Cheered by blacks, booed
by most whites, Monroe's stand against segregation led many in Memphis to
credit his popularity with the desegregation of the city's performance venues.[14]
"I could have done any goddamn thing I wanted," Monroe remembered of
those days. "I was general of a little black army."[15]

By the end of the 1960s, both the territory and the political contexts
had changed. Although legal segregation had ended and Memphis wrestling

incorporated more opportunities for black performers and fans, the turbulent Black Power era produced heightened rhetoric and militant activism that maintained or even deepened racial divides in Memphis and elsewhere. In response, Sputnik Monroe developed a new strategy to recapture his notoriety. He found this opportunity by teaming with the young African-American grappler Norvell Austin.[16] Other interracial teams had appeared in Memphis by the late 1960s, but Austin and Monroe took their gimmick further by presenting themselves as father and son, complete with matching hair and post-match hugs. Even in the aftermath of legal desegregation and cultural progress, this level of intimacy and racial cross-culturation proved too much for a hotly divided audience. As Mark James notes, "Race relations were still strained in Memphis during 1971," so this team "almost had the Memphis fans rioting."[17] Or, at least, the white fans, although the nationalist bent of much Black Power rhetoric may have led to black fans being equally disdainful of the interracial tag team.

Norvell Austin and Sputnik Monroe were not the only wrestlers to foreground Black Power tumult and transformation in their performances. Pioneering heels like Ernie Ladd and Thunderbolt Patterson became the first black wrestlers to directly antagonize white babyfaces and fans with brash words and uncompromising tactics. At the same time, a new group of heroes – like Rocky "Soul Man" Johnson – celebrated their blackness and centralized their racial identity in a manner that exceeded any of their predecessors. Even beyond the scripted in-ring drama, the threat of racial violence shaped the lives of black wrestlers. Johnson, who became the first black regional champion in numerous southern territories, remembered a particularly tense moment against white heel Dick Murdoch, a respected wrestler and real-life member of the KKK. Johnson, also a boxer, recalled having to defend himself when Murdoch dropped the performance and actually tried to physically hurt Johnson during a match. "He didn't like blacks and he kept kicking me hard and punching me and I said 'if you hit me one more time, I'm hitting you back' and he hit me and I knocked him out."[18]

Johnson and Ladd both appeared in Mid-South Wrestling, now controlled by promoter Bill Watts, who purchased the promotion in 1979. Watts, who had tangled with Bobo Brazil in Washington, DC, understood how racially based angles could boost ticket sales, particularly among the often-ignored African-American audience who cheered on Bobo Brazil, Sputnik Monroe and others who fought white supremacy through staged combat and "real" activism. At the dawn of the 1980s, with the support of early booker Ernie Ladd (whom Watts later said "taught me about [being] black" through both his in-ring performances and behind-the-scenes approach), Watts – who had also been influenced by the success of black wrestlers like Art Thomas and Thunderbolt Patterson – pushed an assertive black babyface as the centerpiece of Mid-South.[19]

He chose Sylvester Ritter, a college-educated football player who broke into wrestling as the stereotypical pimp character Big Daddy Ritter and was remade in Mid-South as the Junkyard Dog.[20] Although the presentation of the Junkyard

Dog (or "JYD") evoked certain stereotypes – he wore a collar-and-chain and often danced in the ring – Watts and Ritter crafted a character that could appeal to African-Americans beyond shared skin color. "I knew a black would draw blacks," Watts recalled, "but the real secret was not letting a white man save a black man. I put JYD in situations that were fucking impossible and he always saved himself."[21] This crucial focus on black self-reliance in the face of white antagonism resonated deeply with the African-American fans who filled JYD's matches in New Orleans, Houston, and other Mid-South strongholds.[22]

The climax was JYD's 1982 feud against The Freebirds, a heel team composed of three un-reconstructed white southerners. Taking their name from a song by Southern rock icons Lynyrd Skynyrd, the team waved the Confederate flag and proclaimed their status as rebellious representatives of an untamed South. The angle was hugely successful, leading to unprecedented crowds and unequalled enthusiasm. A gunman leapt into the ring during one contest to defend the JYD, and the culmination match in New Orleans drew 26,000 people, which Greg Klein claims was "the largest indoor crowd in the history of pro wrestling at that time."[23] In the mid-1980s, the Junkyard Dog became one of the highest-paid black athletes in the South.[24]

After the 1984 departure of the Junkyard Dog, who left for the nationally ascendant World Wrestling Federation (WWF), Watts continued to utilize racially charged, regionally specific storylines involving a black hero and white villain. The best of these storylines transcended easy romance or stereotype, instead offering symbolic re-creations of deep and complicated historical dynamics. In 1985, the popular "Hacksaw" Butch Reed – who had earlier played heel in a feud with Junkyard Dog, where he accused the popular JYD of being a racial sellout and challenged him to a series of "Ghetto Street" fights – launched a campaign against the "Nature Boy" Ric Flair, then the world champion, and his henchman "Dirty" Dick Slater.[25] When Reed challenged Flair for the title, the champion – in his tailored suit and bleached blonde hair – refused to fight the hero, yelling "get this monkey out of the ring" to a chorus of boos. Threatened by Reed's challenge, Flair offered money to Dick Slater, a working-class brawler, to injure Reed. Slater was accompanied in this dastardly mission by Dark Journey, a black woman who acted as Slater's valet. At one point, Reed confronted Dark Journey in the ring on Mid-South's television show. As Slater stood nearby, Reed yelled "I'm black and I'm proud of it. I know what I am – the trouble is you don't know who you are. You're trying to be something that you ain't." In response, Dark Journey slapped Reed, leading Reed to warn her that "black men don't treat women like white men when it comes to slapping on them . . . When you put your hands on me again, I'm going to knock you smooth out." The crowd roared its approval. Rather than defend his valet, Slater cowardly hid behind her, begging Reed not to hurt him and promising that he had returned Flair's blood money.[26]

This striking sequence offered a complex staging of defiance and complicity that troubled easy understandings of morality or racial caricature. In this narrative, Reed performed the role of assertive and hardworking black man who worked to achieve success in an unfair and white-dominated world, only to be disrespected and kept down by a conspiracy between a wealthy white man and his working-class employee. At the same time, though, Reed also earned cheers by condemning a black woman for betraying her race by associating with a white man. Reed asserted his masculinity not only by impugning that of Dick Slater, but by threatening Dark Journey with physical violence. Slater's manhood was further challenged by Flair, who employed Slater to keep the black man in line even as he denigrated Slater and abandoned him at the first sign of danger. Historical questions of racial loyalty, class solidarity, labor exploitation, and black women's vulnerability were all articulated in a wrestling performance that exploited these tensions for creative fuel and commercial success.

Still, the sophistication of southern professional wrestling's portrayal of racial violence – or black characters in general – should not be overstated. In the 1980s, numerous southern promoters (including Bill Watts) continued to rely on simplistic black stereotypes that were rooted in the minstrel era and remixed for a contemporary context. Heels like the Zambuie Express and Kamala combined older beliefs in black savagery with post-colonial anxieties over third-world black militancy. Meanwhile, babyfaces like The Bruise Brothers and The PYT Express danced to the ring and spoke in a caricatured dialect. Even Mid-South, which had its greatest success through the explicit promotion of strong black characters in race-based angles, regularly presented such characters as part of their shows. Their audiences dwindled in the late 1980s, which – while not directly traceable to the lack of strong African-American protagonists – nonetheless marked a significant difference from the booming days of the Junkyard Dog.

At the end of the decade, Watts sold Mid-South Wrestling to the Atlanta-based World Championship Wrestling (WCW), by then the most powerful southern-based promotion. WCW occasionally flirted with race-based angles: in 1990, the Junkyard Dog defended Rocky King against the racially tinged threats of Ric Flair and his Four Horsemen stable. (In one televised confrontation, Flair threatened King by saying "you can't moonwalk one foot with a broken leg," referencing the dance popularized by black music star Michael Jackson).[27] But WCW's interest in foregrounding racial violence and promoting a black babyface as the central protagonist unsurprisingly peaked when Bill Watts became the head of the company in 1992.

As he had with Junkyard Dog and Butch Reed, Watts pushed a black hero to the forefront. He chose Ron Simmons, a former college football star who had worked in WCW as one-half of the black tag team Doom. Originally performing in masks, Doom was accompanied to the ring by Nancy Sullivan, a white performer who was known simply (and evocatively) as "Woman." Jim Cornette, the former manager of the Midnight Express who was now working in WCW, admitted that the decision to pair "this beguiling, bewitching, beautiful white woman with these two mysterious black S&M-type [wrestlers]" was consciously designed to push racial buttons, as was the image presented by – as Ron Simmons recalled – Doom being "two big black guys out here who are going to beat up on" their white opponents.[28] Although Doom's run was short-lived, Ron Simmons's athletic background and skill in interviews made him a perfect choice for Watts's plan.[29]

Now unmasked, and wrestling as an "all-American" hero in the model of Art Thomas and others, Ron Simmons soon challenged for the WCW world title. But, like his 1970s forebears Rocky "Soul Man" Johnson and others, Simmons also foregrounded his historical interest in furthering the cause of black progress. In one interview, Simmons declared that "I plan to go where no black man has gone before and that's straight to the top and become the first man to wear that belt." He was then interrupted by villainous manager Harley Race, a former champion who told Simmons that he had no business challenging for the title, especially since – when Race held the title in the 1970s – he had "a boy like you carrying my bag." A chorus of boos rained down as Simmons reminded Race that "you got your year wrong and you got my name wrong. This is almost the year 2000, not the eighteenth century."[30] The crowd greeted Simmons's history lesson with cheers, presaging the ecstatic response when Simmons won the title in June in front of a Baltimore crowd that included a large number of African-American fans.[31]

Even as the national rise of WCW and the WWF hastened the death of territorial promotions, regional wrestling remained prominent in the South into the 1990s. As in earlier eras, race-based angles remained crucial to the creative repertoire. One of the most successful and explosive examples came from the creative mind of Jim Cornette, the white manager who had been instructed to whip black wrestlers in Louisiana and who applied many of Bill Watts's creative strategies to his own promotion, the Tennessee-based Smoky Mountain Wrestling (SMW). Cornette offered a contemporary remix in the form of a heel tag team called The Gangstas. This "stereotype[d] tag team of black criminals" featured Jerome "New Jack" Young and Jamaal "Mustafa Saed" Mustafa, who entered to rap music, traveled with a sizable entourage, and often used weapons.[32] Cornette insisted that The Gangstas address race in their interviews, and the talented New Jack was happy to oblige in comments that condemned America's history of racial violence, called the crowd "rednecks" and racists, and accused SMW's leadership of conspiring to keep them down.[33] Particularly when pitted against heroes like the "Dirty White Boy," The Gangstas were the most hated performers in SMW. While southern audiences may unite behind black babyfaces, they could easily be divided by black heels who offered confrontational and militant performances of contemporary racial anxieties.

WCW had a harder time negotiating this delicate balance, as evidenced by one of its most prominent 1990s tag teams, a duo named Harlem Heat. They were billed as being from "125th Street" (the most famous thoroughfare in the historically black New York neighborhood), given a hip-hop entrance theme, and called Booker T. and Stevie Ray. Harlem Heat tapped into longer beliefs in the danger of southern infiltration by northern blacks, which dated to the slave era and had been a consistent feature of southern racial politics, and also the contemporary tensions of the post–L.A. riots era. This image was strengthened by the managers assigned to perform with them. First was Col. Robert Parker, a strutting buffoon who dressed like a riverboat gambler and spoke with an exaggerated southern accent. Originally, Parker led the team to the ring in chains – thankfully, this idea was quickly abandoned – but the image of two large black men doing the bidding of an archetype of Old South whiteness did not need such obvious coding.[34] Soon, though, Parker was replaced by "Sister Sherri," a white wrestler named Sherri Martel who acted as the team's valet for the rest of their WCW run. As with the earlier pairing of Doom and Woman, Sister Sherri was a white woman who had abandoned her virtue (either forcibly or consensually) in favor of consorting with black men. With both white managers, Harlem Heat reinforced the image of black men as dangerous and disruptive.

This image was crystallized most obviously at the 1996 Hog Wild event in Sturgis, South Dakota, when Harlem Heat challenged white babyfaces The Steiner Brothers. The audience – composed primarily of white bikers – showered Booker T. and Stevie Ray with racial epithets and waved Confederate flags throughout the contest. As journalist David D. notes, "the whole match devolved into a glorified Klan rally."[35] This heated reaction symbolized the broader politics of white backlash that took root in the aftermath of the civil rights movement and was reinvigorated over fears of crime and militancy during the 1980s and 1990s.[36] The team soon broke up, with Booker T. becoming a solo star – and eventual WCW champion – as a babyface.

Meanwhile, Stevie Ray joined the promotion's primary heel faction, the New World Order (NWO). Although the NWO was composed primarily of white wrestlers (including former hero Hulk Hogan), these performers explicitly adopted the characteristics of the non–white urban gangs that became one of the biggest perceived threats to public safety in the 1990s United States. In a similar vein as The Gangstas, the NWO announced their villainy through their rap soundtrack, gang signs, and outfits, and brutalization of opponents with sneak attacks and a variety of weapons. Additionally, since most of the NWO's membership were wrestlers who were either legitimately from the American North or presented as such, the group's battle against a group of white WCW mainstays (like Ric Flair and Sting) took on a distinctly regionalized overtone. The NWO announced that they "were taking over" WCW, while the WCW heroes declared their fight against the NWO to be a battle between an invading army and the forces of tradition. The presence of a few black NWO members – particularly Stevie Ray – reinforced their image as gangland invaders.

Although the NWO fueled an unprecedented moment of success for WCW, the WWF retook its position as the most successful wrestling company in 1998. As WCW struggled to regain its footing, the promotion tried to both expand its audience and reignite its traditional fan base. In 1999, these competing interests led them to partner with Master P, a New Orleans–based rapper and the founder of No Limit Records. WCW's partnership with Master P and his posse of No Limit Soldiers seemingly offered a perfect opportunity to bridge the company's southern roots and national ambitions, as well as to compete with the cutting-edge content of the WWF.

Master P and the No Limit Soldiers made regular appearances on WCW television, heralded by the announcers as major celebrities (which they were) and heroic babyfaces (which they were promoted to be). But the WCW audience – still primarily white and southern, despite the company's attempts to diversify – did not embrace the assertive, camouflaged young black men. Instead, WCW fans rallied around the No Limit Soldiers' main antagonists, a white faction called the West Texas Rednecks. When WCW produced a music video for a country song by the West Texas Rednecks called "Rap Is Crap," which featured the team walking through Nashville and declaring their hatred for hip-hop, the song became a rallying cry for the increasingly popular team.[37] Country music – firmly associated with southern white identity – offered an obvious counterpoint to the rumbling hip-hop of Master P, thus giving white WCW fans a perfect opportunity to crystallize their opposition to the swaggering young African-American men in the No Limit Soldiers. The storyline flopped and the partnership with Master P and No Limit Records dissolved.

Of course, Master P and the No Limit Soldiers were just as southern as the West Texas Rednecks. (The Rednecks' leader, Curt Hennig, was from Minnesota.) But the booing of the black faction symbolized a broader narrative that posed the arrival of hip-hop era blackness (and the black re-migration to the South in the 1990s) as a threat to the supposed "traditions" of the white south.[38] When promoting The Gangstas in the early 1990s in Smoky Mountain Wrestling, Jim Cornette recognized that a heel hip-hop team could be good for business, but WCW failed to properly interpret the allegiances of their fans and thus exploit the partnership with Master P. WCW's fans rejected the promotion of rapping black "soldiers" and claimed white traditionalism as the South's true identity. The failure of the Master P angle was one of the most prominent examples of a broader decline in WCW throughout 1999 and 2000.

WCW closed in 2001, purchased by the WWF. Although the McMahon-led company retained many of WCW's top stars (including Booker T.), the purchase signaled the end of national significance for southern-based professional wrestling.[39] Accordingly, storylines that were based explicitly around the intersections between racial and regional conflict also faded from view. Although the WWE has occasionally been the site of complex racial storylines involving Black Power or gangsta characters, the company has been far less willing to centralize the tense historical relationship between black and white Americans within its storylines in anything more than the most cartoonish fashion. While some southern portrayals unquestionably embody the same stereotypes and outlandish constructs, the South has also been the site of rich and complicated storylines through which wrestlers and fans have engaged the longer history of racial change and conflict in the South and the United States. While not all have been as crude as the instruction to "tell them it's what their grandfathers got," they are all part of a much larger tradition that has structured the form and illuminates its larger context.

Notes

1 Jim Cornette, Shoot interview with RF Video, 2000. In a different interview, Cornette recalls that Mid-South promoter Bill Watts instructed him to threaten two black competitors with tarring and feathering "so that you get a taste of what your grandparents got." He also remembered telling the African-American wrestlers that "we're going to read you *Roots* backwards so it has happy ending." See *Jim Cornette – Timeline: The History of WCW 1989* (Kayfabe Commentaries, 2015).
2 Here, "southern" refers to wrestling promotions and events centered in the southern portion of the United States.
3 One exception is David Shoemaker's recent book, which threads historical context throughout and specifically devotes several pages to a discussion of African-American representations. See Shoemaker, *The Squared Circle: Life, Death and Professional Wrestling* (New York: Gotham, 2013), esp. 125–143.
4 See Eric Lott, *Love and Theft: Blackface Minstrelsy and the American Working Class* (New York: Oxford University Press, 1993) and David Roediger, *The Wages of Whiteness: Race and the Making of the American Working Class* (New York: Verso, 1997).
5 For information on early black wrestlers, see Burkholder's "Black History Month: Pro Wrestling's Black Stars" 2002 series on Wrestleline, http://www.wrestleline.com.
6 Daniel M. Daniel, quoted in Nat Fleischer, *Black Dynamite: The Story of the Negro in the Prize Ring from 1782 to 1938, Volume 1* (New York: C.J. O'Brien, 1938), xi–xii. See also Joe Jares, *Whatever Happened to Gorgeous George?* (Edgewood Cliffs, NJ: Prentice Hall, 1974), 69–70.
7 One of these opponents became so enraged after losing to Small that he shot him after a match in 1892. Dewey Burkholder, "Black History Month: Pro Wrestling's Black Stars, Part 1," Wrestleline, February 5, 2002, http://www.wrestleline.com.
8 Scott Beekman, *Ringside: A History of Professional Wrestling in America* (Westport, CT: Praeger, 2006), 28–30. In Memphis, cards into the early 1960s advertised special "Negro matches" as an attraction. See Mark James, *Memphis Wrestling History Presents: The 1960s: 1960–1969 Record Book* (Memphis: Mark James, 2011).
9 Many black wrestlers competed as foreign villains (usually from Africa or the Caribbean), but those performers who were identified as African-American were usually presented as "good guys."
10 For more on Thomas, see Mike Mooneyham, "Sailor Art Thomas Dies at Age 79," The Wrestling Gospel, March 23, 2003, http://www.mikemooneyham.com/2003/03/23/sailor-art-thomas-dies-at-age-79/.
11 See Kate Masur, *An Example for All the Land: Emancipation and the Struggle for Equality in Washington, D.C.* (Chapel Hill: University of North Carolina Press, 2012).
12 When Jesse Washington was burned alive in Waco, Texas, in 1916, an attendee wrote a postcard telling his friend that he missed the "barbecue." See also Amy Louise Wood, *Lynching and Spectacle: Witnessing Racial Violence in America, 1890–1940* (Chapel Hill: University of North Carolina Press, 2011).
13 *Straight Shootin' Series: Jim Cornette and Bill Watts, Volume 2*, ROH Video, 2006.
14 See Pete Daniel, *Lost Revolution: The South in the 1950s* (Chapel Hill: University of North Carolina Press, 2000), 126; Robert Gordon, *It Came from Memphis* (New York: Atria, 2001, reprint), 32–44.

15 Gordon, *It Came from Memphis*, 37.

16 Later, Austin would be one of the wrestlers whipped by the Midnight Express in Louisiana.

17 James, *Memphis Wrestling History Presents: The 1960s*, 160; Mark James, *Memphis Wrestling History Presents: The 1970s* (Mark James, 2012), 50.

18 Rocky Johnson interview for Hannibal TV/GreatNorthWrestling.Ca, *YouTube video*, October 3, 2014, https://www.youtube.com/watch?v=rRhLqSJNpgk.

19 Bill Watts, interview with RF Video, 2000.

20 For more on the story of Junkyard Dog in Mid-South, see Greg Klein, *The King of New Orleans: How the Junkyard Dog Became Professional Wrestling's First Black Superstar* (Toronto: ECW Press, 2012).

21 Watts quoted in Shaun Asseal and Mike Mooneyham, *Sex, Lies & Headlocks: The Real Story of Vince McMahon and the Rise of World Wrestling Entertainment* (New York: Broadway Books, 2004), 62.

22 One angle involved JYD fighting a group of white wrestlers who mocked JYD by calling him a "monkey" and dressing in a gorilla costume. See David "Masked Man" Shoemaker, "Dead Wrestler of the Week: 'Maniac' Matt Borne, AKA Doink the Clown," *Deadspin*, March 7, 2013, http://deadspin.com/dead-wrestler-of-the-week-maniac-matt-borne-aka-doi-659331900.

23 Klein, *The King of New Orleans*, 72. Such a claim is hard to measure, but there is no question that the JYD/Freebirds angle was hugely successful for its participants and Mid-South Wrestling. As journalist Dave Meltzer notes elsewhere, "it is probable that no city in North America drew as many fans to pro wrestling as New Orleans" during JYD's run. See Dave Meltzer, *Tributes: Remembering Some of the World's Greatest Wrestlers* (Etobicoke, ON: Winding Stair Press, 2001).

24 Meltzer, *Tributes*, 103.

25 Prior to JYD's departure, he feuded with Butch Reed in a series of "Ghetto Street Fight" matches where Reed accused JYD of being a racial sell-out. See *Wrestling Program*, October 23, 1983, 1–2, reprinted in Mark James, *Wrestling Record Book: Houston Programs 1982–1983* (Mark James, 2014), 179–180.

26 "Mid-South Wrestling" *Television Program*, Episode 322, November 1985, accessed through WWEnetwork.com.

27 WCW World Wide, May 26, 1990, accessed https://www.youtube.com/watch?v=Hk AdplMOYOI.

28 "Jim Cornette: Timeline"; Ron Simmons, shoot interview with Highspots.com, 2005.

29 The other half of the team, Butch Reed, did not receive the same boost from his old employer.

30 WCW TV, unknown date, found at https://www.youtube.com/watch?v=AX-03cPJ8P4.

31 WCW "Main Event," Episode 620, August 17, 1992, accessed on WWENetwork.com. The presentation of this match during one of WCW's regular television shows is noteworthy, especially since WCW saved most of its high-profile television matches for pay-per-view events. Additionally, the show's hosts – Eric Bischoff and Teddy Long – talked openly throughout the program about Simmons's defeat of Vader, suggesting that WCW felt the audience would care less about the outcome of the match, and more about the significance of Simmons's victory. Teddy Long, who is black, reiterated this in comments noting that "the one that all the homies in the hood are waiting on is Ron Simmons defeating Big Van Vader for the WCW World Title."

32 Klein, *The King of New Orleans*, 51.

33 Several of The Gangstas' SMW interviews are available on YouTube. For example, see clips at https://www.youtube.com/watch?v=3KW5kj_6jSU, https://www.youtube.com/watch?v=iZGqoknXqx4 and https://www.youtube.com/watch?v=okGyJ-rFZiQ.

34 Shoemaker, "Dead Wrestler of the Week," 140.

35 See D. David, "Vintage Best and Worst: WCW Hog Wild 1996," UPROXX, May 8, 2014, http://uproxx.com/sports/2014/05/vintage-best-and-worst-wcw-hog-wild-1996/.

36 For more on the backlash, see Dan T. Carter, *The Politics of Rage: George Wallace, the Origins of the New Conservatism, and the Transformation of American Politics* (Baton Rouge: Louisiana State University Press, 2000).

37 West Texas Cowboys, "Rap Is Crap," *YouTube video*, https://www.youtube.com/watch?v=HHihfxE0ZTk.

38 See Zandria F. Robinson, *This Ain't Chicago: Race, Class and Regional Identity in the Post-Soul South* (Chapel Hill: University of North Carolina Press, 2014).

39 It can be argued that the creation of the Nashville-based TNA promotion in the early 2000s is an exception to this trend.

Chapter 16

Grappling with the "new racism"

Race, ethnicity, and post-colonialism in British wrestling during the 1970s and 1980s

Nicholas Porter

By the 1970s, professional wrestling was a staple of live entertainment in the UK. Regular events took place up and down the country, drawing audiences to venues in small towns and major cities. At the same time, wrestling was a weekly fixture on television, broadcast into homes throughout the nation. Even as it enjoyed great popularity, wrestling's colourful spectacle, like much of British pop culture at the time, found itself at the conflux of an insular nationalism and multiculturalism that was redefining British society. The seventies and eighties marked a period during which Britain's ongoing, post–World War II racial diversification came to the forefront of public life more than ever before. Wary of this, the country's political powers sought to promote a national identity that effectively marginalised non-white immigrants from former British colonies in the Caribbean, Africa, and Asia. This phenomenon, which intensified with the Conservative politician Margaret Thatcher's ascent to power during the latter half of the seventies and dominance of the entire eighties, was defined by scholar Martin Barker in 1981 as the "new racism."[1] The new racism was striking in that it acknowledged the visible racial diversity of Britain in the seventies and eighties even as it sought to consign immigrants to the periphery. Its implications extended beyond politics to the cultural sphere, where non-white performers in television, film, and theatre struggled for recognition.[2] The inadequate representation and persistent stereotyping of non-whites in British entertainment were topics of debate and the sources of controversy for critics and groups, such as the Campaign against Racism in the Media, who perceived covert racism as endemic within the television industry.[3] As a popular medium, it was inevitable that wrestling would play host to characters who reflected both progressive and regressive attitudes towards Britain's changing demographics.

Wrestlers of African, Caribbean, and Asian descent such as Clive Myers, Caswell Martin, Jackie Turpin, "Jamaica Kid" Lenny Hurst, The Caribbean Sunshine Boys ("Soulman" Dave Bond and Johnny Kincaid), Johnny Kwango, Masambula, Tiger Dalibar Singh, Kashmir Singh, and Honey Boy Zimba were all regulars on wrestling bills throughout Britain during the seventies and eighties.

These men represented a strong diversity within the wrestling ranks, but performed within a space that was indelibly shaped by its larger social context. Every time they stepped into the ring they publicly explored notions of racial identity that were both resistant to and defined by "new racist" sentiments. Largely overlooked within the annals of British popular culture, wrestlers such as Myers, Masambula, and Zimba can be appraised today for their significant yet conflicted contribution to Britain's culture of representation during the seventies and eighties. This chapter will examine how they depicted race and identity in the wrestling ring and assert that their work provides a hitherto unexplored perspective on the plight of multiculturalism during a crucial period in modern British social and cultural history.

Wrestling's *mise-en-scène* was starkly British – it drew on classic traditions of variety show performance and pantomime while echoing the communal appeal of popular sports like football. The settings were often town halls, the symbolic centres of British communities, where the sight of a wrestling ring and colourfully attired wrestlers was jarringly discordant with the bleakness of the building in which they were performing. What wrestling offered these observers was simulated sporting contests that, when done by skilled wrestlers, were exciting and unpredictable, predicated around characters the audience could vigorously support or vocally detest. Performers needed to embody their characters so that wrestling's staged illusion of reality was never violated.[4] To make it appear real, wrestlers needed to master not only the basic mechanics of putting on a match hold-for-hold, but the subtlety of gesture, facial expression, and body language in order to draw the audience into the spectacle.

The audience was typically of the lower-middle and working classes, in which wrestling had strong roots. Many wrestlers were hard- (or broken-) nosed men from the deindustrialising north and there was a general sense that wrestlers were men of the people. The typical audience seen at televised wrestling broadcasts was predominantly white with occasional non-white spectators. Throughout the seventies and eighties, the Britain channelled by the weekly wrestling coverage resounded with the kind of patriotic nationalism that, beyond wrestling, often informed critiques of Britain's diversification. The weekly televised wrestling was awash with garish patriotic overtones: from the ring ropes matching the colour of the Union flag to the relaxed, received pronunciation of commentator Kent Walton, there was never any doubt that the wrestling was suffused with a highly idealised Britishness.

Wrestling's pervasive nationalism was best embodied in the form of Shirley "Big Daddy" Crabtree. The biggest star in British wrestling during the late seventies and early eighties, Crabtree was a larger-than-life man of the people from the working-class North with whom fans across the country could immediately relate. Instantly recognisable by his ring attire that was often emblazoned with the Union flag, Crabtree represented a hybrid of nationalism and working-class whiteness that the more nationalist sections of the public perceived as being so potently under threat from increased immigration and racial diversification.[5] It was perhaps no coincidence that Daddy's celebrity status earned him a fan in

Margaret Thatcher, who became prime minister in 1978 amid a swirl of nation-
alistic euphoria.[6]

In the face of wrestling's overbearing Britishness, the characters performed
by non-white wrestlers typically fell between poles. Many adhered to what
could be described as a classic wrestler archetype. These men opted to downplay
excessive characterisation and exaggerated gestures, instead weaving exciting
matches together from complicated sequences of holds. Their characters could
more generally be considered as representing some variant of "post-colonial,"
"immigrant," or "black British" due to their absence of glaring visual signifiers
of "otherness" beyond their skin colour. The second archetype – the overtly
othered character – was the antithesis of the first. Here, the wrestling character
was an elaborate, often extreme, caricature of a racial and cultural other.[7] In the
context of British wrestling, being an other meant being categorised as different from the white British majority, typically to the extent that the otherness
of the character was blatantly and deliberately broadcast to the audience either
through dress or exaggerated mannerisms.

The overtly stereotyped characters fell within a broad culture of racial stereotyping that was particularly prominent in the seventies. At a time when
racially insensitive programmes such as *It Ain't Half Hot, Mum* and *The Black
and White Minstrel Show* were staples of British entertainment, the presence of
overtly stereotyped characters such as Honey Boy Zimba and Masambula testified to promoters' desire for a colourful cast of characters evoking time-tested
archetypes and served to undermine any progression that the less-stereotyped
performers could make. When Zimba and Masambula stepped into the ring
wearing pseudo-African tribal attire such as faux lion skins, the crowd was left
in no doubt as to their otherness – they were presented as being alien to British
life. Working mostly against white wrestlers in front of largely white audiences,
Zimba and Masambula symbolised an extreme clashing of cultures – denizens
of the old imperial colonies straying waywardly into modern Britain. That wrestling would feature such blatantly colonial characters exposed the susceptibility
for promoting an imagined gulf between island Britain and its former colonies.

Once the bell rang, the overt stereotypes drew upon a range of mannerisms
and techniques that starkly differentiated them from the less-overt types. Typically presented as affable, rule-abiding characters, Zimba and Masambula show-
cased their athleticism not by executing complex chain-sequences of wrestling
holds but by leaping about the ring in a fashion ostensibly disorienting for their
opponents. Their tendency to eschew complicated techniques implied, within
the context of the performance, a lack of grounding in the fundamentals. This
was compounded by a shared tendency among the overtly othered characters
to perform "head butts," one of the most obvious indicators of a wrestler's
unsophistication. The not-so-subtle implication was that characters of African
heritage like Masambula possessed harder skulls than their white opponents.
This suggestion of genetic difference and its insinuation of inferior intelligence
evoked the more sinister undertones of their act and wrestling in general – the
lingering sentiments of colonial superiority.

Masambula and Zimba were exotic, benign, lovable characters – unthreaten-ing figures still rooted in ostensibly uncivilised cultures on the fringe of the British worldview. Billed as being from Gambia and Sierra Leone respectively, there was no missing the signifiers of their difference, especially when they were facing off against generically bland white wrestlers. Regardless of how innocently they were presented to audiences, the underlying impression was that they represented an Africa configured in the British mindset as a dark, distant continent – a collection of former colonies. Masambula, in particular, embraced the role of the primitive other to an extreme degree. In the ring, almost every aspect of his character, from the way he stood to the ungainly man-ner in which he moved around, suggested a man totally out of place. Whereas Zimba's character was not excessively comedic, Masambula's was predicated around his being at odds with the highly technical style of British wrestling. His commitment to providing comic relief went beyond his unusual reper-toire of holds and manoeuvres. One particular television match from 1970, pitting Masambula and Zimba – billed in typical wrestling fashion as "The Black Knights" – against white tag team The Royals, perfectly illustrates his full-bodied approach.[8] When one of his opponents would place Masambula in a hold, he would work his way free not by "reversing" into another hold in the standard fashion, but by crawling on his back to avoid his bemused and amused opponent. In terms of ring presence, Masambula's wide-eyed facial expressions and distinctive vocal style were hallmarks of a natural extrovert. Where other wrestlers symbolised skill and order, moving from hold to hold, Masambula's oeuvre was one of chaos and uncertainty that elicited loud cheers from the audience. To accentuate his character's unorthodox style, he constantly uttered noises that sounded less like a formed language and more like the ravings of a man in a pronounced state of disorientation, as if struggling to process the "developed" society. More incongruity was provided by commentator Walton's casual revelation to viewers that Masambula had, in his pre-wrestling career, worked in the orderly and civil realm of the police force.

By the time wrestling was at the height of its popularity in the late seventies, Britain's colonial empire had effectively been dismantled, with former colonies in Africa, Asia, the Caribbean, and South America gaining independence. In Tony Freeth's estimation, the racist sentiment of the seventies belied the sense that the UK itself had become the British Empire's "last colony."[9] Under the new creed, the perceived inability and unwillingness of immigrants to adapt properly to British society became a central issue, stoked by fears that Britain had been "invaded" not from without but from within.[10] In this context, it's possible to interpret the overtly othered wrestlers as revealing underlying anxi-eties regarding immigrants from the former colonies in Britain. Set against the recent backdrop of decolonisation, Zimba and Masambula functioned as "safe" characters, their supposed cultural differences easily demarcated and emphasised to the extent that they couldn't possibly be mistaken as civilised or equal to the worldly white British wrestlers.

It is telling that, even when the public othering of immigrants was intensifying in the late seventies, the overtly stereotyped characters were outnumbered by non-white wrestlers enacting less exaggerated personae. By the start of the eighties, Zimba and Masambula had fallen from view and wrestlers whose characters were more serious took greater prominence. Notable examples of less overtly othered characters came from a variety of backgrounds. Clive Myers and Caswell Martin were of Caribbean heritage, whereas Tiger Dalibar Singh and Kashmir Singh were of Indian descent. To the audience, these wrestlers occupied a similar status as the majority of white wrestlers and often portrayed the heroic "blue-eye" role, battling villainous "heel" wrestlers to positive responses from majority white audiences. Myers, Martin, and the Singhs came across as serious athletes first and foremost. Like many British wrestlers, they did not exude much personality in the ring – their styles of wrestling were steeped in the British tradition of complex manoeuvres and displays of expert athleticism delivered with a studied unfussiness. Myers, in particular, was capable of wrestling at a heightened pace and filled his matches with segments of technical finesse and non-stop action. His work was essentially similar to that of white stars like Steve Grey, with whom he contested a series of lengthy, exciting matches on television. In his television commentary, Kent Walton generally eschewed any mention of race, emphasising instead these wrestlers' skills, technique, and competitiveness, establishing for the viewer their credentials within the realm of wrestling. The facets of the performance that marked the Caribbean and British-Caribbean wrestlers as having heritage in warmer climes outside dreary Britain were the obligatory mention of one's hometown, or a colourful nickname. So, Myers was introduced as being from Jamaica and Martin from Antigua. Dave Bond and Johnny Kincaid, meanwhile, formed a team known as The Caribbean Sunshine Boys, a name that conveyed the tropical allure of the West Indies.

Wrestlers of Asian descent were similarly able to operate outside of constrictive stereotyping. Tiger Dalibar Singh was a regular on the circuit throughout the late seventies and eighties, while Kashmir Singh began appearing more regularly sometime after Dalibar had become established. To establish his international background, Dalibar was billed from Punjab, India, and regularly introduced on TV as being "one of India's finest wrestlers" or the "champion of India."[11] Once it came time to perform, Dalibar drew from the voluminous repertoire of holds and techniques that formed the basis of British wrestling. Dalibar was a masterful performer, popular with crowds, whose demure ring persona was offset by his supreme aptitude for the technical side of wrestling. There was nothing in his performances to demarcate him from the standard British wrestler – he attained a degree of equality whose heritage was only accentuated by the stereotypical aspects of his "Tiger" moniker. He successfully portrayed the role of an Indian migrant to the UK, only one whose particular occupation was wrestling. Like Dalibar, Kashmir adopted the same style of technical wrestling. He achieved less recognition than Dalibar, but one televised

tag team match, in which Kashmir appeared as a partner for the aging, corpulent figure of Big Daddy, testified to wrestling's notable capacity for combining
disparate characters – in this instance Kashmir's Asian and Daddy's working-
class Englishman – into a besequined microcosm of British multiculturalism.[12]

The ring uniforms of the less–overtly othered wrestlers typically followed the
standard uniform of trunks and boots, and served to demarcate the performers first and foremost as serious wrestlers. Kashmir Singh may have worn a
turban beforehand but once the match began, his sartorial signs of "otherness"
vanished along with any performative cues. Ring attire was a key aspect of a
wrestler's character. For at least one televised match, Clive Myers turned out in
trunks patterned after the Union flag,[13] and in another, wore trunks based on
the black, yellow, and green flag of Jamaica.[14] Within the context of isolationist
Britain, Myers's incorporation of the Jamaican flag suggests a proud investment
in his heritage, identification with his homeland, and a visual marker of his
status as an immigrant to the UK. That he would proclaim his Jamaican background in mid–seventies Britain also hinted at a deliberate attempt to show his
resistance to assimilation. On the contrary, his incorporation of the British flag
invites a number of other readings. By wearing the Union flag so visibly on his
trunks Myers could be seen as playing into a larger narrative in which the old
symbol of British cultural supremacy was not rejected or challenged by a man
from a former colony, but instead accepted and borne publicly into the ring –
Myers depicting a Caribbean who had been assimilated into the white British
mainstream. Alternately, the combination of a non–white wrestler and the British flag testified positively to the ongoing diversification of British society – an
antidote to the stricter nationalism heavily associated with the flag.

Even though they weren't performing overtly othered roles, Myers, Dalibar
Singh and other wrestlers participated in a complex process of give and take
regarding their public identities. Reflecting on his own immigration to the
UK, the Jamaican-born cultural theorist Stuart Hall describes how he had to
resist, as an immigrant, being drawn into the "spectacle of multi-culturalism"
and avoid the pitfalls of being assigned to predefined cultural categories.[15] In
many ways, the wrestlers engaged in a similar project in the ring. By sidestep-
ping the debilitative hallmarks of performed "racial" or "cultural" difference and
instead emphasising their capabilities as wrestlers, it is tempting to argue that
they mirrored popular non–white athletes in major sports by daring to suggest
a greater social equality through athletics. Their work also paralleled the ongoing dilemma faced by minority actors in Britain throughout the seventies and
eighties: how to gain acceptance without being creatively restricted or tokenised
within an overarching white structure. For example, a serious wrestler like Dave
Bond had to endure ring announcers defining him as a "coloured star."[16]

Wrestling's attitude towards race was often so haphazard that characters strad-
dled the line between the less-othered and overtly othered categories. Johnny
Kwango and Jamaica George serve as prime examples of performers whose
characters used aspects of both types to create a mélange of the two. Both

Kwango and George had names that sounded exotic, in contrast to their typical wrestling gear of trunks of boots. Kwango and George were adept technical wrestlers and skilled athletes in the Clive Myers and Caswell Martin sense but they also drew upon the more unorthodox style of Zimba and Masambula, relying on head butts as signature moves. In Kwango's case, this was his major selling point – he was billed as "the King of Head Butts" – and audiences were attuned to recognise the manoeuvre and responded ecstatically when he performed it.[17] George, meanwhile, got to assert his otherness in a different manner. A rare in-character interview before one televised match saw him use an exaggerated Jamaican accent.[18] The overall result was a somewhat incongruous mishmash – unintentional hybrid wrestlers that underscored British wrestling's tenuous position within the larger cultural discourse on race representation. Characters like Kwango and George highlighted the difficulties that arose when more progressive depictions of race were wedded to the same old traits of the colonial other. For each seemingly progressive wrestler of colour on television on a Saturday afternoon, a wrestler portraying an unwieldy stereotype could appear next week.

Wrestling was one of the most blatant examples of British pop culture in which discordant performances of post-colonialism and outdated stereotyping came together during the seventies and eighties. At venues up and down the country during those decades, wrestlers like Clive Myers, Dave Bond, Caswell Martin, Honey Boy Zimba, and Masambula took on characters that highlighted wrestling's skewed attitude towards racial diversity. Some characters evoked the latent "new racism" that was rife in British society, while the work of others was closer to the pioneering non-white athletes and performers who visibly resisted racism and inequality. Their varied exploits in the ring were progressive in some ways and problematic in others, but always relevant to larger issues. There is an element of tragedy in that their chosen medium would suffer just as Britain's entertainment sphere started to better reflect the nation's multiculturalism through the eighties. Having steadfastly refused to update its presentation in the face of diminishing returns, British wrestling declined through the decade until it was axed from television in 1988.[19] Their profession virtually destroyed, the wrestlers receded to the periphery of Britain's cultural memory. But their underappreciated legacy remains compelling. The men whose performed struggles mirrored the very real struggle for acceptance made a small but unheralded contribution to the ongoing discourse on race in modern Britain, one in which the wrestling ring served as an unlikely yet necessary forum for British multiculturalism in the face of marginalisation and suppression.

Notes

1 Martin Barker, *The New Racism: Conservatives and the Ideology of the Tribe*, 2nd ed. (Frederick, MD: United Publications of America, 1982), 20–25. Describing the concept of "new racism," Paul Gilroy writes: "it specifies who may legitimately belong to the national community and simultaneously advances reasons for the segregation or banishment of

those whose 'origin, sentiment, or citizenship' assigns them elsewhere." Paul Gilroy, There Ain't No Black in the Union Jack: The Cultural Politics of Race and Nation, 2nd ed. (Chicago: University of Chicago Press, 1991), 45–46.

2   For more on the television during the seventies and eighties, see Sarita Malik, *Representing Black Britain: A History of Black and Asian Images on British Television* (London: SAGE, 2002) and Gareth Schaffer, *The Vision of a Nation: Making Multiculturalism on British Television, 1960–1980* (London: Palgrave Macmillan, 2014). Personal accounts of life in the entertainment industry are provided by a number of non-white stage and screen actors in Jim Pines, ed., *Black and White in Colour: Black People in British Television since 1936* (London: BFI, 1992).

3   Tony Freeth, "TV Colonialism," in *It Ain't Half Racist, Mum: Fighting Racism in the Media*, ed. Phil Cohen and Carl Gardner (London: Comedia Group, 1982), 27.

4   At several times during the seventies and eighties, exposés appeared in British tabloid newspapers and other media revealing (or confirming) the "truth" about wrestling's predetermined nature to the public. For more on such exposure see Simon Garfield, *The Wrestling*, 2nd ed. (London: Faber and Faber, 2007).

5   Paul Gilroy, *There Ain't No Black in the Union Jack*, 45.

6   Pierre Perrone, "Obituary: Big Daddy," *Independent* (London, UK), December 3, 1997.

7   Within the context of a post-colonial society such as Britain's, the process of "othering" coloniser-colonist relationship. The notion that the coloniser defines their own sense of self-identity through othering is a crucial aspect of the process. Syed Manzurul Islam writes that "the other is never a difference in kind, but rather a conceptual differentiation set in motion by the subject of its own self-realisation: it is the self that others the other for the mediation of its own unity." Syed Manzurul Islam, *The Ethics of Travel: From Marco Polo to Kafka* (Manchester: Manchester University Press, 1996), 81.

8   "World of Sport – Vic Faulkner & Bert Royal vs. Honeyboy Zimba & Masambula pt.1," *YouTube video*, 10:00, from a performance broadcast by ITV on June 6, 1970, posted by "tellumyort," October 1, 2015, https://www.youtube.com/watch?v=G2og3P_Nn8w.

9   Freeth, "TV Colonialism," 27.

10   John Solomos, Bob Findlay, Simon Jones and Paul Gilroy, "The Organic Crisis of British Capitalism and Race: The Experience of the Seventies," in *The Empire Strikes Back: Race and Racism in 70s Britain* (London: Hutchinson, 2007), 23.

11   "World of Sport – 'Tiger' Dalibir Singh vs 'Cowboy' Brett Hart," *YouTube video*, 24:43, from a performance broadcast by ITV on November 18, 1981, posted by "Jonny Tarry," October 3, 2015, https://www.youtube.com/watch?v=oM-uNlZ6G-o.

12   "Big Daddy & Kashmir Singh vs. Rasputin & The Spoiler," *YouTube video*, 14:37, n.d., posted by "Arthur Psycho," October 1, 2015, https://www.youtube.com/watch?v=XHn3n-_1VFM.

13   "Clive Myers vs. Steve Grey," *YouTube video*, 11:07, n.d., posted by "James Payne-Davis," October 1, 2015, https://www.youtube.com/watch?v=_ZUdM4lxa74.

14   "World of Sport – Clive Myers vs. Steve Grey pt.1," *YouTube video*, 10:22, n.d., posted by "tellumyort," October 4, https://www.youtube.com/watch?v=7AaSzaOz4Ps.

15   Stuart Hall, "Old and New Identities, Old and New Ethnicities," in *Culture, Globalization and the World System*, ed. Anthony D. King, 4th ed. (Minneapolis: University of Minnesota Press, 2007), 56.

16   "World of Sport – Tony St. Clair vs. Dave Bond," *YouTube video*, 14:41, n.d., posted by "tellumyort," October 3, 2015, https://www.youtube.com/watch?v=MiW2gDCf7Ak.

17   British Wrestling forum, comment on "Johnny Kwango" thread, posted by "Saxonwolf," March 2, 2006, http://www.britishwrestling.co.uk/forums/topic/johnny-kwango/.

18   "World of Sport – Giant Haystacks vs. Jamaica George," *YouTube video*, 10:06, n.d., posted by "TR25W," October 3, 2015, https://www.youtube.com/watch?v=wg7xjOEq7W4.

19   Joe Moran, *Armchair Nation: An Intimate History of Britain in Front of the TV* (London: Profile Books, 2013), 282.

Additional resources

"Big Daddy & Kashmir Singh vs. Rasputin & The Spoiler." *YouTube video*, 14:37, n.d. Posted by "Arthur Psycho." Accessed October 1, 2015. https://www.youtube.com/watch?v=XHn3n-_1VFM.

"British Wrestling. Giant Haystacks vs. Honey Boy Zimba." *YouTube video*, 7:56, n.d. Posted by "TR25W." Accessed October 2, 2015. https://www.youtube.com/watch?v=RxmNDrja1uM.

"Clive Myers vs. Steve Grey." *YouTube video*, 11:07, n.d. Posted by "james payne-davis." Accessed October 1, 2015. https://www.youtube.com/watch?v=_ZUdM4lxa74.

"Sheik Adnan vs. Lenny Hurst." *YouTube video*, 15:38, n.d. Posted by "Arthur Psycho." Accessed October 3, 2015. https://www.youtube.com/watch?v=thIzZFyXVF4.

"World of Sport – Caswell Martin vs. Dave Bond pt. 1." *YouTube video*, 10:00, n.d. Posted by "tellumyort." Accessed October 4, 2015. https://www.youtube.com/watch?v=ZuhbLJSSaAM.

"World of Sport – Caswell Martin vs. Dave Bond pt. 2." *YouTube video*, 10:01, n.d. Posted by "tellumyort." Accessed October 4, 2015. https://www.youtube.com/watch?v=zVqtY9mP2no.

"World of Sport – Caswell Martin vs. Dave Bond pt. 3." *YouTube video*, 8:03, n.d. Posted by "tellumyort." Accessed October 4, 2015. https://www.youtube.com/watch?v=_t7OU_-DQBg.

"World of Sport – Clive Myers vs. Steve Grey pt. 1." *YouTube video*, 10:22, n.d. Posted by "tellumyort." Accessed October 4, 2015. https://www.youtube.com/watch?v=7AaSzaOz4Ps.

"World of Sport – Clive Myers vs. Steve Grey pt. 2." *YouTube video*, 9:28, n.d. Posted by "tellumyort." Accessed October 4, 2015. https://www.youtube.com/watch?v=-TmjzNMFfII.

"World of Sport – Giant Haystacks vs. Jamaica George." *YouTube video*, 10:06, n.d. Posted by "TR25W." Accessed October 3, 2015. https://www.youtube.com/watch?v=wg7xjOEq7W4.

"World of Sport – Giant Haystacks & Mighty John Quinn vs. Honeyboy Zimba & Dave Bond pt. 1." *YouTube video*, 9:00, from a performance broadcast by ITV on January 9, 1980. Posted by "tellumyort." Accessed October 1, 2015. https://www.youtube.com/watch?v=bSgUIyMXL6s.

"World of Sport – Giant Haystacks & Mighty John Quinn vs. Honeyboy Zimba & Dave Bond pt. 2." *YouTube video*, 4:54, from a performance broadcast by ITV on January 9, 1980. Posted by "telluymort." Accessed October 1, 2015. https://www.youtube.com/watch?v=T959xvo2GoA.

"World of Sport – Johnny Kwango vs. Ivan Penzecoff pt. 1 (75–08–23)." *YouTube video*, 10:30, from a performance broadcast by ITV on August 23, 1975. Posted by "telluymort." Accessed October 4, 2015. https://www.youtube.com/watch?v=-mez2ovf-W4.

"World of Sport – Johnny Kwango vs. Ivan Penzecoff pt. 2 (75–08–23)." *YouTube video*, 10:30, from a performance broadcast by ITV on August 23, 1975. Posted by "telluymort." Accessed October 4, 2015. https://www.youtube.com/watch?v=eNSz3V0Qttg.

"World of Sport – Johnny War Eagle vs. Johnny Czeslaw pt. 1." *YouTube video*, 10:11, from a performance broadcast by ITV on August 2, 1975. Posted by "telluymort." Accessed October 3, 2015. https://www.youtube.com/watch?v=ZeKe8PRfdfc.

"World of Sport – Johnny War Eagle vs. Johnny Czeslaw pt. 2." *YouTube video*, 10:17, from a performance broadcast by ITV on August 23, 1975. Posted by "telluymort." Accessed October 4, 2015. https://www.youtube.com/watch?v=pxpsvjtEpSI.

"World of Sport – Kung Fu & Pete Roberts vs. Johnny Kincaid & I ve Bond pt. 1." *YouTube video*, 10:00, from a performance broadcast by ITV on October 8, 1977. Posted by "telluymort." Accessed October 2, 2015. https://www.youtube.com/watch?v=Mkc33khkhvU.

"World of Sport – Kung Fu & Pete Roberts vs. Johnny Kincaid & Dave Bond pt. 2." *YouTube video*, 10:00, from a performance broadcast by ITV on October 8, 1977. Posted by "telluymort." Accessed October 2, 2015.https://www.youtube.com/watch?v=UDng1B-Akdw.

"World of Sport – 'Tiger' Dalibir Singh vs. 'Cowboy' Brett Hart." *YouTube video*, 24:43, from a performance broadcast by ITV on November 18, 1981. Posted by "Jonny Tarry." Accessed October 3, 2015. https://www.youtube.com/watch?v=oM-uNlZ6G-o.

"World of Sport – Tony St. Clair vs. Dave Bond pt. 1." *YouTube video*, 14:41, n.d. Posted by "tellumyort." Accessed October 3, 2015. https://www.youtube.com/watch?v=MiW2g DCf7Ak.

"World of Sport – Tony St. Clair vs. Dave Bond pt. 2." *YouTube video*, 10:03, n.d. Posted by "tellumyort." Accessed October 3, 2015. https://www.youtube.com/watch?v=q8J0fvdzdsc.

"World of Sport – Vic Faulkner & Bert Royal vs. Honeyboy Zimba & Masambula pt. 1." *YouTube video*, 10:00, from a performance broadcast by ITV on June 6, 1970. Posted by "telluymort." Accessed October 1, 2015. https://www.youtube.com/watch?v=G2og3P_Nn8w.

"World of Sport – Vic Faulkner & Bert Royal vs. Honeyboy Zimba & Masambula pt. 2." *YouTube video*, 9:21, from a performance broadcast by ITV on June 6, 1970. Posted by "telluymort." Accessed October 1, 2015. https://www.youtube.com/watch?v=hwA5DNv-Hd8.

"World of Sport – Vic Faulkner & Bert Royal vs. Honeyboy Zimba & Masambula pt.3." *YouTube video*, 3:59, from a performance broadcast by ITV on June 6, 1970. Posted by "telluymort." Accessed October 1, 2015. https://www.youtube.com/watch?v=YShCW3Fe-UY.

Chapter 17

Some moments of flag desecration in professional wrestling

Morgan Daniels

> When the human body, a nation's flag, money, or a public statue is *defaced*, a strange surplus of negative energy is likely to be aroused from within the defaced thing itself.
>
> Michael Taussig[1]

I

The video I am watching on YouTube right now is shaky and out of focus – all par for the course when it comes to amateur footage of ticketed events sneakily recorded on mobile phones, no doubt, but still, it feels illicit, and disorientingly so. It's like I shouldn't be watching it. But then, the video *does* depict a crime taking place. The scene of this crime is an indoor volleyball arena in São Paulo, which in May 2012 hosted a WWE "house show." Chris Jericho, in the ring prior to a match with CM Punk, holds the Brazilian national flag aloft and slowly shows it to all four sides of the seated audience, receiving cheers and applause. Then he screws it up, drops it on the floor and gives it a kick for good measure. The boos are deafening and sustained – a strange surplus of negative energy? – and, in this video, a man gives Jericho a vigorous thumbs-down, while somebody possibly shouts "Fuck you!"[2]

Though classic heel heat stuff, Jericho's transgression was not comic book villainy – an expected transgression, like hitting an opponent with a chair behind the referee's back – but something that brought the fun of the fair into collision with what I hesitantly and with some dissatisfaction call the "real world," meaning the one with laws and cops who enforce those laws, and where flags often can't be desecrated without repercussions. This real world includes Brazil, in which, since 1971, disrespect toward the national flag has been a criminal act, albeit a minor one, punishable with a fine. I say "albeit a minor one," but it's perhaps the minor-ness that's the point: those witness to desecration surely don't primarily think "That's illegal!" No. The reaction is weirder than that: gut-level, visceral. The crime's minor-ness also doesn't explain why, so WWE.com tells us, law enforcers in São Paulo called a stop to the fight and gave Jericho the chance to apologise to the crowd "or face incarceration." Jericho explained: "I made a bad judgement call in the course of entertaining fans in Brazil."[3]

For Shawn Michaels, this was no bad judgement call, but a controversy defined as such only by overreaction. "Seems to me I'd blame the horrific PC world we've allowed ourselves to be caught up in where you can't 'act' & have it called 'acting,'" he tweeted.[4] He pleads for the privileging of theatre as a space where anything goes: after all, back in 1997, Michaels had his own little flag-denigrating moment while feuding with Bret Hart – a moment far crasser than Jericho's, though not actually illegal. The feud was rather clever; Hart had pulled off a turn as an American-hating heel, remaining a face outside the United States. *Within* the States, the gimmick was definitely "working," Hart wrote – apparently proud that, during this period, he was spat on as he entered the ring and required police escorts when exiting it, speeding out of town to escape enraged Americans "hanging out their car windows, shaking shotguns and half-empty beer bottles."[5] There's that real world again.

So it was that Shawn Michaels entered the Molson Centre in Montreal on November 9, 1997, with the Maple Leaf in hand. First he rubs his groin with the flag, as if somewhat erotically drying himself off after a swim. After some showy muscle-flexing, Michaels shoves it up his nose, throws it down, and – the *pièce de résistance* – starts dry-humping the thing, for *thing* it surely now is. It's almost admirably unpleasant. Bret Hart says that his father Stu "took very real offence to Shawn's actions, as did everyone in the building and all across Canada."[6] Yet according to Michaels, it was Hart himself who had asked whether his opponent might "do something with the flag" for the sake of heat. He continues: "everyone made a big deal about me jerking around the Canadian flag, but like the Sharpshooter, it was his idea."[7]

What does it mean to disrespect a flag in a performance activity, like professional wrestling? No sooner had I begun to ask myself this question than the WWE offered yet another moment of flag desecration. This came courtesy of the Big Show who, during a feud with Rusev, tore down a large Russian flag hanging above the ring (Rusev was working a "Hero of the Russian Federation" gimmick). And though I'm wary of treating iconoclasm as something *built into* wrestling, as a constant that justifies its study due to "real world" ramifications, this latest "moment" was impetus enough to ask whether sporadic flag desecration was somehow *symptomatic* of the type of entertainment put on in the squared circle.[8]

This work has not to do with the performance of nationalism, but with the flag itself, the flag as theatrical prop. It's an impossible ask, because a flag is never *just* a flag: there is always what Taussig calls a "behindedness," meaning baggage, a backstory, a blood price.[9] But I wish to try, all the while considering Kee-Yoon Nahm's simple but essential question: "How does one distinguish between real and theatrical objects?"[10] For that matter, what is iconoclasm, anyway? It's my feeling that these two questions speak to the concerns of thing theory in the same way.

II

Thing theory, which was announced in a now-classic 2001 essay by Bill Brown, riffs on Heidegger's differentiation between *objects* and *things*. If objects are that which we look *through* to gain some knowledge about "history, society, nature, or culture," then things can be described as objects no longer "working for us."[11] An object declaring its thingness might well be quite the banal moment, like a pencil sharpener not sharpening a pencil as well as it used to, or whatever. But Brown turns his attention, too, to contemporary art's engagement with things, such as the surrealists' elevation of found objects.[12] To invoke art is resolutely not to afford primacy to human agency in the mediation of the object/thing dialectic. Things announce themselves. But since Brown sees this announcing as "the story of a changed relation to the human subject," I want to suggest that there *are* human activities, like stage magic, whose practitioners boast a sort of intuitive sense for things and a capacity for bringing out their thingness.[13] Let us call this *thing-work*.

Key is that, as Robin Bernstein argues, *performance* is what separates thing and object. Things, she writes, are performatives because they script movements; they invite humans to move. These movements – *dances with things* – are also performative: "they *think*, or, more accurately, they *are the act of thinking*."[14] So implied is not just that thing-work needs an audience (things require people with whom to dance) but that its definition is *in* the audience, broadly conceived. And iconoclasm, with its (often wrong-headed) questioning of the value of the habituated, might be seen as a type of thing-work. Take Dread Scott's 1989 installation at the School of the Art Institute in Chicago, "What Is the Proper Way to Display a US Flag?" Visitors to the gallery could write their own answers to the question at hand in a guestbook, but they would have to try hard to avoid Old Glory itself, indecorously left on the floor, *begging* to be stood upon. "A flag is not divine, nor should it be sacred," reads one visitor's response. "It is a piece of cloth."[15] A thing.

The reason I claim that asking about props is the same as asking about iconoclasm is because theatre and iconoclasm both, in their own ways, make a mock of the value of objects by virtue of their relationship with an audience playing at not-playing, "knowing what not to know."[16] The former often places great narrative weight on cheap tat; the latter is about asking, "what value?" For play, games, sports, theatre and ritual alike, observes Richard Schechner, objects are "special." He continues:

> Balls, pucks, hoops, batons, bats – even theatrical props – are mostly common objects of not much material value and cheaply replaced if lost or worn out. But during performance these objects are of extreme importance, often the focus of the whole activity.[17]

Extreme importance! Common objects! No wonder the editors of *Performing Objects and Theatrical Things* (2014) describe the questions fundamental to thing-centric study as "necessitat[ing] our self-reflexive awareness as scholars and practitioners."[18] No wonder Andrew Sofer writes that "[p]hysical objects have received short shrift in the study of drama," tracing this neglect back to Aristotle.[19] The thing about things, then, is that it's hard to write about them.

III

At the WWF's fourth Royal Rumble pay-per-view – broadcast on January 21, 1991, four days after the commencement of Operation Desert Storm – Sergeant Slaughter, one-time all-American military hero turned Iraqi sympathiser and thereby heel, defeated the Ultimate Warrior for the world championship. Slaughter wore exotic, curly toed boots for the match that, so the story goes, had been sent to him by Saddam Hussein. Half an hour later, Hulk Hogan gave an interview to "Mean" Gene Okerlund in which he dedicated the upcoming battle royal to "all our boys over there in the Persian Gulf." Okerlund, concernedly fiddling with his earpiece, interrupts his interviewee to bring an "unconfirmed report" that the new world champion was busying himself backstage defacing the American flag. Hogan, who himself spat on and shined his boots with Nikolai Volkoff's USSR flag back in 1985, let rip:

> Mean Gene, let me tell you something . . . if Sergeant Slaughter has gone so far to deface Old Glory, to deface the red, white and blue, brother, I don't care if it's legal or not brother . . . just like Saddam Hussein's reign over Kuwait, brother, it's [Slaughter's reign] gonna be *only temporary*.

The resultant Hogan/Slaughter feud, which reached its peak at WrestleMania VII, saw the latter cut two promos whose thing-work really staggers. Both saw Slaughter interviewed by Okerlund and accompanied to the ring by General Adnan, played by Adnan Al-Kaissy, a real-life school colleague of Saddam Hussein. In the first promo, on 4 March, the General carries a poster of Hulk Hogan:

OKERLUND: Sergeant, do I dare ask: what is the meaning of this?
SLAUGHTER: What is the meaning of *this*? Why, *this* is Americana, is it not?
OKERLUND: Well, this is Hulk Hogan, and he typifies everything that *is* American.
SLAUGHTER: Well, what *you* see, and what *they* see, is the red, the white and the blue of Americana, am I right?
OKERLUND: Yeah, the colour of the Stars and Stripes. The American flag!

After a bit of fumbling, Adnan sets the poster alight. "This is disgusting," intones Vince McMahon on commentary.[20] A week later, Slaughter and Adnan pulled almost the exact same trick, with the prop of choice this time a yellow and red "Hulk Rules" T-shirt on a pole. Slaughter explains:

> In *my* eyes . . . this is nothing more than *a mere piece of cloth*. But in the eyes, and in the minds, and even in the little bitty hearts of millions and millions of Pukamaniacs, this simple piece of cloth symbolises truth, justice, and the Hulk Hogan way, ha, ha, ha![21]

McMahon then adds, ". . . which is an American tradition." As the "U! S! A!" chants dominate, Slaughter quips "Hulk Rules – these are the kind of rules the General and I break!," and takes a lighter to the shirt. It's not a silly or comical moment. I feel it's rather shocking.

The first of three connected points is that, despite Slaughter not once touching Old Glory, we must classify these promos as outstanding examples of flag desecration. This is because a major goal of iconoclasm, the blowing up of ideas about the inherent worth of something revered, is achieved *through* the substitution of the flag for other things, not in spite of it. Slaughter explained that he had originally been asked to burn the Stars and Stripes but opted against it, a wise decision, perhaps, in light of the death threats he was receiving. "So I decided to burn the shirt, and I think it got the job done more than if I went in the other direction."[22] Burning a flag? That's cheap. Ten-a-penny iconoclasm. But burning some tacky merchandise that unmistakeably stands in for the very flag to which allegiance is so regularly pledged? That's iconoclasm twice over: first the sacredness of the object is called into question by the slight-of-hand imbuing of something obviously worthless with the very qualities said to define the original; then the something obviously worthless is destroyed. Extreme importance! Common objects!

Point two: What kind of world is this? What is it about wrestling that allows for signifier no less than signified to be so readily damned? Or, as David Lawton asks in his book on blasphemy: "Does the coarse style of wrestling enable it to offend with vulgar truth?"[23] In Lawton's analysis, wrestling's so-called boundaries between fact and fiction demand urgent inquiry. Again, the performed-to are key. When in one Prime Time Wrestling promo Hulk Hogan led the crowd in a pledge of allegiance to the US flag, for instance, there was "no discernible border . . . between play and reality: otherwise the audience would have felt that they were being called on to travesty the oath."[24] Here was a "particularly clever" and selective agreement wherein and whereby "audience and performers know they are in a symbolic representation of war, not war itself; nobody shoots Sergeant Slaughter because sane people realise he is not Saddam Hussein but stands for him in a linked narrative context."[25]

It was not enough, for Lawton, to shrug off Sergeant Slaughter's promos as fiction, because wrestling is "premised upon its opposite."[26] What was needed was an appreciation of how Slaughter's blasphemy against the American way' was "represented by the oath of allegiance and emblematised by the flag." Blasphemy thus does power's bidding, "conflat[ing] positive and negative, one's reasons for dying and one's reasons for killing ... the undoing of Saddam Hussein is imprinted on Old Glory. It is awesomely simple, circular and closed."[27] Yet while Lawton's reading is obviously brilliant – it clearly *is* the case that transgression is an implied part of a sacred object's meaning – I want to add that bit more on audience (this is point three), something I have claimed as vital for iconoclasm-as-thing-work.

In his survey of secret societies, Michael Taussig retells the story of a young inhabitant of Tierra del Fuego, Isla Grande, who shot dead his brother because he believed him to be a Shoort, a type of spirit-being. After all, he was dressed as such. These spirits, played by the older, "initiated" men of the island, are the stars of a wild performance in a tent, the Big Hut, put on nightly over the course of some months for the benefit of women and children. Taussig sees the islander as unable "to modulate the claims reality makes on illusion": he lacked "performative maturity."[28] Let us ask about the maturity of those witness to flag desecration in professional wrestling.

Adnan Al-Kaissy writes that "political implications and the crazy people who sent us death threats" aside, the Iraqi sympathiser gimmick "was actually really fun to do. To be able to control a crowd like that ... was exciting." "Eventually," however, Al-Kaissy "received a call from someone at the U.S. Department of State" who described the ongoing storyline as "insane." While the official couldn't "legally" stop the act, he pointed out that the wrestling crowd "was unlike any other in the sports/entertainment world" and that a jury would be hard-pressed "to convict someone who tried to beat me up or kill me after what I was doing."[29] But is it the "wrestling crowd" that's performatively immature here?

Though the word "control" is perhaps unfortunate, Al-Kaissy's excitement, like Jericho's apology and Michaels's heat tactics, describes a performance in search of a cool combination of shock and entertainment. The control is reciprocal, and what's more, when the boos start, it's unclear who is shocked (really booing) and who is entertained (playing at booing), with each group likely encouraging the other to boo louder. But in the moment these responses are indistinguishable and thus equally "mature," one in the eye for the apparent distinction between reality and fiction, something that affords reality far too much credit. (In fact this distinction is at stake in the object/thing duality; for Bruno Latour, the seeking of its origins is the very purpose of analysing iconoclasm.)[30] It's not the wrestling crowd that's immature performance-wise. It's the wider audience, those who wouldn't normally give wrestling the slightest notice, like the Department of State, but who suddenly care because of its encroachment upon the real world. Sometimes, as in Brazil, the law of the land, that great arbiter of the real, can put a stop to iconoclasm, within a formally designated, big-P Performance activity or otherwise. Only sometimes, though. Note the Department official's inability to appeal to the law and (thus) his imagining of proceedings in court. (In June 1989, the US Supreme Court's ruling on *Texas v. Johnson*, reaffirmed by *United States v. Eichman* the following year, invalidated the ban on flag desecration maintained in forty-eight states – hence Hogan's "I don't care if it's legal or not brother.")

For W.J.T. Mitchell, the passions roused by images is evidence of magical thinking, making them among "'the most difficult things to regulate with laws and rationally constructed policies – so difficult, in fact, that the law seems to become infected by magical thinking as well."[31] Mitchell suggests, however, that the banning of offensive images is not necessarily wrong, especially those "forced upon the notice of an unwilling public." It is *context* that's important, not content. Art galleries, then, should be treated as "very special places that ought to enjoy the broadest protections from government interference in exhibitions," because only by maintaining a "free space of artistic license . . . can we hope to understand what it is that gives images so much power over people."[32]

Backyard wrestler Mikey Tenderfoot, in interview with Lawrence McBride, sought a similar license. "People get over sensitive to things they might not like," he said. "[Y]ou do one thing and they might take it fifty different ways." Tenderfoot insists: "wrestling at [its] best is an art form." McBride in turn observes that wrestling mixes the very best and very worst parts of culture, making its problems nothing less than those of society.[33] Same with contemporary art, I want to say. Yet what *am* I saying? That we should treat the wrestling arena like the hallowed art gallery? Surely not! But then, witness Bruno Latour:

> Nowhere else [but in contemporary art] have so many paradoxical effects been carried out on the public to complicate their reactions to images [. . .] Generations of iconoclasts smashing each other's faces and works. A fabulous large-scale experiment in nihilism . . . A maniacal joy in self destruction. A hilarious sacrilege.[34]

Nowhere else? Only if we unreservedly consider pro wrestling *as* contemporary art. This description of iconoclasm's ideal lab conditions fits wrestling *exactly*, except in the squared circle the face-smashing and self-destruction are absolutely literal. (Not for nothing does Taussig equate defacement of the human body with defacement of a nation's flag.)

I happened across an old wrestler friend of mine recently, and excitedly told him about my work on iconoclasm. He shrugged. "If you want to get heat, it's *always* going to be better to rip a flag in two than talk shit about someone's country for ten minutes. Simple as that." *Not so simple*, I thought, in awe of the apparent access he had to deeper truths about things and the demands made thereon by performance, no less than vice versa. In fact, it is hard to name or even make-believe a performance activity more thing-centric than wrestling, what with its obsession over foreign objects, and matches whereby to win one must retrieve some item from atop a ladder. The thing's the play, you might say.

Wrestling's weird thing-work thus demands attention from those who, after Dwight Conquergood, seek a turn by performance studies away from scriptocentrism, meaning the particularly Western preference for text-based knowing.[35] And because this weird thing-work can include iconoclastic acts and is motored by real-time engagement with an audience whose suspension of disbelief and capacity for offence is far from uniform, one might, mischievously enough, suggest that the squared circle holds *more* potential for image-testing than the art gallery, in which one always expects a shock or two.[36] Or is that an iconoclastic gesture too far?

Notes

1 Michael Taussig, *Defacement: Public Secrecy and the Labor of the Negative* (Stanford: Stanford University Press, 1999), 1.
2 "Chris Jericho Kicks Brazilian Flag," *YouTube video*, posted by Gokub Gameplays, May 25, 2012, https://www.youtube.com/watch?v=3scYR84eYko.
3 WWE.com. "Chris Jericho Responds to Incident," WWE.com, accessed June 25, 2015, http://www.wwe.com/inside/chris-jericho-responds-to-brazil-incident.
4 Shawn Michaels, Twitter post, May 25, 2012, 6:11 a.m., http://twitter.com/shawnmichaels.
5 Bret Hart, *Hitman: My Real Life in the Cartoon World of Wrestling* (Toronto: Random House, 2007), 421.
6 Ibid., 455.
7 Shawn Michaels and Aaron Feigenbaum, *Heartbreak & Triumph: The Shawn Michaels Story* (New York: Routledge, 2001), 274.
8 See Charles Ford, "Iconoclasm, the Commodity and the Art of Painting," in *Iconoclasm: Contested Objects, Contested Terms*, ed. Stacy Boldrick and Richard Clay (Aldershot: Ashgate, 2007), 75–76.
9 Taussig, *Defacement*, 54.
10 Kee-Yoon Nahm, "Props Breaking Character: The Performance and Failure of Real Objects on the Naturalist Stage," in *Performing Objects and Theatrical Things*, ed. Maris Schweitzer and Joanne Zerdy (London: Palgrave Macmillan, 2014), 187.
11 Bill Brown, "Thing Theory," *Critical Inquiry* 28, no. 1, Things (Autumn 2001): 4.
12 Ibid., 15.
13 Ibid., 4.
14 Robin Bernstein, "Dances with Things: Material Culture and the Performance of Race," *Social Text* 27, no. 4 (Winter 2009): 70.
15 Michael Welch, John Sassi and Allyson McDonough, "Advances in Critical Cultural Criminology: An Analysis of Reactions to Avant-Garde Flag Art," *Critical Criminology: An International Journal* 11, no. 1 (2002): 13.
16 This is Michael Taussig's phrase. He stresses that apparently hidden truths about the inviolate are usually widely known, meaning that we are all putting in quite the convoluted daily performance too, a type of suspension of disbelief. Thus iconoclasm is need of the *theatrical*. See Taussig, *Defacement*, 6.
17 Richard Schechner, *Performance Theory* (New York and London: Routledge, 2003), 11. Emphasis added.
18 Maris Schweitzer and Joanne Zerdy, "Introduction: Object Lessons," in *Performing Objects and Theatrical Things* (London: Palgrave Macmillan, 2014), 2.
19 Andrew Sofer, *The Stage Life of Props* (Ann Arbor: University of Michigan Press, 2003), v.
20 *WWF Prime Time Wrestling*, USA Network, March 4, 1991.
21 *WWF Prime Time Wrestling*, USA Network, March 11, 1991. Emphasis added.

22 Kevin Sullivan, *The WWE Championship: A Look Back at the Rich History of the WWE Championship* (New York: Gallery Books, 2010), 72.

23 David Lawton, *Blasphemy* (Philadelphia: University of Philadelphia Press, 1993), 195.

24 Ibid., 194.

25 Ibid., 197.

26 Ibid., 198–200.

27 Ibid., 200–201.

28 Taussig, *Defacement*, 121.

29 Adnay Al-Kaissy and Ross Bernstein, *The Sheik of Baghdad: Tales of Celebrity and Terror from Pro Wrestling's General Adnan* (Chicago: Triumph Books, 2005), 189.

30 Bruno Latour, "What is Iconoclash? Or Is There a World Beyond the Image Wars?" in *Iconoclash: Beyond the Images Wars in Science, Religion and Art*, ed. Bruno Latour (Cambridge, MA: MIT Press, 2002), 16.

31 W.J.T. Mitchell, *What Do Pictures Want? The Loves and Lives of Images* (London: University of Chicago Press, 2005), 128.

32 Ibid., 142.

33 Lawrence B. McBride, *Professional Wrestling, Embodied Morality, and Altered States of Consciousness* (MA diss., University of South Florida, 2005), 90.

34 Latour, "Iconoclash," 22.

35 Dwight Conquergood, "Performance Studies: Interventions and Radical Research," *TDR: The Drama Review* 46, no. 2 (2002): 145–156.

36 As pointed out in Latour, "Iconoclash," 30.

The game of life

Sharon Mazer

What the world is watching.

WWF (now WWE) slogan circa 1990s

Happy are those epochs that had clear dramas, dreams, and doers of good or evil.

Leonidas Donskis[1]

How safe and comfortable, cosy and friendly the world would feel if it were monsters and only monsters who perpetrated monstrous deeds.

Zygmunt Bauman[2]

Papanui High School, Christchurch, New Zealand. We're here for NWA Emergence on the last Saturday in March 2015. Leaving the late afternoon glow of the car park, we enter the school's all-purpose rectangular room: gym/cafeteria/theatre/auditorium. I'd forgotten this. The slightly musty smell, leftover from the week's adolescent activities and now mixed with the stale cigarette smoke carried in by the punters. The mildly jittery, almost but not quite familial feeling as fifty or sixty people wander in, pay, get hands stamped, suss the dimly lit scene and settle into seats. Grown-ups, some in t-shirts and jeans, others in more heavy metal–esque get-ups, spiky bleached or coloured hair, tattoos, glittery eye shadow and bright lips (on some of the men as well as the women). Children, dressed to match – still surprising to see so many children corralled (not quite successfully) by their parents, offered sodas and sweets, buzzing with excitement.

The ring looks new: shiny black posts and pads, black and white ropes, a clear plastic tarp over the platform. A provisional safety barrier is supported by road cones, black electrician's tape covering their familiar orange patterns – after all, we're still in an earthquake zone.[3] It surrounds the ring and creates a channel leading up to the heavy, dusty maroon curtains that conceal the high school's stage. Some guys in suits are testing microphones. They jump up from their ringside table to lean in behind the curtain, through which we can glimpse half-dressed wrestlers.

The suited announcer begins his welcome: "Ladies and gentlemen, boys and girls. . . ." A heel bursts from behind the curtain. We know he's the heel, of course, because he's dressed in fake bling. He interrupts the suit and grabs the mic to issue the challenge that will lead to the main event. The referee bounds in, an earnest babyface whose exuberance is barely suppressed and makes him appear an easy mark. The early matches are over quickly, but it feels like slow motion watching the youngsters struggle to remember their moves. As the evening progresses, the action accelerates. Sitting close to the ring, we feel the heat and rush of movement – a kinetic contact high that compels even my bemused, somewhat resistant, companion to join in. The wrestlers work us as much as each other. They circle the ring, alternately slapping high-fives with and slinging insults at us, especially the children who are shriekingly suspended between delight and rage. Cell phones and selfies aside, the scene seems the same as it ever was, uncannily preserved and replicated here more than a quarter century and half a world away from my barely remembered first encounters with wrestlers and fans at Gleason's Arena in Brooklyn.[4]

Sometimes it seems that everything I now know about life – especially about academic life – I learnt while sitting on the sidelines of the squared circle. My career as a performance scholar started there, with my first article on professional wrestling appearing in *TDR* in 1990.[5] This chapter is a reflection on wrestling's life lessons: that it's a job; that what makes a good person versus a bad one – what makes one strong or weak – is a matter both of ethics and of contingencies; that regardless, the guy with the money has the power to decide who wins and who loses, and on what terms; that, no longer confined to the squared circle, the sideshow and the street corner, in this globalised, mediatised world, kayfabe has gone mainstream; and that even though the conflict, the (larger-than-)life-or-death struggle we see in the squared circle, is largely a put-on – a performance constructed as much as anything else, in Beckettian terms, to pass the time – even so, we are, in the end, most of us, all in this together.

After so many years, I only rarely watch wrestling. Still, I think about it often, returning in my socio-theatrical imagination to what Angela Carter once called "giants' play."[6] The youngsters I saw strutting their stuff in the Papanui High School gym were not in any way giants, of course. They were kids from the neighbourhood mixing it up with some talent imported from other New Zealand cities. As such, they seemed to be creating performances as much in their own (and our) imaginations as in the lived moment before us. Their surprisingly slight bodies and reedy voices performed as if we were viewing them through an all-encompassing televisual lens: as flickering reflections of the megastars of what is now the WWE.[7] The world was definitely *not* watching us in the Papanui High School gym. But that the wrestlers seemed slight in the shadow of the big leagues made their valour rather poignant and also appealing. They were, in fact, the little guys fighting the good fight not so much against each other but against a world that was unlikely to live up to their dreams.

Writing in 1976, Angela Carter observed the "moral rhythm" of wrestling: "The aggressor, the over-reacher, is foiled by his victim, who in turn becomes the torturer. The serial play of violence denies pain by the sprightly vivacity with which the participants recover from it."[8] Further,

> The bad guy often does win. The morality play element, never very far away in the physical drama of wrestling, does not mean that right inevitably triumphs. Far from it. It's too much like real life for that. Rather, when the bad guy wins the championship, the audience has the positive assurance of its prejudice that he has only done so by low cunning and sleight of hand, although the "mask" or persona of the wrestler bears no connection at all with his actual prowess.[9]

Carter had it half-right. In wrestling, as in life, the audience knows there are two games afoot. The first, the fight in the squared circle, is to be taken at face value; the second, encompassing the arena and the (macro-)world beyond, is the con game, the play on our desire for a fair fight and our sure knowledge of the fix.

Twenty-five years ago, it might have been possible – just – for the illusion of a fair fight to hold, at least while it was happening. No more. Not since 1989 when Vince McMahon, World Wrestling Federation boss, came clean(ish) with the New Jersey State Senate in announcing that professional wrestling is "an activity in which participants struggle hand-in-hand primarily for the purpose of providing entertainment to spectators rather than conducting a bona fide athletic contest."[10] Not that much changed, as a result. Wrestling's audiences continued to play along, to "suspend disbelief," as Peter Kerr writing in the *New York Times* put it, because "Millions of grown men and women just don't want to know."[11] McMahon took a punt on the punters. He broke kayfabe. To say, in public, that wrestling is a fake sport should have cost him audiences and lost him the business. Anyone else would have been ostracised or worse. But not McMahon, the promoter who was by then well on track to creating the monopoly he rules today.

Consider what was going on at the time. In retrospect, it seems it was then that "suspension of disbelief" became a societal norm in the United States, if not elsewhere in the Western world. The end of the 1980s marked the transition from the Reagan years to the presidency of the first George Bush, from "Morning in America" to a "Kinder, Gentler Nation," and saw the final years of Thatcher, but not of Thatcherism. Capitalism was in the ascendancy, globalisation on the horizon. Talk radio dominated the airwaves; cable television was beating down the networks. The Internet was glimmering, but not yet all-consuming. It was a time when scandals, broadcast as spectacles, began to fail to scandalise. (Think of the way the Iran-Contra hearings, for example, generated a lot of heat – at least on television – but didn't change the game.) Politics became sport, became entertainment, became increasingly viewed widely as a fixed fight, the outcome determined by the guys with the money. To protest has become (satisfyingly?) futile. Fast forward to 2016, past the Clinton sex scandal

and the hanging chads of the 2000 election, through 9/11 and the corresponding wars in Afghanistan and Iraq, beyond "truthiness" to the current vast field
of Republican candidates vying less for voters than for the dollars that will be
bestowed by the Koch brothers – or, as seems the case particularly with Donald
Trump, for the vain thrill of seeing themselves in the spotlight.[12]

Watching the "monsters" of the 1980s and 1990s – Macho Man Randy Savage, Ravishing Rick Rude, Jake the Snake, Hulk Hogan, Ric Flair, Rowdy
Roddy Piper, Mr. Perfect, Hacksaw Jim Duggan, The Bushwackers, The Hart
Brothers, et al. – we were proud of being "smart," even as we looked, obsessively
it seemed, to "mark out," to catch a glimpse of the real: anger or fear, pain, blood,
force, victimisation and vindication. The moments when we saw (or thought
we were seeing) the wrestlers shoot their way past the confines of the codified
improvisation were the payoffs for playing along with the con otherwise. Now
even what's set up as spontaneous can be seen to be carefully choreographed as
much, or more, for the absent audience at the other end of the cameras as for
those of us present in the arena. Our performances as spectators are captured,
mixed and edited, packaged and circulated for consumption before our very
eyes. The cycle of reflection, from live to canned to live again, over time effectively erases the rough patches around the edges to create a smooth, continuous
surface of performance. Subtexts are suppressed. The surface is all. And for our
part, we are no longer a public, in the analogue sense. We've been digitalised,
made complicit in our own commodification as producers of data with every
"like" and "share."

The last time I attended a World Wrestling event was at "The Road to WrestleMania" in 2007. For my colleagues and our students this was a big deal, the
WWE's first time ever in Christchurch, New Zealand. Because of my annual
lectures on wrestling in various courses at the University of Canterbury, we
were keenly interested in moving from theory to practice and back again to
theory. None of us had really been keeping up with the game, but we gamely
played along. In spite of our relative ignorance, it didn't take long – a matter of
seconds, really – each time a wrestler appeared, to figure out where he (and we)
stood and to perform in accord with the script. We revelled in the high-pitched
atmosphere: especially the diversity of the spectators, from rowdy university
students and families with kids racing around to older more staid observers, and
every kind of person in between, it seemed. We indulged in the junk food, fin-
gered the merchandise, and played hide-and-seek with our film camera when
the ushers came around. Even though in our imaginations we were commit-
ting acts of performance ethnography, the experience was more Artaudian than
Brechtian – more visceral, more of contagion than of detached analysis, no
sitting back and smoking (not that smoking is allowed any longer). We had fun.

Still. Perhaps I'd been away too long, but for me the wrestlers no longer
looked like Angela Carter's "giants." They were big, huge in fact. There were
some overblown costumes, but a surprising number of the wrestlers were down
to their skivvies. There were dramatic entrances complete with fireworks and

smoke. There were grand claims and challenges. The audience was alternately insulted and schmoozed. On the surface, it was the same as it's ever been. But the iconography seemed off. Nostalgia aside, there was something missing. The wrestlers' personae seemed much of a muchness, only tangentially connected to anything recognisably social. What did they stand for? What were they representing beyond demonstrating themselves to be with us or against us? We couldn't really tell.

It is tempting to assert that wrestlers cannot be larger than life if life ceases to be their point of reference. But what if this slippage is more than a change in the way the performance is being practiced? What if it is, in fact, a sign of a loss of tangibility in the social order? What's left of the contest between good and evil, in wrestling as in life, if the distinctions are detached from ideology, if they become completely arbitrary – reduced to a matter of liking those who play for rather than against the code of likeability?[13]

The main event was Mr. Kennedy versus the World Wrestling Champion Batista. Mr. Kennedy was the heel. How did we know? He grabbed the mic from the announcer, and shouted at us: "Crusaders suck! . . . All Blacks suck! . . . New Zealand is Australia's BITCH!" This was a really cheap trick.[14] This was no "morality play." This was just plain rude. Attack our local rugby team, blaspheme the national stars, then emasculate the country – we hate you, we so so so hate you. By the time Mr. Kennedy was on the turnbuckle, the spectators were fully riled up. But the confrontation was clearly manufactured and fully contained, both by the Māori wardens[15] who stood, backs to the ring, staring us down (and occasionally turning to catch a look at the action) and by the conventions that simultaneously licenced and limited our outcries. The only thing truly, if only momentarily, unpredictable was an attempt to resist the script, stirred by seven or eight young men in the row behind us, fuelled it seemed by equal parts beer and camaraderie, and perhaps (it might be admitted) by vague feelings of disappointment and boredom: "Come on, Mr. Kennedy, you can do it . . . Ken–ned–dy, Ken–ned–dy, Ken–ned–dy." We picked it up and as much from academic curiosity as commitment to the cause, tried to carry it forward. "Ken–ned–dy, Ken–ned–dy, Ken–ned–dy." The chant grew, tentatively, and spread in odd patches around us. And then it collapsed. The boys shrugged. We turned our backs to them and reabsorbed ourselves into the mass. Batista won. With and without us, on side and not, the game went on.

To us it looked like the main event, in particular, the words and choreography, had been put through a sieve, with any extemporaneous impulses strained out and the performance thus purified. This is how the WWE manufactures a consistent "entertainment" that can be transported from the global to the local and then back again. Along with the wrestlers, our spectatorial selves were stripped of specificity and our contrary acts edited into conformity for incorporation into the mediatised spectacle. What the world was watching was us watching in a loop that seems endless, sealed against protest. We had felt the stirrings of discontent, small but visceral in the margins of the arena, trivial and irrational as it might seem, and so we joined the boys behind us in acting back, challenging the narrative flow of the event and our place within it. And even though our challenge to the prevailing values of the arena quickly collapsed, the act was more important, more felt and somehow more significant, than its failure. Almost ten years on, I'm told the WWE now experiments with ways of engaging the malcontents on the fringes, using social media. But this seems counterproductive. One of the very real pleasures peculiar to wrestling is being cranky about the way the promoter is taking the game.

The gaps, fissures and ruptures in the apparent seamlessness of the professional wrestling event, like other genres of popular performance (and I believe in life), are not necessarily to be found in grand gestures, which themselves can so quickly be absorbed into the dominant discourse. Resistance is not futile, but it is smaller than we would like to believe. It is not necessarily contagious, and it generally doesn't look heroic. Nor is it moral *per se*. (We were, after all, siding with a convincingly antagonistic heel.) It is not even persuasive, at least not at first encounter. Resistant spectators double up. They can be seen to play along at the same time that they, sometimes, play against the otherwise smooth surface of the performance. They are not necessarily "emancipated" from the spectacle, but neither are they completely enthralled.[16] In acting back, we recognise that what we see is not as it appears to us. We are at least that smart.

So too in universities, where being, and acting, smart is the name of the game. Performing as an academic requires a peculiar balance of bluster (think Hulk Hogan) and ferocity (think Stone Cold Steve Austin) with guilelessness (think Bushwackers, maybe, or Hacksaw Jim Duggan). In the golden, olden days of professional wrestling, we used to see the occasional "Professor." Appearing in academic robes (topped with mortarboard and tassel), sporting horn-rimmed glasses and a hectoring tone, professional wrestling's Professor appears as an obvious throwback to Il Dottore of Commedia dell'Arte – a stock character with a long history, whose earliest manifestations can be found in Greek and Roman comedy. In Commedia, Il Dottore appeared as a pompous old man noted for his propensity to wrest the stage from the other characters and bring the plot to a standstill with his nonstop rattling on of a kind of polyglot gibberish, including bits of bastardised Greek and Latin, until finally, he would be lifted up and carried off still carrying on chattering until beyond hearing. In some scenarios, Il Dottore could take on key characteristics of the Miles Gloriosus, the vain and boastful soldier whose valour would comically wilt at the first sign of a real fight.

Contemporary wrestling's Professor upholds such traditions. He is almost invariably a heel, whose posturing pontifications – parodies of academic jargon – are aimed at the audience at least as much as toward his opponent and the referee, and are turned to prevarications the instant he is forced to disrobe and prove himself in action, usually by clinging to the ropes while continuing to lecture and hector.[17] While there are aspects of travesty in such performances, they are not so farfetched as I would like to believe. Universities are, after all, built more on talk than walk, even in the more "practice-led" disciplines. Academic robes are not everyday wear as they were in the time of Il Dottore, of course; they appear anachronistically, the more flamboyant versions somehow adding an aspect of camp to the *Pomp and Circumstance*. However, day-to-day performances of academia often belie the plain dress. The heels are generally in suits, bureaupathological administrators carrying calculators and spreadsheets, wielding agendas and cumbersome processes, and a thinly masked contempt – many of them – for academics whom they cast as sentimental and unrealistic. In the opposing corner are lecturers, who may stand up but often waffle away the point of contention in earnest efforts to appear reasoned. We're supposed to be smart, but often we are made to feel like marks. Cynicism versus idealism, with the real powers-that-be safely tucked away in council rooms and ministries of education.[18]

All of this is by way of saying that while universities are staged as meritocracies – may the best idea win! – academic processes can be seen as highly codified exchanges between antagonists whose postures are value-laden and whose differences can sometimes appear more metaphoric than tangible. Not for nothing does my current dean frequently repeat the axiom that in universities the battles are so intense because the stakes are so low. Not surprising that the phrase "imposter syndrome" arises from the academic environment. No wonder that the idea of simulation, raised by Jean Baudrillard as a critique of contemporary capitalist society, can seem to refer to the way "shared governance" has become more show than reality. In fact, in *The Transparency of Evil: Essays on Extreme Phenomena*, Baudrillard discusses "the fate of value" and adds: "Properly speaking there is now no law of value, merely a sort of epidemic of value, a sort of general metastasis of value, a haphazard proliferation and dispersal of value."[19]

Increasingly, in New Zealand as elsewhere, decisions are made behind closed doors in advance of the consultative processes and debates that appear to determine what courses will be taught, how research is to be developed, and the shape and scope of the institution's profile. Call it "kayfabe creep," maybe. The shifts have been in plain sight, directed by the guys with the money and driven, we are told, by government policies, economic exigencies and – closer to home for me, of course – earthquakes. The evacuation of the real from university decision-making means that the performances we see (and give) are more extreme, more vehement for being less likely to produce meaningful results. What was once a kind of rough theatre[20] – albeit more dialogic and sedentary than physically engaged, but nonetheless intimate, performed by and for the people in the room – has become polished, slippery and very much conscious of an audience beyond.

The effect, in the university as in professional wrestling, is something more than "a-morality play." It's moral blindness, a product of idealism as much as of capitalism, what happened when the relativism that underscored identitarian politics in the 1980s gave way to "saming" and then was consumed by the mass mediatisation of individuality in the twenty-first century. In *Moral Blindness: The Loss of Sensitivity in Liquid Modernity*, Leonidas Donskis begins his dialogue with Zygmunt Bauman by observing:

> Everything is permeated by ambivalence; there is no longer any unambiguous social situation, just as there are no more uncompromised actors on the stage of world history.[21]

He adds: "Happy are those epochs that had clear dramas, dreams, and doers of good or evil."[22] Indeed, Bauman replies:

> How safe and comfortable, cosy and friendly the world would feel if it were monsters and only monsters who perpetrated monstrous deeds.[23]

They're not talking about professional wrestling, of course, although they could be. What they're articulating, in part, is the erosion of the social aspect of identity, the sense that members of communities – including academics – can play distinctive, significant roles in building local bulwarks against the incursions of the global. They are not optimistic. Donskis says:

> The capitalization of universities and the de facto libertarian model of their development, imposed from above by the state bureaucracy, is something so grotesque that the great liberals – above all, the liberal economists and political thinkers – never even dreamt of it. It is academic capitalism without freedom, a species of technocratic and bureaucratic tyranny implemented in the name of freedom and progress. At the same time it is a technocratic simulacrum of the free market, in which competition is fabricated from criteria chosen so tendentiously that certain favoured institutions are guaranteed to win.[24]

In fact, here as elsewhere, universities appear to have been thrust into an epic battle between the arts and the STEM (science, technology, engineering, mathematics) disciplines. We can and do take sides, at faculty meetings and in public fora, but not only is it not a fair fight, it's not even a real fight.

How are we to act when we find ourselves working and living in "a world of intermittent human ties and of inflated words and vows"[25] – a world that looks much like the world of wrestling wrought small and intimate? This is, for me, a critical question. I was fortunate to begin watching wrestling when it first hit the big time, and when performance studies was emerging as a discipline to be reckoned with. I remain fascinated with the way professional wrestling plays with morality at the same time that it is widely viewed as an immoral performance practice, vulgar in its conceits and fundamentally dishonest because of the fix. It is indeed a con game, but one that plays with open cards. In his recent *New York Times* review of Penn and Teller's new show on Broadway, Ben Brantley observes:

> It's hard to hear a pop star's hit record now without thinking of the technology that smoothed and sweetened the vocals, or to listen to a politician without imagining a team of speechwriters, or to watch special effects in an action movie without wondering about green screens. As much as we may be amused or even enthralled by such spectacles, it's become a point of honor to know that they're only illusions.[26]

We go to the arena, as we go to the theatre, to be amused and also to be acculturated. We go to universities to be smart. But it doesn't really work that way, does it? Wrestling is a symptom both of social malaise and of social vitality, a performance in which our desire for revolution is played out against the apparent inevitability of our acquiescence. The true tension is between the cynicism that tells us it's all a game owned by the guy with the money at the expense of the rest of us and the optimism that keeps us in it, keeps us trying to find a way to be more smart than mark, and barring that, at least to acquire the self- and social-awareness to see how we are made into marks, and with that knowing to learn to act outside the box, to break free of the squared circle, of its ethos and of the dominant culture pro wrestling so richly represents.

Author's note

With apologies to Milton Bradley, who created the original "Checkered Game of Life" in order "to forcibly impress upon the minds of youth the great moral principles of virtue and vice" (quoted in Jill Lepore, "The Meaning of Life," *New Yorker*, May 21, 2007). Parts of this chapter were first presented as "Acting Back" for PSi13 (November 2007), and in "What's Live Got to Do With It?" for a Comparative Media Studies Colloquium at MIT (April 29, 2007), available as a podcast at http://cmsw.mit.edu/sharon-mazer-whats-live-got-to-do-with-it/. Thanks to Colin for coming along.

Notes

1 Zygmunt Bauman and Leonidas Donskis, *Moral Blindness: The Loss of Sensitivity in Liquid Modernity* (Cambridge: Polity Press, 2013), 5.
2 Ibid., 23.
3 Christchurch was struck with a series of devastating earthquakes that began on September 4, 2010 and climaxed with the deaths of 183 people on February 22, 2011. Aftershocks continue, more than 14,000 to date. Much of the city was destroyed or demolished, and the rebuild will be ongoing for decades. Orange road cones and visibility vests are integral to the post-earthquake landscape. See Sharon Mazer, "Quake City," *Performance Research* 20, no. 3 (June 2015): 163–172.

4 For a peek at the current incarnation of the Johnny Rodz School of Unpredictable Wrestling, see the World of Unpredictable Wrestling website: http://wuwonline.com/.

5 Sharon Mazer, "The Doggie Doggie World of Professional Wrestling," 34, no. 4 (Winter 1990): 96–122. Also Sharon Mazer, *Professional Wrestling: Sport and Spectacle* (Jackson: University Press of Mississippi, 1998).

6 Angela Carter, "Giants' Playtime," in *Shaking a Leg: Collected Journalism and Writings* (London: Vintage 1998): 332–336. Originally published in *New Society* (1976).

7 See WWE website: http://www.wwe.com/.

8 Carter, "Giants' Playtime," 334.

9 Ibid., 335.

10 Quoted by Peter Kerr, "Now It Can Be Told: Those Pro Wrestlers Are Just Having Fun," *New York Times*, February 10, 1989, accessed June 21, 2015, http://www.nytimes.com/1989/02/10/nyregion/now-it-can-be-told-those-pro-wrestlers-are-just-having-fun.html. That knowledge of professional wrestling's artifice doesn't necessarily impinge on the watcher's pleasure is evidenced in this popular clip of a Japanese wrestler mixing it up with a mannequin: "Endless Canadian Destroyer from Kota Ibushi vs. Yoshihiko, DDT," October 25, 2009, accessed June 20, 2015, https://www.youtube.com/watch?v=qsMECSKzdSQ&feature=youtu.be.

11 Ibid.

12 See Jedd Legum's recent observation that Roland Barthes's famous essay on professional wrestling (in *Mythologies* 1957) may "hold the key to understanding Trump's appeal" in "This French Philosopher Is the Only One Who Can Explain the Trump Phenomenon," *Think Progress*, September 14, 2015, accessed December 22, 2015, http://thinkprogress.org/politics/2015/09/14/3701084/donald-trump/. For my own discussion of the proximity of American politics to professional wrestling, see Sharon Mazer, "Los verdaderos luchadores no usan mascaras" ("Real Wrestlers Don't Wear Masks"), *Luna Cornea* 27 (2004): 270–275, 323–325.

13 Here, I'm recalling the question that circulates during presidential elections: "which candidate would you like to have a beer with?"

14 In fact, I heard in the moment, an echo of the time, more than twenty-five years ago, I saw Linda Dallas grab the mic to shout "Brooklyn sucks!" at the spectators watching a Johnny Rodz show in Gleason's Arena. Same trick, same effect, albeit with a more sexually charged response from the crowd. See "The Doggie Doggie World of Professional Wrestling," *TDR: The Drama Review* 34, no. 4 (1990): 100.

15 For the definition, history and current status of Māori wardens see, for example: *Te Kaunihera Māori o Aotearoa/New Zealand Māori Council* (http://www.maoricouncil.com/wardens) and *Te Puni Kōkiri* (http://www.tpk.govt.nz/en/whakamahia/maori-wardens).

16 See Jacques Rancière, *The Emancipated Spectator*, trans. Gregory Elliott (London and New York: Verso, 2009).

17 When I was first doing my research, I had the pleasure of seeing Laurence deGaris (aka Larry Brisco), who was then working on a PhD in sports sociology, take up the mantle of the Professor on occasion at Gleason's in a performance that was as much observed, it seemed, as stock. See Laurence deGaris, "Sometimes a Bloody Nose Is Just a Bloody Nose: Play and Contest in Boxing, Wrestling, and Ethnography," *Sport in Society* 13, no. 6 (2010): 935–951; and Laurence deGaris, "Experiments in Pro Wrestling: Toward a Performative and Sensuous Sport Ethnography," *Sociology of Sport Journal* 16 (1999): 65–74.

18 There are many academic fora and blogs in which one can bear witness to colleagues who, taking on cartoonish personae, eloquently and vehemently lament the decay of tertiary education. See, for example, my own current favourite, College Misery (http://collegemisery.blogspot.co.nz/).

19 Jean Baudrillard, *The Transparency of Evil: Essays on Extreme Phenomena*, trans. James Benedict (London and New York: Verso, 1993): 5. Italics in original.

20 See Peter Brook, *The Empty Space* (New York: Simon and Schuster, 1968).
21 Ibid., 5.
22 Ibid.
23 Ibid., 23.
24 Ibid., 137–138.
25 Ibid., 217.
26 Ben Brantley, "Review: 'Penn & Teller on Broadway' Explores the Illusions of Technology," *New York Times*, July 12, 2015, accessed July 13, 2015, http://www.nytimes.com/2015/07/13/theater/review-penn-teller-on-broadway-explores-the-illusions-of-technology.html.

Bibliography

Adelman, Rebecca A. and Wendy Kozol. "Discordant Effects: Ambivalence, Banality, and the Ethics of Spectatorship." *Theory & Event* 17, no. 3 (2014).

Aiba, Keiko. "Japanese Women Professional Wrestlers and Body Image." In *Transforming Japan: How Feminism and Diversity Are Making a Difference*, edited by Kumiko Fujimura-Fanselow, 268–283. New York: Feminist Press, 2011.

———. *Joshi puroresura no shintai to jenda-kihanteki onnarashisa wo koete (Body and Gender of Women Pro-Wrestlers in Japan: Beyond "Normative" Femininity)*. Tokyo: Akashi Shoten, 2013.

Al-Kaissy, Adnan and Ross Bernstein. *The Sheik of Baghdad: Tales of Celebrity and Terror from Pro Wrestling's General Adnan*. Chicago: Triumph Books, 2005.

Allen, Robert C. *Horrible Prettiness: Burlesque and American Culture*. Chapel Hill: University of North Carolina Press, 1991.

Anae, Nicole. "Poses Plastiques: The Art and Style of 'Statuary' in Victorian Visual Theatre." *Australasian Drama Studies* 52 (2008): 112–130.

Anderson, Ole and Scott Teal. *Inside Out: How Corporate America Destroyed Professional Wrestling*. Gallatin, TN: Crowbar Press, 2003.

Angle, Kurt, interview with Rob Feinstein. *Kurt Angle Shoot Interview*. DVD. Directed by Rob Feinstein. Langhorne, PA: RF Video, 2008.

"Annual Report." Form 10-k. World Wrestling Federation Entertainment, Inc. *Edgar Online*, April 30, 2000. Accessed October 22, 2014. http://yahoo.brand.edgar-online.com/display filinginfo.aspx?FilingID=1361985–1136–235098&type=sect&TabIndex=2&companyid=7520&ppu=%252fdefault.aspx%253fcik%253d1091907.

Anzaldúa, Gloria. *The Gloria Anzaldúa Reader*. Edited by AnaLouise Keating. Durham and London: Duke University Press, 2009.

Arroyo, Jossianna. "Mirror, Mirror on the Wall: Performing Racial and Gender Identities in Javier Cardona's You Don't Look Like." In *The State of Latino Theater in the United States: Hybridity, Transculturation, and Identity*, edited by Luis A. Ramos-García, 152–171. New York: Routledge, 2002.

Arroyo, Jossianna. "Sirena canta boleros: travestismo y sujetos transcaribeños en *Sirena Selena vestida de pena*." *CENTRO: Journal of the Center for Puerto Rican Studies* XV, no. 2 (2003): 39–51.

———. *Travestismos culturales: literatura y etnografía en Cuba y Brasil*. Pittsburgh: University of Pittsburgh International Institute of Iberoamerican Literature, 2003.

Asseal, Shaun and Mike Mooneyham. *Sex, Lies & Headlocks: The Real Story of Vince McMahon and the Rise of World Wrestling Entertainment*. New York: Broadway Books, 2004.

Auslander, Philip. *Liveness: Performance in a Mediatized Culture*, 2nd ed. London: Routledge, 2008.

———. *Performing Glam Rock: Gender & Theatricality in Popular Music*. Ann Arbor: University of Michigan Press, 2006.

Bakhtin, Mikhail. *Speech Genres and Other Late Essays*. Translated by Vern W. McGee. Edited by Caryl Emerson and Michael Holquist. Austin: Texas University Press, 1986.

Barker, Martin. *The New Racism: Conservatives and the Ideology of the Tribe*, 2nd ed. Frederick, MD: University Publications of America, 1982.

Barthes, Roland. *Mythologies*. Translated by Annette Lavers. New York: Hill and Wang, 1972.

Bateman, Oliver Lee. "Capitalism, Violence and Male Bodies: The Strange Saga of Vince McMahon." *The Good Men Project*, October 25, 2013. Accessed 15 July 2015. http://good menproject.com/featured-content/capitalism-violence-and-male-bodies-the-strange-saga-of-vince-mcmahon/.

———. "Male Bodies and the Lies We Tell About Them: The Making and Faking of Professional Wrestling." *Good Men Project*, May 3, 2013. Accessed January 15, 2016. http://goodmenproject.com/featured-content/male-bodies-and-the-lies-we-tell-about-them-the-making-and-faking-of-professional-wrestling/.

Baudrillard, Jean. *The Transparency of Evil: Essays on Extreme Phenomena*. Translated by James Benedict. New York: Verso, 1993.

Bauman, Zygmunt and Leonidas Donskis. *Moral Blindness: The Loss of Sensitivity in Liquid Modernity*. Cambridge: Polity Press, 2013.

Beck, Ethel. "Hey Lady! Catch Ricki Starr!" *Kansas City Sunday Herald*. August 16, 1959.

Beckett, Andy. *When the Lights Went Out: Britain in the Seventies*. London: Faber and Faber, 2010.

Beekman, Scott M. *Ringside: A History of Professional Wrestling in America*. Westport, CT: Praeger, 2006.

Bennett, Susan. *Theatre Audiences: A Theory of Production and Reception*. London: Routledge, 1997.

Berger, John. *Ways of Seeing*. London: BBC and Penguin Books, 1972.

Berger, Phil. "Ricki Starr, 'I Consider Wrestling an Art.'" *Wrestling World Magazine*, December 1965.

Bernstein, Robin. "Dances with Things: Material Culture and the Performance of Race." *Social Text* 27, no. 4 (Winter 2009): 67–94.

Binner, Andrew. "The Rise of Mixed Martial Arts." Accessed June 10, 2015. http://www.alja zeera.com/sport/othersports/2014/04/rise-mixed-martial-arts-201441094427103582.html.

Blau, Herbert. *The Audience*. Baltimore: Johns Hopkins University Press, 1990.

Bordo, Susan. *Unbearable Weight, Feminism, Western Culture and the Body*. Berkeley and Los Angeles: University of California Press, 1993.

Bourdieu, Pierre. *Distinction: A Social Critique of the Judgement of Taste*. Cambridge, MA: Harvard University Press, 1984.

Bradburne, James. *Blood: Art, Power & Pathology*. London and New York: Prestel, 2002.

Brannon, Robert. "The Male Sex Role – And What It's Done for Us Lately." In *The Forty-Nine Percent Majority*, edited by Robert Brannon and Deborah David, 1–40. Reading, MA: Addison-Wesley, 1976.

Brantley, Ben. "Review: 'Penn & Teller on Broadway' Explores the Illusions of Technology." *New York Times*, July 12, 2015. Accessed July 13, 2015. http://www.nytimes.com/2015/07/13/theater/review-penn-teller-on-broadway-explores-the-illusions-of-technology.html.

"Brock Lesnar's Apology." *RAW*, June 22, 2015. Accessed June 30, 2015. https://www.you tube.com/watch?v=XnYq_kgdA_Q.

Brook, Peter. *The Empty Space*. New York: Simon and Schuster, 1968.

Brown, Bill. "Thing Theory." *Critical Inquiry* 28, no. 1 (Autumn 2001): 1–22.

Budd, Michael Anton. *The Sculpture Machine: Physical Culture and Body Politics in the Age of Empire*. New York: New York University Press, 1997.

Burkholder, Denny. "Black History Month: Pro Wrestling's Black Stars." February 5, 2002. Accessed January 15, 2015. http://www.onlineonslaught.com/columns/circa/200202 bhm1.shtml.

Burnett, Cora. "Whose Game is it Anyway? Power, Play and Sport." *Agenda* 49 (2001): 71–78.

Butler, Judith. *Excitable Speech*. London: Routledge, 1997.

———. *Gender Trouble: Feminism and the Subversion of Identity*. New York: Routledge, 1990.

Cadena-Roa, Jorge. "Strategic Framing, Emotions and Superbarrio: Mexico City's Masked Crusader." *Mobilization: An International Quarterly* 7 (2002): 201–216.

Carro, Nelson. *El Cine de Luchadores*. México, DF: Filmoteca de la UNAM, 1984.

Carter, Angela. "Giants' Playtime." *Shaking a Leg: Collected Journalism and Writings*, 332–336. London: Vintage 1998. Originally published in *New Society* (1976).

Carter, Dan T. *The Politics of Rage: George Wallace, the Origins of the New Conservatism, and the Transformation of American Politics*. Baton Rouge: Louisiana State University Press, 2000.

Center for Contemporary Cultural Studies. *The Empire Strikes Back: Race and Racism in 70s Britain*. Birmingham: Center for Contemporary Cultural Studies, 1982.

Child, Ben. "Dwayne 'The Rock' Johnson Named Highest Grossing Actor of 2013." *Guardian*, December 18, 2013. Accessed January 16, 2015. http://www.theguardian.com/ film/2013/dec/18/dwayne-the-rock-johnson-highest-grossing-actor-2013.

Chow, Broderick D.V. "A Professional Body: Remembering, Repeating, and Working Out Masculinities in Fin-de-Siècle Physical Culture." *Performance Research* 20, no. 5 (2015): 30–41.

———. "Work and Shoot: Professional Wrestling and Embodied Politics." *TDR: The Drama Review* 58, no. 2 (2014): 72–86.

Chow, Broderick and Eero Laine. "Audience Affirmation and the Labour of Professional Wrestling." *Performance Research: A Journal of the Performing Arts* 19, no. 2 (2014): 44–53.

Coddington, Anne. *One of the Lads: Women Who Follow Football*. London: HarperCollins, 1997.

Connell, R.W. *Gender & Power: Society, The Person and Sexual Politics*. Stanford: Stanford University Press, 1987.

Conquergood, Dwight. "Performance Studies: Interventions and Radical Research." *TDR: The Drama Review* 46, no. 2 (2002): 145–156.

Crawley, Sara. L., Lara J. Foley and Constance L. Shehan. *Gendering Bodies*. Lanham, MD: Rowman & Littlefield, 2008.

Criollo, Raúl, José Xavier Nava and Rafael Avina. *¡Quiero ver sangre!: Historia ilustrada del Cine de luchadores*. Mexico, DF: UNAM, 2012.

The Crow. Directed by Alex Proyas. 1994. London: EIV, 2003. DVD.

Daniel, Pete. *Lost Revolution: The South in the 1950s*. Chapel Hill: University of North Carolina Press, 2000.

David, D. "Vintage Best and Worst: WCW Hog Wild 1996." Accessed August 5, 2014. http:// uproxx.com/sports/2014/05/vintage-best-and-worst-wcw-hog-wild-1996/.

Davis, Danny. "Interview with Jim Ross." *Ross Report*. Podcast audio. May 27, 2015. http:// cdn46.castfire.com/audio/522/3426/25262/2497032/2497032_2015-05-21-003132- 7770-0-8544-2.64k.mp3.

DeGaris, Laurence. "Experiments in Pro Wrestling: Toward a Performative and Sensuous Sport Ethnography." *Sociology of Sport Journal* 16 (1999): 65–74.

———. "Sometimes a Bloody Nose is Just a Bloody Nose: Play and Contest in Boxing, Wrestling, and Ethnography." *Sport in Society* 13, no. 6 (2010): 935–951.

Dell, Chad. *The Revenge of Hatpin Mary: Women, Professional Wrestling, and Fan Culture in the 1950s.* New York: Peter Lang, 2006.

Deller, Jeremy. *Jeremy Deller: Joy in People.* London: Hayward Gallery, 2012.

———. "So Many Ways to Hurt you, The Life and Times of Adrian Street, 2010." Accessed June 1, 2015. http://www.jeremydeller.org/SoManyWays/SoManyWaysToHurtYou_Video.php.

Demedeiros, James. "Welcome to John Cena's World." *Men's Fitness.* Accessed July 15, 2015. http://www.mensfitness.com/life/entertainment/welcome-to-john-cenas-world.

Dias, Belidson and Susan Sinkinson. "Film Spectatorship between Queer Theory and Feminism: Transcultural Readings." *International Journal of Education through Art* 1, no. 2 (2005): 127–141.

Diaz, Kristoffer. *The Elaborate Entrance of Chad Deity.* New York: Samuel French, 2011.

Dolan, Jill. *The Feminist Spectator as Critic.* Ann Arbor: University of Michigan Press, 1991.

———. *Theatre & Sexuality.* Basingstoke: Palgrave Macmillan, 2010.

Duncan, Margaret Carlisle and Barry Brummett. "The Mediation of Spectator Sport." *Research Quarterly for Exercise and Sport* 58, no. 2 (1987): 168–177.

Dunn, Carrie. *Female Football Fans.* Basingstoke: Palgrave Pivot, 2014.

———. "Sexy, Smart and Powerful: Examining Gender and Reality in the WWE Divas' Division." *Networking Knowledge* 8, no. 3 (2015). http://ojs.meccsa.org.uk/index.php/netknow/article/view/378.

———. *Spandex, Screw Jobs and Cheap Pops: Inside the Business of British Professional Wrestling.* Worthing: Pitch, 2013.

"Dusty Rhodes Talks about 'Hard Times.'" *Mid-Atlantic Wrestling*, October 29, 1985. Accessed June 30, 2015. https://www.youtube.com/watch?v=9py4aMK3aIU.

Dworkin, Shari L. and Faye Linda Wachs. *Body Panic, Gender, Health, and the Selling of Fitness.* New York: NYU Press, 2009.

Dyer, Richard. *White.* London: Routledge, 1997.

Edwards, Lisa. "Postmodernism, Queer Theory and Moral Judgment in Sport: Some Critical Reflections." *International Review for the Sociology of Sport* 44 (December 2009): 331–344.

Ehara, Yumiko. *Jenda chitsujo* (Gender Order). Tokyo: Keiso Shobo, 2001.

Elias, Norbert and Eric Dunning. *Quest for Excitement: Sport and Leisure in the Civilizing Process.* Oxford: Basil Blackwell, 1986.

"Endless Canadian Destroyer from Kota Ibushi Vs Yoshihiko, DDT 10/25/2009." Accessed June 20, 2015. https://www.youtube.com/watch?v=qsMECSKzdSQ&feature=youtu.be.

English, Arkady. "What is it Like to See Professional Wrestling Live?" August 1, 2013. http://www.quora.com/What-is-it-like-to-see-professional-wrestling-live.

Entin, Esther. "All Work and no Play: Why Your Kids are More Anxious, Depressed." *Atlantic*, October 12, 2011. http://www.theatlantic.com/health/archive/2011/10/all-work-and-no-play-why-your-kids-are-more-anxious-depressed/246422.

Fair, John D. *Mr. America: The Tragic History of a Bodybuilding Icon.* Austin: Texas University Press, 2015.

Fascinetto, Lola Miranda. *Sin Máscara Ni Cabellera: Lucha libre en México hoy.* Mexico City: Marc Ediciones, 1992.

Figueira, Dorothy M. *The Exotic: A Decadent Quest*. New York: State University of New York Press, 1994.

Finnegan, William. "The Man without a Mask: How the Drag Queen Cassandro Became a Star of Mexican Wrestling." *New Yorker*, September 1, 2014. Accessed March 28, 2015. http://www.newyorker.com/magazine/2014/09/01/man-without-mask.

Fisher, Jennifer. *Nutcracker Nation*. New Haven: Yale University Press, 2007.

Fleischer, Nat. *Black Dynamite: The Story of the Negro in the Prize Ring from 1782 to 1938, Volume 1*. New York: C.J. O'Brien, 1938.

Ford, Charles. "Iconoclasm, the Commodity and the Art of Painting." In *Iconoclasm: Contested Objects, Contested Terms*, edited by Stacy Boldrick and Richard Clay, 75–92. Aldershot: Ashgate, 2007.

Freeman, Elizabeth. "Time Binds, or, Erotohistoriography." *Social Text* 23, no. 3–4 (Fall–Winter 2005): 57–68.

———. *Time Binds: Queer Temporalities, Queer Histories*. Durham and London: Duke University Press, 2010.

Freeth, Tony. "TV Colonialism." In *It Ain't Half Racist, Mum: Fighting Racism in the Media*, edited by Phil Cohen and Carl Gardner. London: Comedia Group, 1982.

Garfield, Simon. *The Wrestling*. London: Faber and Faber, 2007.

Gauntlett, David. *Media, Gender and Identity: An Introduction*. London and New York: Routledge, 2002.

Giddens, Anthony. *Modernity and Self-Identity: Self and Society in the Late Modern Age*. Cambridge: Polity Press, 1991.

Gill, Rosalind, Karen Henwood and Carl McLean. "Body Projects and the Regulation of Normative Masculinity." *Body & Society* 11, no. 1 (2005): 37–62.

Gilroy, Paul. *There Ain't No Black in the Union Jack: The Cultural Politics of Race and Nation*, 2nd ed. Chicago: University of Chicago Press, 1991.

"Glamor Approach Versus Rough Guys On Mat Card Here Saturday." *Lexington Dispatch*, November 16, 1956.

Goldust and Stardust. Interview by Chris Jericho." *Talk is Jericho*. Podcast audio, August 6, 2014. http://podcastone.com/pg/jsp/program/episode.jsp?programID=593&pid=426708.

Gordon, Robert. *It Came From Memphis*. New York: Atria, 2001.

Gray, Peter. "The Decline of Play and the Rise of Psychopathology in Children and Adolescents." *American Journal of Play* 3, no. 4 (Spring 2011): 443–463.

Griffin, Marcus. *Fall Guys: The Barnums of Bounce: The Inside Story of the Wrestling Business, America's Most Profitable and Best Organized Sport*. Chicago: Reilly Lee, 1937.

Gutierrez, Lucas. "Cassandro 'El Exótico': El Liberace de la lucha libre." *FriendlyLife*, September 26, 2014. Accessed March 28, 2015. http://friendlylife.com/espectaculos/18076.

Hackenschmidt, George. *The Way to Live in Health and Physical Fitness*. London: Athletic, 1911.

Hackett, Thomas. *Slaphappy: Pride, Prejudice, and Professional Wrestling*. New York: HarperCollins, 2006.

Hall, Stuart. "New Ethnicities." In *Black British Cultural Studies: A Reader*, edited by Houston A. Baker Jr., Manthia Diawara and Ruth H. Lindbourg, 163–172. Chicago: University of Chicago Press, 1996.

———. "Old and New Identities, Old and New Ethnicities." In *Culture, Globalization and the World System*, edited by Anthony D. King, 41–68. 4th ed. Minneapolis: University of Minnesota Press, 2007.

Halbert, Christy. "Tough Enough and Woman Enough: Stereotypes, Discrimination and Impression Management Among Women Professional Boxers." *Journal of Sport and Social Issues* 21 (1997): 7–36.

Hardt, Michael and Antonio Negri. *Commonwealth*. Cambridge, MA: Belknap Press of Harvard University Press, 2009.

Hargreaves, Jennifer. "Where's the Virtue? Where's the Grace? A Discussion of the Social Production of Gender Relations in and through Sport." *Theory, Culture & Society* 3, no. 1 (1989): 109–121.

Harris, Keith, "Tyler Reks: 'WWE Wrestlers Break their Bodies to Barely Pay their Bills.'" *Cageside Seats*, posted December 17, 2014. Accessed July 15, 2015, http://www.cagesideseats.com/wwe/2014/12/17/7412959/tyler-reks-wwe-wrestlers-break-their-bodies-to-barely-pay-their-bills.

Hart, Bret. *Hitman: My Real Life in the Cartoon World of Wrestling*. Toronto: Random House, 2007.

Harvey, David. *Spaces of Hope*. Edinburgh: Edinburgh University Press, 2000.

Haywood, Chris and Máirtín Mac an Ghaill. *Men and Masculinities: Theory, Research and Social Practice*. Buckingham: Open University Press, 2003.

Healy, Patrick. "Like the Movie, Only Different: Hollywood's Big Bet on Hollywood Adaptations." Movies. *New York Times*, August 1, 2013. Accessed June 2, 2015. http://www.nytimes.com/2013/08/04/movies/hollywoods-big-bet-on-broadway-adaptations.html.

HeelZiggler. Twitter Post, May 18, 2015, 9:12am. https://twitter.com/HEELZiggler/status/600333063739027457.

Heidegger, Martin. *Being and Time*. Translated by Joan Stambaugh. New York: State University of New York Press, 1996.

Herbert, Grahame. "10 Things WWE mean by the 'Reality Era.'" *WhatCulture.com*. Accessed April 20, 2015. http://whatculture.com/wwe/10-things-wwe-mean-reality-era.php.

Herzfeld, Michael. *Cultural Intimacy: Social Poetics in the Nation State*. New York: Routledge, 1997.

Hill, Annette. "The Spectacle of Excess: The Passion Work of Professional Wrestlers, Fans and Anti-Fans." *European Journal of Cultural Studies* 18, no. 2 (2014): 174–189.

"History." *Feld Entertainment*. Accessed 21 March 2014. https://www.feldentertainment.com/History/.

Hitchcock, John. *Front Row Section D*. Middletown, DE: TV Party! Books, 2015.

Hoechtl, Nina. "El Teatro Maya como travestismo cultural: Una lectura performativa y descolonizadora de su arquitectura" *Extravío. Revista electrónica de literatura comparada*, 7. Universitat de València, 2015. http://www.uv.es/extravio.

———. *If Only for the Length of a Lucha: Queer/ing, Mask/ing, Gender/ing and Gesture in Lucha Libre*. PhD diss., Goldsmiths, University of London, 2012.

———. "Lucha libre: un espacio liminal. Lis exótiquis "juntopuestas" a las categorías clasificadoras, unívocas y fija." In *La memoria y el deseo. Estudios gay y queer en México*, edited by Rodrigo Parrini, 223–251. México, DF: PUEG-UNAM, 2014.

Hofman, Sudie. "Rethinking Cinco de Mayo." *Zinn Education Project*, May 5, 2012. Accessed March 15, 2015. http://zinnedproject.org/2012/05/rethinking-cinco-de-mayo/.

Holling, Michelle A. and Bernadette Marie Calafell. "Identities on Stage and Staging Identities: ChicanoBrujo Performances as Emancipatory Practices." *Text and Performance Quarterly* 27, no. 1 (January, 2007): 58–83.

Hollywood, California Program. July 21, 1958 "Tricky Ricki Starr Owes Mat Skill to Ballet."

hooks, bell. "Eating the Other." *Black Looks: Race and Representation.* Cambridge: South End Press, 1992.

Howard, Brandon. "2015 Year-End Stats: Star Ratings, TV Ratings, Attendance & more! (WWE, NJPW, NXT, ROH)." *Voices of Wrestling,* Last modified January 13, 2016. Accessed January 16, 2015, http://www.voicesofwrestling.com/2016/01/13/2015-year-end-stats-star-ratings-tv-attendance-wwe-njpw-nxt-roh/.

Hozic, Aida. *Hollyworld: Space, Power, and Fantasy in the American Economy,* Ithaca: Cornell University Press, 2001.

Huggan, Graham. *The Post-Colonial Exotic: Marketing the Margins.* London and New York: Routledge, 2001.

Hunt, Leon. *British Low Culture: From Safari Suits to Sexploitation.* London and New York: Routledge, 1998.

Hutcheon, Linda. *The Politics of Postmodernism.* London: Routledge, 2002.

Ichikawa, Koichi. *Ninkimono no shakai shinirishi* (Social-Psycho History of Stars). Tokyo: Gakuyo shobo, 2002.

Ingraham, Paul. "Pain is Weird." *PainScience.com.* Accessed June 12, 2015. https://www.pain science.com/articles/pain-is-weird.php.

Irigaray, Luce. *This Sex Which is Not One.* Ithaca: Cornell University Press, 1985.

Islam, Syed Manzurul. *The Ethics of Travel: From Marco Polo to Kafka.* Manchester: Manchester University Press, 1996.

James, Mark. *Memphis Wrestling History Presents: The 1960s: 1960–1969 Record Book.* Memphis, TN: Mark James, 2011.

———. *Memphis Wrestling History Presents: The 1970s.* Memphis, TN: Mark James, 2012.

———. *Wrestling Record Book: Houston Programs 1982–1983.* Memphis, TN: Mark James, 2014

Jares, Joe. *Whatever Happened to Gorgeous George?* Edgewood Cliffs, NJ: Prentice Hall, 1974.

Jenkins, Henry. *The Wow Climax: Tracing the Emotional Impact of Popular Culture.* New York: New York University Press, 2007.

Jericho, Chris. "Talk is Jericho EP74 Matt and Jeff – The Hardy Boyz Pt 1." Podcast audio. PodcastOne, September 17, 2014. http://podcastone.com/pg/jsp/program/episode.jsp?programID=593&pid=442593.

Jim Cornette – Timeline: The History of WCW 1989. 2015, Kayfabe Commentaries.

John, Cena. Twitter Post, September 2, 2013, 7:26am. https://twitter.com/johncena/status/374538722249015296.

Johnson, Joe. "WWE Will Face Most Hostile Audience Yet in Chicago on Monday Night RAW." WWE. *Bleacher Report,* February 27, 2014. Accessed November 10, 2015. http://bleacherreport.com/articles/1976031-wwe-will-face-most-hostile-audience-yet-in-chicago-on-monday-night-raw.

Johnson, Reed. "Lucha VaVoom and Cirque Berzerk are L.A.'s Theatre of the Odd." *Los Angeles Times,* July 19, 2009. Accessed April 7, 2015. http://articles.latimes.com/2009/jul/19/entertainment/ca-alternative19.

Johnson, Steve. Obituary of Starr, Accessed January 16, 2015, http://slam.canoe.com/Slam/Wrestling/2014/10/01/21978411.html.

Jones, Chris. "Lucha va vaVoom! Mexican Wrestling is Blended with Burlesque, Heavily Spiced with Irony." *Chicago Tribune,* May 09, 2005. Accessed April 15, 2015. http://articles.chicagotribune.com/2005–05–09/features/0505090016_1_wrestling-mexican-announcers.

Kamei, Yoshie. *Joshi puroresu minzoku shi: Monogatari no hajimari* (Ethnography of Women Pro Wrestling: The Beginning of the Story). Tokyo: Yuzankaku, 2000.

Kammers, Marjolein, Frédérique de Vignemont and Patrick Haggard. "Cooling the Thermal Grill Illusion through Self-Touch." *Current Biology* 20 (2010): 1819–1822. http://dx.doi.org/10.1016/j.cub.2010.08.038.

Kanamoto, Megumi. Tamio Yokozawa, and Masuo Kanamoto. "Shintai ni taisuru sougo ninshiki ni kansuru kenkyu" (Study of Mutual Perception Toward the Body) *Jochi Daigaku Taiiku* (Sophia University Studies in Physical Education) 32 (1999): 1–10.

"Karis Wilde." *Frontiers Media*, June 30, 2011. Accessed March 28, 2015. "https://www.frontiersmedia.com/uncategorized/2011/06/30/karis-wilde/.

Kato, Kiyotada, Tadaaki Yajima and Kazumasa Seki. "Gendai nihonjin seinen no shintaibikan ni tsuite – Daigakusei no chosa kara." (Beautiful Body Image Perceived by Contemporary Japanese Youth: From a Perception Survey of University Students) *Waseda daigaku taiiku kenkyu kiyo* 22 (1990): 13–20.

Keller, Gary D. *Hispanic and United States Film: An Overview and Handbook.* Tempe, AZ: Bilingual Press, 1994.

Kerr, Peter. "Now it Can be Told: Those Pro Wrestlers are Just Having Fun." *New York Times*, February 10, 1989. Accessed June 21, 2015. http://www.nytimes.com/1989/02/10/nyregion/now-it-can-be-told-those-pro-wrestlers-are-just-having-fun.html.

Kershaw, Baz. "Oh for Unruly Audiences! Or, Patterns of Participation in Twentieth-Century Theatre." *Modern Drama* 42, no. 2 (2001): 133–154.

Kimmel, Michael (ed.). *The Politics of Manhood.* Philadelphia: Temple University Press, 1995.

———. *Revolution: A Sociological Interpretation.* Philadelphia: Temple University Press, 1990.

Klein, Greg. *The King of New Orleans: How the Junkyard Dog Became Professional Wrestling's First Black Superstar.* Toronto: ECW Press, 2012.

Lamoureux, Christophe. *La Grand Parade du Catch.* Toulouse: Presses Universitaires du Mirail, 1993.

Lang, Derrik J. "Clinton, Obama and McCain on WWE's 'Monday Night Raw.'" *USA Today*, April 22, 2008. Accessed January 10, 2015. http://usatoday30.usatoday.com/life/television/news/2008-04-21-candidates-WWE_N.htm.

Lash, Scott. "Reflexive Modernization: The Aesthetic Dimension." *Theory, Culture & Society* 10, no. 1 (February 1993): 1–23.

Latour, Bruno. "What is Iconoclash? Or is there a World Beyond the Image Wars?" In *Iconoclash: Beyond the Images Wars in Science, Religion and Art*, edited by Bruno Latour, 16–38. Cambridge, MA: MIT Press, 2002.

"La Versión Completa." *YouTube video*, posted by "La Cueva de Camaleooon." February 6, 2007. Accessed September 24, 2015. https://www.youtube.com/watch?v=sOlxABydPP4.

LeBar, Justin. "Breaking Down Why Royal Rumble 1992 Was Pinnacle of Storied Event." Accessed June 29, 2015. http://bleacherreport.com/articles/1902849-breaking-down-why-royal-rumble-1992-was-pinnacle-of-storied-event.

Legum, Jedd. "This French Philosopher Is The Only One Who Can Explain The Trump Phenomenon." *ThinkProgress*, September 14, 2015. Accessed December 22, 2015. http://thinkprogress.org/politics/2015/09/14/3701084/donald-trump.

Lemish, Dafna. "Girls Can Wrestle Too: Gender Differences in the Consumption of a Television Wrestling Series." *Sex Roles* 38, no. 9–10 (1998): 833–849.

Leng, Ho Keat, S.Y. Kang, C. Lim, J.J. Lit, N.I. Suhaimi and Y. Umar. "Only For Males: Gendered Perception of Wrestling." *Sport Management International Journal* 8, no. 1 (2012): 44–53.

Lepore, Jill. "The Meaning of Life." *New Yorker*, May 21, 2007. Accessed October 6, 2015. http://www.newyorker.com/magazine/2007/05/21/the-meaning-of-life.

Levi, Heather. "Lean Mean Fighting Queens: Drag in the World of Mexican Professional Wrestling." *Sexualities* 1, no. 3 (1998): 275–285.

———. *The World of Lucha Libre. Secrets, Revelations, and Mexican National Identity.* Durham: Duke University Press, 2008.

Levine, Lawrence W. *Highbrow/Lowbrow: The Emergence of Cultural Hierarchy in America.* Cambridge, MA: Harvard University Press, 1988.

Lieberman, Evan. "Mask and Masculinity: Culture, Modernity, and Gender Identity in the Mexican Lucha Libre Films of El Santo." *Studies in Hispanic Cinemas (New Title: Studies in Spanish & Latin American Cinemas)* 6 (2009): 3–17.

"Live Nation Entertainment, Inc." *Yahoo Finance.* Accessed December 10, 2014. http://finance.yahoo.com/q/pr?s=LYV.

Lott, Eric. *Love and Theft: Blackface Minstrelsy and the American Working Class.* New York: Oxford University Press, 1993.

Luchini. "How about Wyatt Lanterns?" http://www.wrestlingforum.com/general--wwe/885409--how--about--wyatt--lanterns.html.

Lyons, John. Advocate Sports Editor, "Cowboy Helps Ricki Starr Win." *Victoria Advocate,* December 3, 1953.

Mad Max. Directed by George Miller. 1979. Burbank: Warner Home Video, 2006. DVD.

Malik, Sarita. *Representing Black Britain: A History of Black and Asian Images on British Television.* London: Sage, 2002.

Masur, Kate. *An Example for All the Land: Emancipation and the Struggle for Equality in Washington, D.C.* Chapel Hill: University of North Carolina Press, 2012.

Matysik, Larry. *Drawing Heat the Hard Way: How Wrestling Really Works.* Toronto: ECW Press, 2009.

Mazer, Sharon. "The Doggie Doggie World of Professional Wrestling." *TDR: The Drama Review* 34, no. 4 (1990): 96–122.

———. "Los verdaderos luchadores no usan mascaras"; "Real Wrestlers Don't Wear Masks." *Luna Cornea* 27 (2004): 270–275; 323–325.

———. *Professional Wrestling: Sport and Spectacle.* Jackson: University Press of Mississippi, 1999.

———. "Quake City." *Performance Research* 20, no. 3 (June 2015): 163–172.

———. "Skirting Burlesque." *Australasian Drama Studies* 63 (October, 2013): 24–32.

McBride, Lawrence B. *Professional Wrestling, Embodied Morality, and Altered States of Consciousness.* MA diss., University of South Florida, 2005.

McClintock, Anne. *Imperial Leather: Race, Gender and Sexuality in the Colonial Contest.* London and New York: Routledge, 1995.

McCullough, Lissa. "Silence." In *The Routledge Encyclopaedia of Postmodernism,* edited by Victor E. Taylor and Charles E. Winquist. London: Routledge, 2001.

McKibbin, Tony. "The Well-Being of Friendship: Frances Ha." *Experimental Conversations* 13 (Winter 2014). http://www.experimentalconversations.com/article/4/.

Meade, Lawrence. "Ricki Starr Gets His Kicks for Victory." *Chicago Daily Tribune,* October 24, 1959, A4.

Meltzer, Dave. *Tributes: Remembering Some of the World's Greatest Wrestlers.* Etobicoke, ON: Winding Stair Press, 2001.

Messner, Michael, Carlisle M. Duncan and C. Cooky. "Silence, Sports Bras, and Wrestling Porn: Women in Televised Sports News and Highlights Shows." *Journal of Sport and Social Issues* 27 (2003): 38.

Messner, Michael, M. Dunbar and D. Hunt. "The Televised Sports Manhood Formula." *Journal of Sport and Social Issues* 24 (2000): 380.

Michaels, Shawn and Aaron Feigenbaum. *Heartbreak & Triumph: The Shawn Michaels Story*. New York: Routledge, 2001.

"Mid-South Wrestling." *Television Program*, Episode 322, November 1985. Accessed January 15, 2015. WWEnetwork.com.

Miller, Henry. *Air Conditioned Nightmare*. New York: New Directions, 1945.

Miller, Shane Aaron. "Making the Boys Cry: The Performative Dimensions of Fluid Gender." *Text and Performance Quarterly* 30, no. 2 (April 2010): 163–182.

"Mistico CMLL en Comercial del PAN." *YouTube video*, posted by "CMLLeLoMejor." April 24, 2009. Accessed January 11, 2015. https://www.youtube.com/watch?v=a-nUv189UlM.

Mitchell, W.J.T. *What Do Pictures Want? The Loves and Lives of Images*. London: University of Chicago Press, 2005.

Miyadai, Sinji, H. Ishihara and A. Ootsuka. *Zoho sabukarucha shinwa kaitai* (Enlarged ed. Dismantling the Myth of Sub-Culture: Transformation and the Current Situation of Girls, Music, Manga and Sexuality and Current Situation). Tokyo: Chikuma Shobo, 2007.

Möbius, Janina. *Und unter der Maske . . . das Volk. LUCHA LIBRE – Ein mexikanisches Volksspektakel zwischen Tradition und Moderne*. Frankfurt/Main: Vervuert Verlag, 2004.

Molloy, Molly. "The Mexican Undead: Toward a New History of the 'Drug War' Killing Fields." *Small Wars Journal*, August 21, 2013. Accessed June 30, 2015. smallwarsjournal.com/printpdf/14461.

Mondak, Jeffrey J. "The Politics of Professional Wrestling." *Journal of Popular Culture* 23, no. 2 (1989): 139–150.

Mooneyham, Mike. "Sailor Art Thomas Dies at Age 79." March 23, 2003. Accessed January 15, 2015. http://www.mikemooneyham.com/2003/03/23/sailor-art-thomas-dies-at-age-79/.

Moran, Joe. *Armchair Nation: An Intimate History of Britain in Front of the TV*. London: Profile Books, 2013.

Morocco. Directed by Josef von Sternberg. 1930. London: Universal, 2008. DVD.

Morse, Ann. "Arizona's Immigration Enforcements Laws." *National Conference of State Legislatures*, July 28, 2011. Accessed August 8, 2015. http://www.ncsl.org/research/immigration/analysis-of-arizonas-immigration-law.aspx.

Morton, Gerald W. and George M. O'Brien. *Wrestling to Rasslin': Ancient Sport to American Spectacle*. Bowling Green, OH: Bowling Green University Popular Press, 1985.

"Muldoon Denounces Bouts in Civic Centre." *New York Times*, May 15, 1931. Accessed May 15, 2015. http://query.nytimes.com/mem/archive/pdf?res=9C06EED71F38E03ABC4D52DFB366838A629EDE.

Mulvey, Laura. "Visual Pleasure and Narrative Cinema." In *Film Theory and Criticism: Introductory Readings*, edited by Leo Braudy and Marshall Cohen, 833–844. New York: Oxford University Press, 1999.

Muñoz, José Esteban. *Disidentifications: Queers of Color and the Performance of Politics*. Minneapolis: University of Minnesota Press, 1999.

Murphy, Patrick, John Williams and Eric Dunning (eds). *Football on Trial: Spectator Violence and Development in the Football World*. London: Routledge, 1990.

"Nacho Libre (2006) – Box Office Mojo." *Box Office Mojo*. Internet Movie Database. Accessed September 24, 2015. http://www.imdb.com/title/tt0457510/?ref_=ttfc_fc_tt.

Nahm, Kee-Yoon. "Props Breaking Character: The Performance and Failure of Real Objects on the Naturalist Stage." In *Performing Objects and Theatrical Things*, edited by Maris Schweitzer and Joanne Zerdy, 187–199. London: Palgrave Macmillan, 2014.

Nathanson, Donald. Foreword to *Queer Attachments: The Cultural Politics of Shame*, by Sally Munt, xiii–xvi. Farnham: Ashgate, 2008.

Newton, Esther. *Mother Camp: Female Impersonators in America*. Chicago: University of Chicago Press, 1979.

"The Nexus' WWE Debut." *RAW*, June 7, 2010. Accessed June 20, 2015. https://www.youtube.com/watch?v=vVVtqoqzgNw.

Ngai, Sianne. "Theory of the Gimmick." *Wissenschaftskolleg zu Berlin*. Accessed July 6, 2015. http://www.wiko-berlin.de/en/fellows/fellowfinder/detail/2014-ngai-sianne/.

Noland, Carrie. *Agency and Embodiment: Performing Gestures/Producing Culture*. Cambridge, MA: Harvard University Press, 2009.

Ogawa, Hiroshi. "Aidoru kashu no tanjyo to henyo" (Birth and Transformation of Idol Singers), in *Gendai no ongaku* (Modern Music). Tokyo: Tokyo Shoseki, 1991.

O'Hagan, Sean. "Interview: Marina Abramovic." *Guardian*, October 3, 2010. Accessed January 15, 2015. http://www.theguardian.com/artanddesign/2010/oct/03/interview-marina-abramovic-performance-artist

Oppliger, Patrice. A. *Wrestling and Hypermasculinity*. Jefferson, NC and London: McFarland, 2003.

Park, Alice. "Science of Pain: Healing the Hurt – Finding New Ways to Treat Pain." *TIME Magazine* 21 (March 2011): 30–35.

Pérez, Emma. *The Decolonial Imaginary: Writing Chicanas into History*. Bloomington and Indianapolis: Indiana University Press, 1999.

———. "Queering the Borderlands: The Challenges of Excavating the Invisible and Unheard." *Frontiers: A Journal of Women Studies* 24, no. 2/3 (2003): 122–131.

Perrone, Pierre. "Obituary: Big Daddy." *Independent* (London, UK), December 3, 1997.

Petten, Aaron J. "The Narrative Structuring and Interactive Narrative Logic of Televised Professional Wrestling." *New Review of Film and Television Studies* 8, no. 4 (2010): 436–447.

Pines, Jim, ed. *Black and White in Colour: Black People in British Television since 1936*. London: BFI, 1992.

Polhemus, Ted. "The Performance of Pain." *Performance Research: On Ritual* 3, no. 3 (2008): 97–102.

Predator. Directed by John McTiernan. 1987. London: Twentieth Century Fox, 2003. DVD.

Puchner, Martin. *Stage Fright: Modernism, Anti-Theatricality and Drama*. Baltimore: Johns Hopkins University Press, 2011.

PWTorch.com. "NEWS: British Star Ricki Starr Dies at 83, WWE Issues Statement." Accessed June 1, 2016. http://pwtorch.com/artman2/publish/Other_News_4/ article_81014.shtml#.VDvsGdR4.

Rancière, Jacques. *The Emancipated Spectator*. Translated by Gregory Elliott. London and New York: Verso, 2009.

Reynolds, R. D. *Wrestlecrap: The Very Worst of Professional Wrestling*. Toronto: ECW Press, 2003.

Richardson, Niall, "The Queer Activity of Extreme Male Bodybuilding: Gender Dissidence, Auto-Eroticism, and Hysteria." *Social Semiotics* 14, no. 1 (2004): 49–65.

Rickard, John. "'The Spectacle of Excess': The Emergence of Modern Professional Wrestling in the United States and Australia." *Journal of Popular Culture* 33, no. 1 (1999): 129–137.

"Ricki Starr Turned from Ballet to Mat." *Reading Eagle*, February 27, 1957.

Robinson, Zandria F. *This Ain't Chicago: Race, Class and Regional Identity in the Post-Soul South*. Chapel Hill: University of North Carolina Press, 2014.

Robson, Garry. *"No-One Likes Us, We Don't Care": The Myth and Reality of Millwall Fandom*. Oxford: Berg, 2000.

Rocky Johnson interview for Hannibal TV/GreatNorthWrestling.Ca. Accessed January 15, 2015, https://www.youtube.com/watch?v=rRhLqSJNpgk.

Rodriguez, Clara E. *Heroes, Lovers, and Others: The Story of Latinos in Hollywood*. Washington, DC: Smithsonian Books, 2004.

Roediger, David. *The Wages of Whiteness: Race and the Making of the American Working Class.* New York: Verso, 1997.

Ronay, Barney. "How Wrestling is Taking Over the Movies." *Guardian*, September 2, 2010. http://www.theguardian.com/film/2010/sep/02/wrestling-movies.

Royal Rumble 1992. Accessed January 2015. WWE Network.

Rubenstein, Anne. "El Santo: Many Versions of the Perfect Man." In *The Mexico Reader*, edited by Joseph Gilbert and Timothy J. Henderson, 570–578. Durham: Duke University Press, 2003.

Rubin, Gayle. "The Traffic in Women: Notes on the 'Political Economy' of Sex." In *Toward an Anthropology of Women*, edited by R. R. Reiter, 157–210. New York: Monthly Review Press, 1975.

Runnels, Dustin. "The Man Behind the Paint: Inside the Bizarre Career of Goldust." Edited by James Wortman. *WWE.com*, October 20, 2013. http://www.wwe.com/inside/goldust-rhodes-retrospective-interview-26157145.

The Running Man. Directed by Paul Michael Glaser. 1987. London: Universal, 2010. DVD.

Russell, Gordon, V. Horn and M. Huddle. "Male Responses to Female Aggression." *Social Behavior and Personality* 16, no. 1 (1988): 51–57.

Sammond, Nicholas. *Steel Chair to the Head: The Pleasure and Pain of Professional Wrestling.* Durham: Duke University Press, 2005.

Savran, David. "The Curse of Legitimacy." In *Against Theatre: Creative Destructions on the Modernist Stage*, edited by Alan Ackerman and Martin Puchner, 189–205. New York: Palgrave Macmillan, 2006.

———. *Highbrow/Lowdown: Theatre, Jazz, and the Making of the New Middle Class.* Ann Arbor: University of Michigan Press, 2010.

Scarface. Directed by Brian de Palma. 1983. London: Universal, 2004. DVD.

Scarry, Elaine. *The Body in Pain: The Making and Unmaking of the World*, Oxford and New York: Oxford University Press, 1985.

Schaffer, Gavin. *The Vision of a Nation: Making Multiculturalism on British Television, 1960–1980.* London: Palgrave Macmillan, 2014.

Schneiderman, R. M. "Better Days, and Even the Candidates, Are Coming to W.W.E." *New York Times*, April 28, 2008. Accessed June 22, 2015. http://www.nytimes.com/2008/04/28/business/media/28wwe.html.

Schulman, Michael. "Generation LGBTQIA." *New York Times*, January 9, 2013. Accessed August 3, 2015. http://www.nytimes.com/2013/01/10/fashion/generation-lgbtqia.html?_r=0.

Schweitzer, Maris and Joanne Zerdy. "Introduction: Object Lessons." In *Performing Objects and Theatrical Things*, edited by Maris Schweitzer and Joanne Zerdy, 1–20. London: Palgrave Macmillan, 2014.

Sedgwick, Eve Kosofsky. "Queer and Now." In *Tendencies*, 1–22. Durham: Duke University Press, 1994.

Serrels, Mark. "How do Pro Wrestlers Use Twitter?" *Gizmodo.com.au*. Accessed June 1, 2015. http://www.gizmodo.com.au/2011/10/how-do-pro-wrestlers-use-twitter/.

Shapiro, Gregg. "'Sunset Boulevard' Still a Camp Classic." *Wisconsin Gazette*, February 21, 2013. Accessed January 16, 2016. http://www.wisconsingazette.com/dvds/sunset-boulevard-still-a-camp-classic.html.

Shoemaker, David. *The Squared Circle: Life, Death, and Professional Wrestling.* New York: Gotham Books, 2013.

Siska, William. "Metacinema: A Modern Necessity." *Literature Film Quarterly* 7, no. 4 (1979): 285–290.

Slotkin, Richard. *Regeneration through Violence: The Mythology of the American Frontier, 1600–1860.* Norman: University of Oklahoma Press, 1973.

Smith, R. Tyson. *Fighting for Recognition: Identity, Masculinity, and the Act of Violence in Professional Wrestling.* Durham: Duke University Press, 2014.

———. "Pain in the Act: The Meanings of Pain Among Professional Wrestlers." *Qualitative Sociology* 31, no. 2 (2008): 129–148.

———. "Passion Work: The Joint Production of Emotional Labour in Professional Wrestling." *Social Psychology* 71, no. 2 (2008): 157–176.

Snowden, Jonathan. "Inside WWE: An Exclusive Look at How a Pro Wrestling Story Comes to Life." Longform. *Bleacher Report,* January 21, 2015. Accessed January 21, 2015. http://bleache rreport.com/articles/2283701-inside-wwe-an-exclusive-look-at-how-a-pro-wrestling-story-comes-to-life.

Sofer, Andrew. *The Stage Life of Props.* Ann Arbor, MI: University of Michigan Press, 2003.

Somerville, Siobhan B. *Queering the Color Line: Race and the Invention of Homosexuality in American Culture.* Durham: Duke University Press, 2000.

Sontag, Susan. "Notes on Camp." In *Against Interpretation and Other Essays,* 275–292. London: Penguin, 2009.

———. *On Photography.* London: Penguin, 1979.

———. *Regarding the Pain of Others.* London: Hamish Hamilton, 2003.

Soulliere, Danielle. "Wrestling With Masculinity: Messages About Manhood in the WWE." *Sex Roles* 55 (2006): 1–11.

Stallman, Richard. "Un nuevo sistema fácil para conseguir neutralidad de género en la lengua castellana." 2011. Accessed March 23, 2012. http://stallman.org/articles/castellano-sin-genero.html.

Steele, George, interview by Sean Oliver. *Kayfabe Commentaries Timeline Series: 1986 WWE as told by George "The Animal" Steele.* DVD. Directed by Sean Oliver. Bayonne, NJ: Kayfabe Commentaries, 2012.

Steichen, James. "Are HD Performances 'Cannibalizing' the Metropolitan Opera's Live Audience?" *OUPBlog,* August 13, 2013. Accessed April 3, 2014. http://blog.oup.com/2013/08/hd-broadcast-cannibalization-met-operas-live-audience/.

Stonley, Peter. *A Queer History of the Ballet.* London and New York: Routledge, 2007.

Straight Shootin' Series: Jim Cornette and Bill Watts, Volume 2, ROH Video, 2006.

Street, Adrian Street. *Imagine What I Could Do To You.* Createspace Independent, 2013.

———. *I Only Laugh When It Hurts.* Createspace Independent, 2012.

———. *My Pink Gas Mask.* Createspace Independent, 2012.

———. *Sadist in Sequins.* Createspace Independent, 2012.

———. *So Many Ways To Hurt You.* Createspace Independent, 2012.

———. *Violence Is Golden.* Createspace Independent, 2015.

Stromberg, Peter G. *Caught in Play: How Entertainment Works on You.* Stanford: Stanford University Press, 2009.

Sugawara, Toshiko. "Daigakusei no shintai ishiki ni tsuite—danshi shintai ishiki no gonindo" (Body Awareness of University Students: The Degree of Erroneous Recognition Among Male University Students) *Toyo Daigaku Kiyo Kyoyokatei hen (Hokentaiku)* 1 (1991): 23–39.

Sullivan, Kevin. *The WWE Championship: A Look Back at the Rich History of the WWE Championship.* New York: Gallery Books, 2010.

Sunset Boulevard. Directed by Billy Wilder. 1950. Paramount, 2003. DVD.

Tanaka, Reiko. "Wakai jyosei no soshin zukuri ni kansuru shakaigaku teki kosatsu: jyoshi-gakusei kunin no jirei wo tooshite" (A Sociological Study of Young Women's Efforts to become Thin – Nine Case Studies of Female College Students) *Taiikugaku kenkyu* 41 (1997): 328–339.

Taussig, Michael. *Defacement: Public Secrecy and the Labor of the Negative.* Stanford: Stanford University Press, 1999.

Te Kaunihera Māori o Aotearoa / New Zealand Māori Council. http://www.maoricouncil.com/wardens.

Te *Puni Kōkiri.* http://www.tpk.govt.nz/en/whakamahia/maori-wardens.

They Live. Directed by John Carpenter. 1988. London: Momentum, 2002. DVD.

Timeshift. "When Wrestling Was Golden: Grapples, Grunts and Grannies." Directed by Linda Sands. BBC4, December 13, 2012.

"Top 20 Knockouts in UFC History." *YouTube video*, 7:25. Posted by "UFC – Ultimate Fighting Championship." November 12, 2013. https://www.youtube.com/watch?v=LWE79K2Ii-s.

truk83. "How about Wyatt Lanterns?" July 18, 2013, 12:43 AM http://www.wrestlingforum.com/general--wwe/885409--how--about--wyatt--lanterns.html.

Tumblety, Joan. *Remaking the Male Body: Masculinity and the Uses of Physical Culture in Interwar and Vichy France.* Oxford: Oxford University Press, 2012.

UFC.com. "UFC Rules and Regulations." Accessed April 23, 2015. http://www.ufc.com/discover/sport/rules-and-regulations#1.

"Ultimate 8: Heavyweight Knockouts." *YouTube video*, 4:50. Posted by "UFC – Ultimate Fighting Championship." October 17, 2013. https://www.youtube.com/watch?v=Oe2YF56JklQ.

University College London. "Acute Pain is Eased with Touch of a Hand." Accessed May 5, 2015, UCL.ac.uk. https://www.ucl.ac.uk/news/news-articles/1009/10092401.

Vasquez, Angélica Cuellar. *La Noche Es de Ustedes, El Amanecer Es Nuestro.* Mexico City: UNAM, 1993.

Vintage Muscle Mags. Accessed June 18, 2015. http://vintagemusclemags.com/.

Wakin, Daniel J. and Kevin Flynn, "A Metropolitan Opera High Note, as Donations Hit $182 Million." *New York Times*, October 10, 2011. Accessed April 3, 2014. http://www.nytimes.com/2011/10/11/arts/music/metropolitan-operas-donations-hit-a-record-182-million.html.

Wall, Patrick. *Pain: The Science of Suffering.* London: Phoenix. 1999.

Warde, Alan. "Cultural Capital and the Place of Sport." *Cultural Trends* 15, no. 2/3 (June/September 2006): 107–122.

WCW "Main Event." Episode 620, August 17, 1992. WWENetwork.com.

WCW World Wide, May 26, 1990. Accessed January 15, 2015. https://www.youtube.com/watch?v=HkAdplMOYOI.

West Texas Cowboys, "Rap Is Crap." Accessed January 15, 2015. https://www.youtube.com/watch?v=HHihfxE0ZTk.

"Who We Are." *Ticketmaster.* Accessed December 10, 2014. http://www.ticketmaster.com/about/about-us.html.

Williams, Joe. "The Hippo Hippodrome." *Judge*, reprinted in *Literary Digest*, 41. February 6, 1932.

Willis, Paul. *Learning to Labor: How Working Class Kids Get Working Class Jobs.* Farnborough: Saxon Press, 1977.

Wilshire, Bruce. "The Concept of the Paratheatrical." *TDR: The Drama Review* 34, no. 4 (1990): 169–178.

Wood, Amy Louise. *Lynching and Spectacle: Witnessing Racial Violence in America, 1890–1940*. Chapel Hill: University of North Carolina Press, 2011.

"World Wrestling Entertainment, Inc. (WWE)." *Yahoo! Finance*. Accessed June 26, 2015. http://finance.yahoo.com/q?s=WWE.

"Wrestling Placed Under New Status." *New York Times*, April 9, 1930. Accessed May 15, 2015. http://query.nytimes.com/mem/archive/pdf?res=9902E5DE1F39E03ABC4153DFB26 6838B629EDE.

WWE. "Corporate Overview." *WWE.com*. Accessed November 2, 2015, http://corporate. wwe.com/company/overview.

———. "The Undertaker throws Mankind off the top of the Hell in a Cell (1998)." Accessed January 15, 2015, http://www.wwe.com/videos/the-undertaker-throws-mankind-off-the-top-of-the-hell-in-a-cell-king-of-the-ring-16346646.

"WWE CM Punk Go to Sleep Finisher Tribute." *YouTube video*, 2:15. Posted by "WrestlingReels." May 20, 2012. Accessed January 16, 2015. https://www.youtube.com/watch?v= cGIJktgQrK0.

WWE.com. "Goldust's WWE Debut." *YouTube video*, 16:18. September 30, 2013. https:// www.youtube.com/watch?v=3j9KFh_5cDs.

———. "Goldust vs. Razor Ramon." *Royal Rumble*, January 20, 1996. WWE Network. http://www.wwe.com/wwenetwork.

———. *WrestleMania XI*. April 2, 1995. WWE Network. http://www.wwe.com/wwenetwork.

———. "WWE Parents Overview." Accessed May 2, 2015. http://corporate.wwe.com/par ents/overview.jsp.

———. "10 Baddest WWE Magazine Covers." Accessed January 13, 2016, http://www. wwe.com/inside/magazine/10baddest.

WWE Sheamus. Twitter Post, November 20, 2014, 8:08am. https://twitter.com/wweshea mus/status/535464740269883393.

Yomota, Inuhiko. *Kawaii ron* (On Kawaii) Tokyo: Chikuma shobo, 2006.

YouTube and Chicago Film Archives. "Haystack Calhoun vs. Buddy Rogers." Accessed June 3, 2015. https://www.youtube.com/watch?v=zcP6KizyhXc.

Zombie Princess. "How about Wyatt Lanterns?" http://www.wrestlingforum.com/general--wwe/885409--how--about--wyatt--lanterns.html.

Zweininger-Bargielowska, Ina. "Building a British Superman: Physical Culture in Interwar Britain." *Journal of Contemporary History* 41, no. 4 (2006): 595–610.

———. *Managing the Body: Beauty, Health and Fitness in Britain, 1880–1939*. Oxford: Oxford University Press, 2010.

Index

In-ring names of wrestlers are listed as they would be on the card, e.g. "Rowdy" Roddy Piper. All other names are listed surname first, e.g. Butler, Judith.